IN FAVOR OF DECEIT

Aifa at Dawn, 1980

Ellen B. Basso

IN FAVOR OF
DECEIT

A Study of Tricksters
in an Amazonian Society

The University of Arizona Press, Tucson

The University of Arizona Press

Copyright © 1987
The Arizona Board of Regents
All Rights Reserved

The book was set in 10/12 Linotron 202 Palatino.
Manufactured in the U.S.A.

Library of Congress Cataloging-in-Publication Data

Basso, Ellen B., 1942–
　In favor of deceit: a study of tricksters in an Amazonian society　Ellen B. Basso.
　　p.　cm.
　Bibliography: p.
　Includes index.
　ISBN 0–8165–1022–9 (alk. paper) : $40.00
　1. Apalakiri Indians.　2. Indians of South America—Brazil—
Legends.　3. Trickster—Brazil.　4. Deception.　I. Title.
F2520.1.A63B365　1987
398.2′08998—dc19　　　　　　　　　　　　　　　87–18784
　　　　　　　　　　　　　　　　　　　　　　　　　CIP

British Library Cataloguing in Publication data are available.

Contents

Preface

A major impediment to our understanding of South American Indians—to their ideas about personhood and society, their senses of history, and the meaning of these in relation to their experiences of the sensory world—is the rarity of adequately collected and translated texts through which native voices can be directly heard. This scarcity is as much a consequence of the serious difficulties most have encountered with learning South American languages as it is of the research interests that are brought to bear. The South American ethnographer frequently faces the difficult task of having to learn a language that has never been adequately described, having, in other words, to puzzle out its mysterious grammar while hoping to translate successfully what people are saying. And, when "what people are saying" involves a complex and subtle interplay of didactic, poetic, rhetorical, and psychodynamic functions all created within a dialogical, interactive context, such as we now understand to occur in storytelling throughout the New World, serious problems of analysis and interpretation encompass those of grammatical description. Together, ethnographers and native authorities work with many simultaneously overlapping dimensions, not the least of which is a continuous struggle to overcome mutual confusion.

This is the second in a series of books concerned with the vital, continuously evolving forms of Kalapalo narrative art. It is the result of a longstanding collaboration I have enjoyed with Kalapalo storytellers, translators, and commentators, men and women who, as long as I have known them, have wanted to make known to outsiders so much that is crucial to understanding their lives. As an occasional participant in those Kalapalo lives, I am much concerned with what can be learned from their narratives, for it is through narratives, above all, that Kalapalo represent themselves, both collectively and as individuals.

In 1961, land around the headwaters of the Xingu River in the northern region of the state of Mato Grosso, Brazil, was set aside as an Indian reserve, known as the Parque Nacional do Xingu. What lands the Kalapalo, a Carib-speaking community of approximately 300 persons, occupied until 1961 fell outside this reserve. They were persuaded to abandon their old settlements to the south and move within the Park boundaries. While their new settlement, which they called Aifa (which means both "Finished" and "Ready"), was located far downstream, several days' canoe travel to the north, they have continued to travel back to the old places to farm and to gather piqui fruit from old orchards. Their population has risen dramatically since this move north, in part because of access to medical care and especially anti-malarial campaigns, but also because of greater protection from epidemic diseases, which killed many people in the past. Even today, the Kalapalo and their neighbors are exceptional in Brazil in living apart from the surrounding rural society, though that society threateningly encroaches on the very boundaries of the Park. While the proximity of outsiders has made the Kalapalo increasingly knowledgeable about the nation in which they live, they are still able and concerned to pursue their traditionally defined goals in the artificial isolation of the reserve.

This book, of course, could hardly have been written without the desire of all those storytellers (*akiñotoi*) to make Kalapalo oral tradition known to the outside world, and who allowed me to tape and publish their performances. Many of them number among the most elderly members of the community, and are considered knowledgeable by virtue of sheer experience and the fact that they all learned from distinguished teachers. Here, as they wanted me to, I say something about these people by way of acknowledgment.

During my stay among the Kalapalo, Ulutsi was the principal hereditary leader (*anetu*) of Aifa. Though no longer in his prime, and having suffered for many years from a series of family tragedies that left him increasingly withdrawn from community life, Ulutsi was still thought of by most of his people as the person who could be counted on most for stories about the distant past, and the one who was most concerned with preserving esoteric ritual matters. As leader, Ulutsi was expected to live simply, but he seemed to carry this asceticism further than the other old people did. Long without a wife, he slept on what must have been the most decrepit hammock in Aifa, depending upon his daughter and his grandsons' wives for food. Had he not suffered yet another shock when a young granddaughter died suddenly in April 1979, I would have had the opportunity to hear many more stories from him than I did, for he subsequently retreated into a melancholic daze from which he was barely recovering during my most recent visit in 1982.

When I was escorted into Aifa early in 1979, at the height of the rainy season, the house of Kambe, where I was asked to live, was overcrowded with his nervous, forever-agitated family: children crying, women shrieking at them and each other, men sullen and withdrawn. The old house was cramped and very dirty, smelling of rotten manioc and the resinous wood smoke of many family hearths, but to Kambe and his younger wife Kafagagu (grandmother or mother to most of these people), all this was a positive sign of the size and vigor of their family. While Kafagagu was usually involved with her family, Kambe's older wife Kofoño (all of whose children had died many years ago) was much more of a companion to the old man, and it was she who traveled with him on most occasions. Kambe was Ulutsi's constant rival for leadership of the Kalapalo, and had a decided advantage because of the productive and organizational skill these two wives contributed. Kambe and his adult children were the most rapid speakers of all the Kalapalo, and this rapidity of speech made him seem all the more nervous. But despite the difficulties we all had in understanding his tapes, he was regarded as a master of narrative whose stories were the most precise and reflective of Kalapalo tradition. Kambe told us he had learned storytelling from his father-in-law Mugika, the leader of the previous Kalapalo settlement, Kanugidyafïtï.

Hobbling bravely between his manioc fields and home, Kakaku, though his left knee was badly swollen by arthritis, still worked long hours and fished avidly. He was particularly fond of stories about the disgusting Dawn People, of which he and his son-in-law Aipatsi had a great store, and he seemed to enjoy joking with the young men more than any other older person in Aifa. He was leader of the former Carib-speaking settlement known as Dyagamï (whose dialect closely resembles Kalapalo), and he understands his stories to reflect Dyagamï tradition.

Kudyu's parents were members of yet another Carib-speaking group, the Kuikuro. By the early sixties, Kudyu was married to a widow whose Kalapalo husband had been killed by a jaguar. When I knew him he had already adopted a distinctly Kalapalo intonation in his speech, but, like the other Kuikuro speakers living among the Kalapalo, was still identified as a Kuikuro. Kudyu was one of the most important musicians in the community. An especially gifted speaker, his stories were distinguished by their clarity of explanatory detail and a mastery of onomatopoeia. His performances were also exceptional for the elaborate body language that accompanied them. A natural actor, he was stimulated to greater heights of performance by large audiences.

Very much in contrast to Kudyu was Muluku. Shy, overly respectful of things and people in the outside world of Brazilians, careful to preserve tradition, and very conscious of himself as the bearer of that tradition, Muluku was a younger hereditary leader. His father, Mugika, had been a master narrator, from whom many of the present storytellers received their knowledge. Somewhat ill at ease, Muluku used words sparingly, haltingly, and with few accompanying gestures. Muluku's stories are therefore, in general, the least performed of all.

Kwatagi was a "knower," a *fuati* or shaman, who frequently experienced visions of powerful beings. This intense relationship with the other world did not prevent him (or other shamans, including Agakuni) from concerned reflection and comment upon the world of Brazilians, a world he found simultaneously attractive and absurd. While he was not known as a storytelling expert, his narratives were lively and to the point, the kind of performances I came to expect from most older Kalapalo.

Agakuni was an important Kalapalo shaman, who had trained a number of younger men, and who had a reputation beyond the Kalapalo settlement as a curer and a seer. He was a stocky and pugnacious man who had developed the art of mimicry to an exquisite degree. Agakuni's stories were among the most performed, since he, even more than Kudyu, was especially keen to take on the voices of his characters. Sitting close to his listener, his stories unfolded with great excitement and bodily tension, which were quickly communicated to those around him.

Aside from the storytellers, to single out people for acknowledgments would be contrary to the Kalapalo way of representing as a community effort their own hospitality and efforts to teach me about themselves. What I must acknowledge, as always, is their constant and sympathetic sharing of the good things of their lives with me, and their continuing to allow me to learn from them in so many different and lasting ways.

I am also deeply grateful to my friend and colleague Professor Roque de Barros Laraia of the Universidade de Brasilia and to the officials of the Conselho Nacional de Desenvolvimento Científico e Technologico and the Fundação Nacional do Indio, for their considerable assistance in furthering my research in Brazil.

I also thank William Hanks, Jonathan Hill, Susan Phillips, Joel Sherzer, and Greg Urban for generously sharing their expertise in the study of language and culture, and Lee Fratt for her perseverance on my behalf in the University of Arizona library.

My stay among the Kalapalo from 1978 to 1980 was supported by a National Science Foundation Research Grant (BNS 78-00849) and the University of Arizona. A grant from the Wenner-Gren Foundation for Anthropological Research, Inc., supported my travels during 1982. A grant from the Faculty of Social and Behavioral Sciences of the University of Arizona allowed me to complete the manuscript more comfortably than otherwise during the summer of 1985.

A portion of Chapter 3, including the analysis of an earlier translation of "Fitsagu the Cuckoo," first appeared as "Quoted Dialogues in Kalapalo Narrative Discourse" in *Native South American Discourse,* edited by Joel Sherzer and Greg Urban (Mouton de Gruyter, 1986).

Translating Kalapalo Narratives

Among the Kalapalo, stories are told almost anyplace, and at any time. Personal narratives are told in conversational contexts but also in public, somewhat formal situations. They often occur in the setting representing community interest, outside in the central plaza (*fugombo*) around which the communal family houses are located. There, one hears meticulously detailed narratives of journeys made by hereditary leader-messengers who have returned home from inviting a neighboring settlement to a ceremony. There, too, a person who has come to visit after a long absence will tell of intervening events. Hunters, fishermen, traders, people who have traveled great distances, and shamans, all narrate their experiences in public places—especially when the experiences are unusual and worthy of being incorporated into the commonly held knowledge that over time becomes the substance of more traditional storytelling. Myths, that is, narratives of very ancient times in which the Dawn People (*angifolo*) figure, are also told by hereditary leaders inside the centrally located ceremonial house. Because this house is the repository of flutes women are not allowed to see, men alone hear stories this way. Women and small children tend to hear myths inside their houses, especially when they are narrated at night. Less formal, gossipy narratives (which listeners consider rather unreliable) are embedded in conversations of all kinds held in more private settings: whispered inside a house, told by a woman to her friends working in the manioc fields, or to a party of travelers canoeing along a stream, or even in the plaza, when only a few trusted friends are listening.

What makes narratives special to the Kalapalo is the formal, dialogical nature of the telling. One of the listeners, the person to whom the story is being told or "given," is made a "what-sayer" (*tiitsofo*), who responds (*etiitsa*) in one of several conventional ways after each of the narrator's pauses. The most common of these responses are monosyllabic expletives that indicate to the narrator the nature of the listener's reception of the story (awe, excitement, interest, or boredom), or simply that the listener is paying attention. Second, the responder may from time to time repeat significant words from the narration, signaling an understanding that they are significant; these words tend to be repeated once more by the narrator, to validate the listener's comprehension of their importance. The result is a text pervaded by repetition of words, phrases, and grammatical forms in rephrasings, a kind of parallelism that is an important emergent feature of Kalapalo narrative performances. It is also a feature that creates the greatest aesthetic difficulty for English-speaking readers, who are unused to such repetition in written texts. Finally, at certain major breaks in the story, the what-sayer can ask questions, and probably should, since those who don't are prompted to do so by the speaker. A woman telling me a story about some men who had visited her community long ago stopped at one point and said, "Ask me, 'What are their names?'" When I answered, "What are their names?" she listed them with apparent satisfaction and had me repeat them until I seemed to know them well. Only then did she continue her narrative.

In these ways, the responder contributes substantially to the construction of the narrative: by marking structural units or segments, by signaling politely to the speaker that the images he or she is constructing are understood, appreciated, and agreed with, and by diverting the speaker into new channels of detail and explication that might not be strictly pertinent to the story but enhance the listener's understanding while confirming the expertise of the narrator.

Kalapalo narratives are performed to varying degrees of elaborateness. The more public the context and the more traditional the content, the more elaborate the performance tends to be and the more authoritative the text is considered. Kalapalo evaluate performances primarily on how successfully the speaker conveys the content. A good storyteller, the Kalapalo say, is a person who keeps repetition to a minimum, and does not bore or embarrass the listener with excessive personal opinions or digressions. But a Kalapalo performance also necessarily involves the responder. The narrator, and anyone else who might be interested in hearing the narrative, judge the what-sayer according to how alert the responses are and how much they are in keeping with the rhythms of the narrator's telling. These rhythms are created by the patterns of intonational contouring, which result from the pauses after lines to allow for the what-sayer's response, repetition of significant lines, and modulation of the voice in keeping with the segmenting processes.

In this book, I present translations of stories that were in the main told to me directly. My translations are arranged to indicate the small-est segment, that is, line structure, as suggested by the patterns of dialogic interaction between the narrator and me, acting as the re-sponder. Each line break indicates a brief pause that was followed by my reply. A narrator's qualifications, elaborations, and ornamentation of the content appear after the main subject, usually spoken in in-creasingly softer tones of voice, with a summary or conclusion spoken more loudly. I have attempted to convey this quality of Kalapalo nar-rative by placing lines on the page according to tone of voice. Lines that appear toward the right of the page were uttered in a relatively soft voice. Those appearing at the left (which also introduce or con-clude a major segment) were spoken in a relatively loud and emphatic voice. Occasional double spaces between clusters of lines indicate an important thematic shift in the story, somewhat equivalent to chapters or stanzas. These are used when the storyteller concludes a segment with a formulaic remark such as: "Then they remained there." The new segment usually begins with a similar formula: "Then . . ."; "Be-cause of what (had happened to them). . . ."

The consecutive numbering of lines serves as a guide to a notes sec-tion that follows most of the stories. These notes clarify species iden-tification, place names, celestial phenomena, and particular features of performance such as gestures or changes of voice that could not be conveniently shown in the body of the translation. Asterisks in a story text indicate material that is explained in the notes to that story.

In the original narrative performances, storytellers frequently used gestures to accompany or substitute for verbal description. Where this was so, I have often supplemented the original Kalapalo to in-clude what was being described. For example, while telling me the story "Kwatïngï," Kambe pointed to a place in the sky just above the western horizon while saying, "The sun was here as they approached Faukugu." I translate this simultaneously verbal and visual event as: "The sun was here in the western sky as they approached Faukugu."

Kalapalo rarely label feelings in narratives. They prefer to modulate tone of voice when quoting the speech of a character to describe an emotional state more dramatically. For example, in "Kwatïngï," a woman angrily dismisses her sister, who has refused to heed her warning. I closely translate her remark, "Go ahead then, drink if you wish," adding, to show how Kambe's voice changed at that point, "Her sister spoke angrily to her" (line 919). An interesting example in the same story of how emotion can be described more literally is line 1383.

Kalapalo pronouns and pronominal prefixes to transitive verbs are often sufficient for distinguishing characters from each other in terms of focality, topical newness, subject-object relations, and spatial-temporal relations. Consequently, there are far fewer instances of personal naming in these stories than an English reader would anticipate. But since in English there are so few third-person pronouns (compared with fourteen Kalapalo possibilities), I often had no choice but to insert names despite their absence in the original.

Kalapalo narratives are replete with sound symbols. Onomatopoeia usually accompanies or substitutes for descriptions of activities involving inanimate objects. Kalapalo speakers do not describe inanimate objects as agents of transitive verbs. They are of course acted upon, and onomatopoeia seems to highlight the object at the expense of the agent by suggesting motion, even though involuntary. A good example from the story "Kwatïngï" is the description in lines 872–876 of a woman climbing a palm tree in order to cut some young shoots off the plant. Notice how rarely Kambe mentions the name of the tree, and how I have had to include it in the translation. I preserve onomatopoeia while describing the action more explicitly than in the original. Without such an elaboration of the original text, it would be almost impossible for the reader to understand what was taking place.

As she crept up,   872
itsaingalefa
  puh puh puh   873
  puh puh puh (sound of her lower limbs hitting the tree trunk as she climbed)
    as she crept up the trunk of the burity palm,   874
    itsaingalefa,
tsuk she cut it off. *Tsuk, tooh, tsuk.* The burity shoot landed upright.   875
tsuk itsaketifeke. tsuk, tooh, tsuk tsatsegate itsainga.
    (*tsuk* = sound of knife; *tooh* = sound of palm shoot landing in a muddy lake bottom)
  Tsiuk uuh,   876
  Tsiuk uuh,
    (*tsiuk* = sound of knife; *uuh* = sound of palm shoot sinking into the muddy bottom)
    it stuck out from among the water plants. The burity shoot stuck out.   877
    tatsegate ikai, idyika, itate itatsegate.

Some of the most frequently used forms have lost their original onomatopoetic significance. The sound of bare feet on a path (represented by *ti ti ti* or *titititi* when a person is hurrying along) is used generally to refer to animate motion away from a particular place (though it may be an alligator or a tapir rather than a human being who is doing this). The sound *tikii*, which represents the sound of thatch brushing against the shoulders of a person bending over to enter the low doorway of a house, more generally is used in stories to refer to someone's arrival, even if it be at a location out of doors.

Sound symbols other than onomatopoeia include animal and bird calls, human expletives, songs of powerful beings, and, above all, quoted speech. Kalapalo use three types of quotation indicators that also emphasize to the listener who among various characters is speaking. The form *nïgifeke* (to which may be added the particle *ti,* indicating that what is quoted is hearsay) indicates conversational speech between the focal character and another person present; the second person is usually named by the narrator early on in the conversation. I translate these forms as "said," "answered," "replied," or occasionally "went," if a narrator rushes his use of the expression. The forms *kilï* or *kita,* which are intransitive verbs, simply mean "spoke up" and "was talking," respectively, and are used to introduce a new speaker as a conversation begins, especially when that person is different from the focal character. Finally, the form *taifeke* indicates non-conversational speech such as proclamations, oratorical declamations, and song texts. I translate this as "declared" or "proclaimed."

Sound symbols are important because they underscore the categories of entities involved in specific communicative relationships. These relationships are as much interpersonal forms of consciousness as they are sound-centered events. In mythic narratives especially, sound symbols represent ideas about relationships, activities, causalities, processes, goals, and states of mind. I have tried to maintain as much of the importance of sound symbols in Kalapalo narrative as possible, though of course there is no substitute for the actual performance, when the listener is made aware of a dense texture of multiple presences engaged in the events of the story.

A Guide to Pronouncing Kalapalo Words

The following phonetic symbols have been used to write Kalapalo words:

Vowels

a, as in oper*a* (low front open)
e, as in b*e*st (middle open)
e, as "oe" in French *coeur* (middle closed)
i, as in s*ee*m (high front open)
i, as in sh*ou*ld (middle open)
o, as in *o*ld (middle rounded)
u, as in m*oo*n (high back rounded)
Vowel nasalization is indicated by a tilde (as in ũ).
Nasalization usually occurs in a stressed syllable.

Consonants

d, as in English (voiced alveolar stop)
dy, somewhat as in the name Na*di*a, but with more breath (voiced alveopalatal fricative)
f, pronounced while blowing air through loosely opened, untouching lips (voiceless bilabial fricative)
g, as in English but slightly farther back in the mouth (voiced glottal fricative)
h, as in English (voiceless glottal fricative)
k, as in *c*offee (voiceless velar stop)
l, as in English but tongue is held slightly longer and farther back in mouth (voiced alveolar lateral)

m, as in English (voiced bilabial nasal)
n, as in English (voiced alveolar nasal)
ñ, as in Spanish mañana or Portuguese li*nh*o
ng, similar to si*ng*, but pronounced farther back in mouth (voiced palatal nasal). This sound is often followed by a syllable beginning with g, hence the common written form ngg; normally, there is a syllabic break between ng and g.
p, as in English (voiced bilabial stop)
s, as in English (voiceless alveopalatal fricative)
ts, as in ca*ts* (voiceless dental affricate)
t, somewhat softer than *t*ooth (voiceless alveolar stop)
w, as in *w*ent (voiced bilabial semivowel)
zh, as if pronouncing *sh*oe farther back in mouth (voiced alveopalatal fricative)

Where only two syllables occur in a word, stress is usually on the first syllable. In noncompound words of more than two syllables, the second syllable of the word is normally stressed. Nasalized vowels also indicate stressed syllables.

IN FAVOR OF DECEIT

Chapter 1

An Elusive Intelligence

Among the Kalapalo, narrative traditions are a vital, dynamic, and productive art form, an elaborate means of preserving, reworking, and sharing between generations knowledge, insight, and understanding of their world. By *oral traditions* I mean the narratives (*akiña*) Kalapalo tell about both relatively recent, personal experiences and events connected with a magically distant, "mythological" past. These stories are a complex mix of imaginative, technical, and morally instructive content, through which we come to admire their remarkably precise and detailed awareness of life, their reflections and speculations on the implications of natural events, and, above all, their insights and their fantasies—both dreamlike and nightmarish—on human existence. Traditional narratives are thus the essential key for entry into the poetic world of the Kalapalo. This is very much a psychological world concerned with the evolution of feeling, with motivation and the formulation of goals, in which ideas about the nature of different kinds of beings and presences, their relationships and activities of thought, are conceived, represented, and (through performance) rendered apparent.

The discursive, narrative representations of personality development that constitute mythological stories of lives anticipated, remembered, and imagined, are important objects for interpretive scrutiny and linguistic analysis. Kalapalo myths contain considerable suggestive thematic content in the form of ideas about personality processes, character development, consistencies, and changes, and the relations of these to such things as initiation seclusion, marriage, dietary and medical practices, traveling, musical ritual, and mourning. In a sense, Kalapalo myths are "studies of self," representing personal motives, choices, interpretations, and goal orientation, and, as such, are especially open to methods that unite a linguistic focus on narrative discourse with a psychoanalytically informed, interpretive focus on symbolic forms. I first examined some of the possibilities for anthropology created by such a fusion of perspectives in my first book on Kalapalo performances, *A Musical View of the Universe* (University of Pennsylvania Press, 1985). They are explored further in this book with a new set of Kalapalo narratives.

On and off since 1966, I have listened to Kalapalo tell stories, and have been repeatedly impressed with their fascination with illusion and deception. As they describe the actions of a variety of characters (some *itseke* or powerful beings, some *kuge* or human beings, some— the *angifolo* or Dawn People—combining the attributes of both), Kalapalo storytellers illustrate a distinctive view of the dubious quality of human experience and understanding. There is a sense in these stories of reality developed through paradox and contradiction, an emphasis on transiency and multiple identities and powers, that suggests a skeptical view of a fixed and invariant sensory universe, one that differs markedly from our own concern to keep separate genuineness, naturalness, normality, honesty, and the morally good on the one hand, and deception, falsehood, paradox, and evil on the other.

Rather, Kalapalo understand the special quality of human life to be our ability to create illusions through verbal and visual fabrications. Through these fabrications, many of the forms and processes of experience are constituted and made intelligible. "Illusionary consciousness" (as I call both the processes and resulting understandings) is what makes people distinctive, accounting for their curiosity, their dreaming and inventiveness, their sly cunning, and most of all their love of intrigue and chicanery. While people also have a more detached, focused, anticipated, detailed, and concretely sensory "material consciousness," which they share with other living forms, it is their ability to create subjective illusions that separates humans from the rest of the natural world.

For the Kalapalo, the manner of seeing influences the kind of understanding that takes place. For this reason, they often allude to instances of material and illusionary consciousness by using visual imagery. Thus, the fixed, direct gaze and a lively, healthy, alert state of material consciousness are contrasted with the sideward glance and the oblique view, dreaming, and the hallucinatory vision of the narcotized shaman and the perilously sick, all instances of illusionary consciousness. But, more narrowly, the activities involving illusion (and especially "deception," as I translate the Kalapalo root *augï*, usually represented in the form *auginda*) are most directly associated with our ability to speak, and with the genealogical connections between various primordial tricksters and human beings, who have descended from them. These tricksters are, more than anything else, verbally deceptive beings. For the Kalapalo, language is inseparable from people's illusionary sensibility, and especially from their ability to deceive one another. It is the ability to speak, in other words, that makes human relationships ambiguous. People are often perceived to mask their feelings and identities in the course of their pursuits, and their goals, moreover, are imaginatively constructed within a verbal mode.

Ultimately, this prejudice in favor of deceit affects the ways Kalapalo perpetuate their distinctly Kalapalo way of living out their lives. As I will explain, Kalapalo deceit has less to do with truth or falsehood than with enactment of an illusionary relationship. Such a relationship does not depend upon validation and acceptance of responsibility, and may actually exist independently of them. In other words, illusionary relationships involve legitimate assertions of personal difference and of independence from society.

The Kalapalo idea of language as illusion and human thought as illusionary contributes to their sense of the inseparability of language and emotion in the operations of human life. All the stories that I present in this book, and the frequent and diverse deceptions by Kalapalo in daily life that I describe, express a view of emotions as *enacted and transacted through* language, rather than "expressed" or "represented by" language. This view of emotions has implications for understanding how, when people talk to one another in particularly creative ways, personal selfhood becomes socially contextualized.

Some of the stories I examine in this book suggest deep satisfaction with what is beautiful and harmonious in the world, a world of predictable, repeatable, successful events and actions. Others are sassy kinds of joking stories that show an ironic, mocking, rebellious push toward disorder. There are also melancholy myths that sadden and depress, showing the listeners a fantasy world of fear, hatred, and murderous violence directed against innocence. In others, careful, tightly controlled gestures lead to sudden, irrevocable decisions to act made in sorrow and defiance. And just as these stories seem to cover the broad range of feelings we would expect in a people's language arts, the characters are far from being mere representations of a few stereotyped ideas of feeling. Instead, individuals are plausibly motivated by emotions, and act in concrete, carefully situated dilemmas.

The stories in the narrative tradition that I present in translation in this book contain Kalapalo insights into deceptive forms of speech, various points of view taken by tricksters and by the targets of their deceit, numerous means of developing deceptions, and many artful ways of accomplishing or thwarting them. I offer here interpretations of the Kalapalo trickster traditions considered in their broader social milieu, side by side with the actual narratives, stories that continue to amuse, instruct, and direct the Kalapalo audiences, who love to listen to them, over and over. My approach, being discourse-focused and socially contextualized, is different from virtually all previous studies of tricksters, since I am above all concerned to show the connections between the content of trickster stories, their tellings, and lives as actually lived; each is an inseparable dimension of a single process during which meaning, at once personal and social, is constructed.

The widespread occurrence of trickster characters in folklore has long been an intriguing puzzle to anthropologists and folklorists, who have written insightfully—but exceedingly sporadically—about these mythological figures. Their interest in fact is closely linked to the origins and subsequent theoretical trends of American anthropology. The writings of Franz Boas and of Robert Lowie, and the famous collaborative work of Paul Radin, Karl Kerenyi, and Carl Jung are enduring classics, works that must be understood in the context of a special concern with the development of traditions among North American Indians. Like many of us working with myths today, these writers sought understanding of the specific historical and psychological processes out of which particular traditional images arose, images they tended to overgeneralize by using capitalized titles to designate them: Trickster, Coyote, Raven (names taken from original, specific characters in several mythological traditions).

Writers were impressed then, as now, by the contradictions in Trickster's moral character, by what Boas called the "troublesome psychological discrepancy" between the apparently incongruous attributes of the "culture hero" (who makes the world safe and secure for human life) and the "selfish buffoon" (who ludicrously attempts the inappropriate). These epithetical roles subsumed personal habits and proclivities. On the one hand are Trickster's creative insight and inventiveness in the service of human beings; on the other are his compulsive and thoughtlessly excessive behavior, his lust, gluttony, and, especially, his greed for unsuitable objects and relationships. The earliest explanations for this strange mix were framed in terms of a universal history of religion, and later, a universal human psychology. The anthropologist Daniel Brinton claimed that Trickster represented a "degeneration" and "debasement" of an original heroic deity. Arguing against this view, Boas and Lowie suggested that the trickster was a character type older than the serious culture hero, who began to appear in the traditions of more "advanced" societies only when it came to be appreciated that beneficial actions could proceed from an altruistic disposition. They argued that when people expected action to follow only from egocentric motives, a character who benefited human beings would not be associated with altruistic behavior. Thus, Boas suggested, benefits to human beings could only be created incidentally, almost by chance, by selfishly motivated action, not by altruism.

Paul Radin, agreeing with Boas's historical explanation, sought a closer understanding of the stories themselves by considering the specifically psychological implications of Trickster's strange character. Radin was especially interested in the Winnebago Trickster's uncontrolled impulses, which created the world and were portrayed as the source of all its confusion. While at first he paid careful attention to the ethnographic details in the stories, Radin's final conclusions were Jungian in both style and substance. Trickster, Radin suggested, represented an "absolutely undifferentiated human consciousness" not yet evolved into a rational capacity for distinguishing right from wrong. As for the stories themselves, he said, the frequent descriptions of Trickster behavior markedly contradicting the values of the society suggested that the tales were satirical forms of social protest.

In sum, these early attempts to understand Trickster focus upon "themes" and "elements" of character—what makes Trickster different from others—rather than upon the continuities, cohesions, and overall developmental changes in Trickster's experiences and actions.[1] Almost all recent writers have followed this approach, trying to systematize further the characteristics of trickster themes. While they have cast on these most elusive intelligences several thoughtful insights into the symbolic references of tricksters' ambiguities, these newer studies have a comparative focus, shared with the Boasians, that assumes a comprehensive class of characters who can be fairly easily identified in traditions around the world (or, more modestly, on a single continent). The capitalized title of Radin's Winnebago character (Trickster) has become a lower-cased label (trickster) for a category. The category includes a variety of figures, from many different places, who in some way conform to a particular type definition. The definition varies significantly from author to author. But as T. O. Beidelman points out, whatever the definition of such a class of mythological characters might be, we are invariably restricted by a functional theory of the significance of a few attributes of a character's demeanor or identity. These are usually the more sensational attributes, those that are—at least to an outsider—strikingly antisocial, marginal, or ambiguous.

It is true that tricksters are, in Kerenyi's words, the "spirit of disorder, the enemy of boundaries." But by singling out the paradoxical, we tend to distort—indeed, to fragment—the intelligence of these characters and to emphasize only those mythological scenes and activities in which the trickster's actions are most peculiar. As a consequence, the comparative studies of recent years are as restricted to interpretations of sensational themes and shocking images in myth as were the earlier studies.[2]

It is not that I disagree with the idea that tricksters are liminal characters that transform our modes of perceiving reality, or that they represent the deepest dilemmas of social life and express antisocial feeling. (As Jung put it, tricksters represent the *shadow* aspect of human feeling and experience.) Nor do I dispute the idea that tricksters' excessive bodily appetites, solitary habits, and profound inventiveness represent Freudian conflicts between sexuality and aggression on the one hand and civilization on the other. The reader will find most, if not all, the material in this book supporting these generalities. My point is that any such propositions reflect a vision of reality that is developed far from day-to-day experience, arising from very general theories about human psychology, and about myths and their symbolic functions. These ideas are given priority over the actual settings and activities with which the images in question are concerned. For tricksters, as for the crazily convoluted adventures they involve themselves in, a very different perspective is needed.

Clearly, we need to look more carefully at trickster stories, not just trickster images, of trickster action rather than trickster characters. We need to look especially at the manner in which a trickster's action, enacted and transacted, is developed as a biographical narrative. We should ask about the manner in which a trickster's psychological states are conceived and rendered apparent in discursive ways, and the interpersonal and interactive dimensions of such states. Especially important are the developmental aspects of the narratives: on the one hand, the changes in the characters' responses to the many recurrent situations of decision and choice, and, on the other, the continuities and repetitions in the characters' experiences. Given the speech-centeredness of the events in which tricksters are so often involved, what can be said about the verbal (syntactic, pragmatic, and especially strategic and discursive) continuities in a trickster's action?

Textual analysis of trickster stories has to be complemented by synthetic methods. We must search out the locally relevant contexts in which tricksters derive much of their significance, interpret the intentions behind the telling of trickster stories, and work toward understanding the relationships between such mythological characters and the day-to-day understanding and patterning of experience of the people who tell them. It is there, in the seemingly picayune details of living in a particular way in a certain time and place, that tricksters have the greatest interest and importance.

For Radin, the Winnebago Trickster is a desocialized being, who has broken all ties with human society, and who becomes almost fully undifferentiated and instinctual. Yet, Trickster is a historical character, insofar as he eventually learns (at the end of the cycle) who he is; in the words of the account, "He suddenly recollected the purpose for which he had been sent to the earth by Earthmaker." Radin is also plainly interested in Trickster as the source of interpersonal values and of the varying qualities of human personality:

creator and destroyer, giver and negator, he who dupes others and who is always duped himself. He wills nothing consciously. At all times he is constrained to behave as he does from impulses over which he has no control. He knows neither good nor evil yet he is responsible for both. He possesses no values, moral or social, is at the mercy of his passions and appetites, yet through his actions all values come into being. But not only he, so our myth tells us, possesses these traits. So, likewise, do the other figures of the plot connected with him: the animals, the various supernatural beings and monsters, and man.

Assuming the basic accuracy of Radin's characterization of this particular trickster, we might shift our focus away from the presence or absence of values and the pervasive ambiguity and liminality of Trickster, to address more concretely how his curiously depersonalized self can constitute a kind of personality. What are the implications of his undertaking contradictory and incompatible courses of action, of shifting between radically different feelings and attitudes? Does Trickster in fact act in such ways without experiencing distress or a sense of dilemma or absurdity? We might also ask how the Winnebago (and characters in Winnebago myths) compromise or solve problems resulting from those contradictory and incompatible courses of action. Is there any sense of conflict in such a trickster, or does he experience no sense of disorder, personal or otherwise? Here, the question is not about guilt or moral sensibility. I am concerned with the consequences of the ability of a trickster (or a person) to act inconsistently and experience inconsistencies, in other words, to actively participate in dissolving or scattering the self in order to achieve a new personal understanding, a new identity. Does this capacity for inconsistent action imply that the Winnebago Trickster essentially disclaims responsibility for his action? And, if so, how is his disavowed action represented? (Perhaps the change of Trickster to a body part—or, as with a particular Kalapalo trickster, to be simultaneously himself in one place and an animal in another—is such a representation.) Where else in Winnebago culture is disclaimed action found? Are Winnebago tricksters (Trickster and Hare) completely free and uninhibited experimenters?

To answer such questions, we might look more closely at traditional Winnebago culture. We might look further, if we could, at Winnebago understandings of creative imagination, of poetic and shamanistic processes, and of dreaming. For example, a most prominent cultural theme involved the development of an adult identity through fasting in puberty, which was connected with quests for visions and protective guardians. The young seeker was forced to live outside the family camp, lonely and fearful (at least as described in personal narratives) of sudden encounters with powerful beings. The grandmother (like the grandmother of the Winnebago trickster Hare) seemed to have figured in major ways as a personal guide and guardian during these experiences. Later, men sought visions of protective beings and hoped to be endowed by them with powers to be used in war. Could there have been expectations that during these crucial life events the world suddenly lost its normal structure, or that a destructured world came into being, and with it the self of the seeker became deconstructed? To what extent were the orgies of self-abandonment connected with war-bundle rituals attempts to reclaim these experiences of a destructured world? If we could answer these questions, we might understand more clearly the various ways personal Winnebago events achieved significance through the sacred trickster narratives.

To achieve deeper understanding of tricksters, then, we need to look at social life and at how personality processes are culturally constituted, particularly those personal events that are strikingly difficult and worrisome, or even traumatic. But even this is not enough. We have to focus attention on what are clearly special qualities of intelligence in the actions of these preeminently deceitful characters. As we shall see, the playful subterfuges of Kalapalo tricksters, their wildly speculative thought, concrete inventiveness, fascination with tinkering, and seemingly capricious and uninhibited experimentation are often belied by the careful planning and cunning foresight that accompany their experiments. The very attributes that make such tricksters inventive heroes and clownish fools in the first place are, after all, natural necessities of human intelligence, operating in practical, concrete, face-to-face relations that people negotiate all the time, sometimes with considerable immediacy.

I think it is generally true that deceptions, while often meticulously conceived in advance away from the scene where they will be enacted, and sometimes requiring elaborate staging and costuming, actually occur very quickly, and have to be perceived and interpreted moment-to-moment. Their penetration and interpretation thus require complementary wisdoms. For the shame and embarrassment that are felt, both by someone who has experienced being tricked and a trickster who has known failure, are grasped in a rapid moment of understanding and insight. Consequently, tricksters and their tricks are best engaged at close quarters, with the observer's attention sharply focused on the details of process and strategy.

Chapter 2

The Human Pedigree

At the center of the Kalapalo idea that deception and language some-how go together is the figure of Taugi, the most important Kalapalo trickster, though by no means the only one. Taugi is one of the chief characters in a distinctive cycle within Kalapalo mythology. This set of stories (called "stories about Kwatïngï" and "stories about Taugi") can be arranged in a linear, temporal order, beginning with the birth of the creator known as Kwatïngï, Taugi's grandfather, and ending with Taugi's creation of human beings. The stories also detail the adjust-ments Taugi makes to the earthly environment to make it a suitable setting for the successful reproduction of human life. The cycle un-folds the drama of the formation of characteristically human qualities of thought, as the Kalapalo understand them. This is accomplished through a narrative accumulation of the various feelings and powers of different mythic personages who make up the human pedigree. These feelings and powers, passed down from one generation of Dawn People to the next, culminate in the blossoming forth of human-ity in all its peculiar, passionate complexity.[1]

Stories About Kwatïngï

The cycle begins with the story called "Dyekuku's Daughter." A maiden, the daughter of the Trees Dyekuku and Agenggi, is confined in puberty seclusion, and has been mysteriously impregnated by Adyuakuegï the Fishing Bat, a powerful being (*itseke*) who lives in per-petual darkness in a region "beyond the sky." Kwatïngï, the child of this union between the Tree Woman and the Bat, figuratively unites human vitality and the physical changes that occur during human life, on the one hand, with motility on the other. During his infancy, Kwatïngï, though obviously alive, cannot move. In order to do so, he must be made to recognize his father. Most of the story recounts the steps taken by Dyekuku to make this happen. The reader will immediately notice the repetition of events in the central portion of the story. The sameness of these events is important and necessary for Kalapalo listeners because successful, goal-oriented action requires repetition of the action. In their stories, the fifth occurrence leads to final accomplishment. Thus, in "Dyekuku's Daughter," the messengers find the boy's father on their fifth excursion.

After the old leader Ulutsi told me this story, his nephew Muluku told me something more of the significance of the Tree People. He explained that as the first Dawn People were trees, so our lives begin in childhood like resilient sprouts; we grow towards "firmness," "ripening," and strength in adulthood; and end with an increasing "over-ripeness" and decay during old age. But, of course, growth and decay are characteristics we share with other living things; humans are also mobile. To this end, Fishing Bat, the symbol of mobility, is made to acknowledge his son, and Kwatïngï, who has been motionless, in turn recognizes and publically identifies his father.

Bat, the husband of the first bride, endowed her parents, Dyekuku and Agenggi, with color, setting a precedent and a very high standard for the payment that should be given for a young woman. The gift also has special aesthetic meaning for the Kalapalo. Much of their habitat consists of what they call *oti,* or "grasslands" (known in Brazil as *campo cerrado*), characterized by low scrub forests and extensive areas of open country that flood periodically. The beauty of the *cerrado* lies not in the topography of the landscape, which is exquisitely flat, nor in the light, which is harsh during the dry times of year and dim during the rainy season. After sunrise, the eye sees a shadowless and dull uniformity in the color values of plants, soil, and sky. Only water, abundant and flowing, sparkles in this landscape. Rather, the *cerrado*'s peculiar interest lies in its great variety of species; the different nests of wasps and bees and termites; the variety of birds, all with differing survival strategies. Especially fascinating are the forms and cycles of plant life that go through complex seasonal changes, from flowering and leafing, to fruiting and the falling of the leaves. Anything that interrupts the pervasive dullness of color is bound to capture the imagination, and this is just what seems to occur to the Kalapalo when they observe the magnificent floral displays of crimson, yellow, and purple that transform the cerrado trees at the end of the dry season. This is the time of year when, as the Kalapalo say, "the hands of Duck [the stars Castor and Pollux] are rising up ahead." This gesture signals the approach of the rains and the imminent appearance on the southwestern horizon of "Duck" itself (the stars Procyon and Canopus).

Ulutsi

Dyekuku's Daughter

Told by Ulutsi at Aifa. August 15, 1980.
Asterisks (*) in text refer to notes on pages 21–22.

There was a maiden, a maiden.
   "I'm going to bathe," she told her mother.
   A maiden.
It was late at night, it was very dark.
She appeared there, at the bathing place.   5
Someone touched her there.
   But she didn't realize it,
      she didn't realize it.
         No.
He had come quickly to her   10
   and *pupupu!* he flew away.
She had been made love to when he did that,
   she had been made love to very quickly,
      but she didn't see who had been there,
        no.   15
Because of what had happened to her,
   her parents began to notice a change in her appearance.
      She had become pregnant because of what had been done
      to her.
   "Something is wrong with our daughter," her parents said.
      Her mother, and her father as well.   20
Dyekuku is her father.
Agenggi is her mother.
Their daughter doesn't have a name,
   she's just called "Dyekuku's daughter."
      "Dyekuku's daughter," they say.   25
She was a maiden then.
Someone had come to her,
   he had done that quickly.
Her parents hadn't seen
   and she herself didn't know about him.   30
   She didn't know about Adyuakuegï the Fishing Bat.
He was the one who had been able to come to her that way,
   to her.
Now she was pregnant.
   She had been made pregnant.   35
She didn't know what had happened,
   no.
He had been invisible,
   he had.
   She had been impregnated so quickly.*   40

Following that it was fully developed.
    She didn't know anything about it,
        nor did her parents know,
           her parents.
    Her mother said,   45
      "How did this happen to you?
        You seem to have been made pregnant."
      "I don't know."
      "It seems to be so.
        Yes. It seems to be so."   50
      "Yes, it does."
      "What sort of person was it who touched you,
        what sort of person?"
      "I don't know.
        I don't know who, Mother," she answered.   55
      "No, you don't."
It was fully developed.
      By then it had developed fully.
    "Our daughter has just been made pregnant,"
      she said to her husband.   60
        "I see."
    By then it was fully developed.
    She called her mother to her.
      "My stomach is ready now to give birth.
      I'm in great pain."   65
        "All right."
When it was ready she gave birth.
    She gave birth,
      she gave birth.
Something came,   70
      a boy emerged.
        He emerged,
          he emerged.
    A boy,
      a penis on him.   75
        A boy.
Then she picked him up and nursed him.*
    He didn't move at all.
      The boy didn't walk,
        not at all.   80
    "There's something wrong with our grandson."
    He didn't move at all.
      He seemed to be dead.
        Nothing happened.

Then he continued to exist as if he were dead. 85
  "What's the matter with your son,
    why doesn't he walk?"
  "I don't know."
  "Who was it who came to you before to lie down with you?"
  her father asked.*
  "I don't know, I don't know. No. 90
    I don't have any idea what happened to me before,
      I don't know."
  "All right, you don't."
"We should take your son outside now so he can be seen,
    your son. 95
  You must do this because your son isn't walking.
    He doesn't walk."
  "All right," she answered.
"We should take our grandchild outside now so he can be seen,
    our grandchild. 100
      I want our grandchild to walk right now.
  Let's try to discover exactly who it was who made our daughter
  pregnant before.
    Let's do it right now!"
  "All right."
Then her father came out to the plaza. 105
  "Children," he told the others,
    "We still don't know anything about just who touched our
    daughter before,
      Children.
  Something must be done about it since your nephew doesn't
  seem to move for us at all," he said to his people.
  "That must be done so that afterward your nephew will really
  walk. 110
    I want your nephew to walk right now!" he told them.
      "I want it done, for their poor son's sake!"
  "All right!" they answered,
    "Let's do it!"
The next day, 115
    to another settlement.
  To one of human beings,
    to human beings.
  Well, "What are you here for?"
  "I've come here to get you, to get you." 120
  "You have? For what reason?"
  "Someone just asked me to get you.
    He doesn't know who made his daughter pregnant,
      he doesn't know.

Because she wants her son to walk,   125
    I've come to all of you.
Because his mother really wants to have everyone do
something,
    all of you are going to do it.
He doesn't walk.
    So later, when he is with her his father will call to him.   130
After, when he is with her.
    His father will call to him.
        He will call him away from their daughter."
"All right.
    Come on, let's all go!"   135
Then the next day they presented themselves.
    "Hoh hoh hooh!"*
His mother had brought him into the plaza.
As they arrived,
    "Hoh hoh hoh!"   140
Now, they came, approaching the others!
    "Hoh hoh hooh!"
        They had arrived!
    "Hoh!"
    "Let's go!"   145
Each one of them had small arrows,
    they had small arrows which Dyekuku had made for them.
        Yes, small arrows.
They held them up to the boy.
    He sat over there across from them,   150
        in the plaza.
    "Hoh!" So they came there.
"Come get these, my little one," someone said.
    "Come get these."
    "Come get these."   155
        Iiiiii although each one tried to make him move,
            nothing happened.
He didn't walk.
    "Come get these."
    "Come get these."   160
He didn't move toward them at all,
    no.
    There was only one person who could do it.
"No, they just can't do it!"
    ("Now who can it be?")   165
"You may leave now.
    Go away.

Because of this I sent for you.
I'm doing this for our grandson."
    "All right."   170
The next day,
        to yet another settlement of human beings.
    Afterward, the messenger presented himself.
    "What are you here for?"
    "I've just come to get you, to get you.   175
        Our parent sent me."
    "Very well, what does he want?"
    "The one who filled his daughter's womb is a person who
    doesn't walk.
        He doesn't walk!
            Not at all!   180
    Your appearance before him . . . your appearance before him
    is because of his relatives . . . his grandparents wanting him
    to walk,
        wanting him to walk.
            That's why I've come to get you now.
    Hoping that he will walk, his grandfather has made some small
    arrows.
        They were made to be given to everyone.   185
    Showing them to the boy, each man will go toward him.
        'Go ahead,' his grandfather will say to everyone.
    The boy will be seated opposite everyone with our daughter
    while each man comes into the plaza.
    Then while her son sits with her, he will be called away.
        He will be called away from Dyekuku's daughter," the
        messenger told them.   190
            "All right! Come on, let's do it just as you say!"
Again they presented themselves.
    The next day they appeared again.
        They arrived when the sun was here.*
    He, the son was there with his mother.   195
"Uuh hoh hoh!"
        They all came toward him.
One by one they stepped forward.
    "Come get these, my little one." "Come get these, my little
    one."
    "Come get these." "Come get these."   200
Nothing happened!
    Nothing.
"Now, have we done all we could?"
    "Well, you should leave.

It isn't any of your people, none of your people.
  Go away, it isn't your people."
"What sort of person was it who touched his daughter before?"
they asked each other. "I don't know." "It wasn't any of you so
go away."
After that they left right away.
  Those who had presented themselves went away.
The next day the messenger appeared once again
somewhere else,   210
    at another place again.
  "Hoh!" to that place again.
"Why are you here?"
"I've just come to get you, to get you."
"Why are you doing this?"   220
"What's-his-name's, Dyekuku's, solution for his grandson,
Dyekuku's.
His grandson's solution.
  That boy is someone who doesn't walk, he's a person who
  doesn't walk."
  "Very well, very well."
"Take these small arrows of his.   225
  They're to be shown to him, to him."
    "All right!"
"Everyone will show them to him, and after they are shown,
  tigitigitigi* perhaps the boy will move, he will move."
    "All right!"   230
"Because of that everyone will call him away from her.
  While he sits with her,
    he'll be called away from Dyekuku's daughter," the
    messenger told them.
"All right! Come on, let's go as you say!"
And again people presented themselves as before.   235
  The boy was across from them again in his place.
    He sat with his mother.
  "Ah hoh!" to that place.
"All right, my little one, come get these."
"Come get these." "Come get these." "Come get these."   240
  But nothing happened,
    nothing.
"Why is he still just the way he's been?" his relatives asked each
other.
"From just where could the person who touched our daughter
before have come?" they continued,
  "From just where could the person who touched our
  daughter before have come?"   245

The next day a messenger appeared again.
    "All right, go once again."
      To another place,
        to another place.
    And once again, 250
      "Why are you here?"
      "I have come to get you, I have."
      "You have? For what reason?
      "Dyekuku's solution for his grandson. He doesn't walk at all.
      Because he must have him walk . . . 255
        because he must have him walk he wants all of you to
        present yourselves there," the messenger told them,
          "so let's all go now."
      "All right!" 260
      "He'll be called away from his mother."
      "All right!"
      "We should all go now," the messenger said to them.
      "There are some small arrows there for you to take along, some
      small arrows."
      "All right."
They approached once again.
    "Hoh hoh!" they appeared once again, "Ahaah hoh!" 265
      There were so many people!
      So they presented themselves once again.
    So, once again to him,
      once again opposite him.
      "Take these, my little one," someone said. 270
      "Take these." "Take these," someone said. "Take these,"
    someone said. "Take these."
Nothing happened!
    Nothing.
    "What's wrong with him? What's wrong with him?
    From where could the person who touched our daughter have
    come?" 275
      "What sort of person is he?"
    "No one knows."
"All right, go right away to the Other Side.
    The Other Side.
    To him." 280
      "All right!"
    "To Adyuakuegï the Fishing Bat."
      "All right!"
    The messenger came there.

Then, the Other Side.   285
    "So, why are you here?"
    "I've come to get you all, I have."
    "You have? For what reason?"
    "Dyekuku's very solution for his grandson."
    "This is it, this is it. This is the correct place, Children.   290
    This is the correct place.
    Yes, yes, it was I who came to her before.
        It was I who came to her before," he told them,
            "Come on, let's all go as you say."
    Small arrows were given to him to take along.   295
        "All right!"
"Hoh hoh!" once again they appeared.
    Once again they appeared,
        well, they all arrived.
As they came,   300
    tigitigi, he began to shake himself.
        "Hoh hoh!"
            Now, our son sat with his mother.
Fishing Bat came toward him,
    "Hoh!" they came,   305
        and as they came the boy sat there . . .
            Now, he stood up!
                He stood right up.
Yes, tigitigi, tigitigitigitigi . . .
        finally!   310
    Tigitigitigitigi
"He really walked,
    our grandson really walked!" they said.
    Tigitigitigitigi
        as the other came tigi tigi tigi tigi   315
            HE DIDN'T STOP AT ALL!
Fishing Bat showed the boy the small arrows.
    He himself showed them to him.
    Pok! his mother pulled him back.
    As he came to get the arrows pok!   320
        she pulled him back,
        and so he went more slowly tigi tigi tigi.*
"That person over there is the one who touched our daughter
before, he is.
    I'm sure he is. When our child was secluded before," her
    mother told Dyekuku.
        "That person over there was the one who came to our
        daughter before, that person over there."   325
            "All right."

Then he learned all about what that person had done.
  "I was the one who did that before, who came to her before.
  That's why you didn't know what sort of person it was who
  impregnated your daughter," Fishing Bat told them.
"He's certainly the one.   330
    Their own leader did that.
  He himself was certainly the one who came to her before,
    he, before."
  "Yes he was,
    he was."   335
"You may go if you wish. You will leave with my daughter.
  You will go to your own place,
    you will go to your own place.
      At last!" he told him.
"You may go if you wish. You will leave with my daughter.   340
  You will go to your own place,
    you will go to your own place.
  My young relative," he said,
    "Take your sister away,
      take your sister away."   345
  "Well, I will, I will."
"All right now."
  After he said that to her father,
    he gave him a toucan feather headdress.
  "Go ahead, you must be sure to take this."   350
    He gave it to her father.
  "Go ahead, take this,"
    he gave a cacique feather headdress to her mother,
      to Agenggi.
  "Go ahead now," *pok*. The headdress fell before her.   355
    "Very well!"
  "Go ahead now," to someone else, *pok*. The thing fell before
  another person.
  Still another person, another relative,
    to Agate.
  "Very well," it was taken.   360
  Then *pok*, a cacique feather headdress fell before yet another
  person.
  "Here, take this. It represents my sister."
    "Very well."
      To Afigu.
  Another toucan feather headdress.   365
    "Take this."

Because of that Angakwaumbungu is a magnificent color.
Next, "Go ahead," "Very well."
    A toucan feather headdress as before.
Since then Sike is like the others.   370
    Teh he he's a beautifully red color!
He's a relative.
    He's another brother of her father.
That was all.*
Someone else still,   375
    to another person, look.
    He was given *ugi,* the leader's seat.
    It was made from a turtle shell.
        It was a deception indeed.*
"Well, that's all. I must be going now."   380
    "Go away. Go, go.
        Go with your son."
            "All right."
They began to leave, they went away.
    They went far away to the Other Side.   385
"Our daughter, you will leave us."
"All right, I will leave you."
"I was the one who spoke to you before about doing this so we
could animate our child,
    since he didn't move before,
    unlike a human being,"   390
        her father said, he told her.
            "All right!"
Then they went on.
    So, they went on right after all that happened.
        They went on.   395

It's over.
    That's just what happened.

Notes to "Dyekuku's Daughter"
lines
32–40   Ulutsi refers to the ability of powerful beings to impregnate women
        immediately, in contrast with the need for a human male repeatedly
        to donate semen, which eventually coagulates into an embryo.
77   A sign that the mother of a child whose father is unknown will rear
        her newborn. Had she not picked him up, the infant would have
        been buried alive.
89   "To lie down with," a euphemism for sexual relations used in formal
        "controlled" speech, particularly among relatives by marriage and
        by dignitaries such as Ulutsi, who told this story.

137   The greeting cheer of visitors, which is responded to in kind by their hosts.

194   That is, early in the morning, after dawn.

229   Ulutsi moves his upper body in a stiff shaking motion, as an infant might when grasping a rattle.

322   As a consequence of this pulling back, human children take a long time learning to walk.

349–374   The wealth that was given in payment by Fishing Bat to his parents-in-law and their siblings was red and yellow feather headdresses, from which resulted the magnificent flowers of the trees of the central Brazilian *cerrado*, whose red, yellow, and magenta blooms distinguish the landscape from the end of the dry season (Kofongo), to the time of heavy rains (Tute). Each of the names Ulutsi mentioned, Dyekuku, Agenggi, Agate, Afigu, and Sike, designates a particular species of tree with brilliantly colored blooms.

377–379   Dyekuku's youngest brother demanded payment, and was given a leader's stool. Rather than having been carved from a valuable hardwood, the stool was the turtle shell from which the feathers for the ornaments had been plucked. This sequence is an allusion to the Kalapalo notion that turtles formerly were feathered creatures.

In his maturity, Kwatïngï initiated the powerful processes that resulted in human life as the Kalapalo now know it. The long and intricately detailed story called "Kwatïngï" describes how he made women from wood, giving them in marriage to the Black Jaguar as substitutes for his own daughters. These events led to the birth of the twins Sun (*Giti*) and Moon (*Ngune*), or, to use their adult names, Taugi and Aulukuma, and eventually to Taugi's creation of human beings. There are a number of striking and distinctive characters in this rich and complex story, which is told most elaborately by the older hereditary leaders (*anetau*). As representatives of their people, these elders offer up something of an origin myth, which includes an explanation of why different groups of people behave toward each other as they do. Versions of "Kwatïngï" turn up in all published collections of myths from the Upper Xingu Basin. As a story concerned with the origin of human beings, "Kwatïngï" provides a referenced grounding for successful relations between Kalapalo and other Upper Xingu residents, as well as between the Xinguanos and foreign visitors.

The harsh vigor and concentrated drama of the opening section of the story pits the obtuse ferocity of the Jaguar against the intelligent sensitivity of Kwatïngï. The transitional journey of his surrogate daughters made of wood is highly repetitive (much like "Dyekuku's Daughter") and helps to clarify the intentions behind their father's earlier activities. Like all Kalapalo journeys, this one contrasts two settings for varieties of consciousness: the focused, yet detached materiality connected with learning about the pleasures and hazards of hunger, thirst, and sexual desire, versus the peculiarly hallucinatory and histrionic events in the settlement of the Jaguar, involving deception, death, and mourning. A series of outbursts between the twins Sun and Moon bring the story to a close. Together, these events lead the listener through many distinct moods, senses of place, and a wonderful variety of personages. The Kalapalo title makes clear, though, that even when Kwatïngï is not the focal character within a restricted course of action, he is the instigator of all the story's action, action that demonstrates the myriad possibilities that emerge from his shiningly creative, imaginative intelligence.

Certain psychological elements, especially recognizable in the longer, more detailed stories, are always important within the overall explanatory framework, the patterning of events, and the narrative structure of a Kalapalo story. How the storyteller develops these elements constitutes the particular narrative movement from the initial situation to the final resolution—predictable or mildly unexpected, successful or not. This situation tends to be one from which an uncertainty arises about the consequences of a local character's feeling. Normally, the uncertainty comes from the fact that the feeling in question (a man's confusion about who impregnated his daughter, for example) needs reformulation and channeling as an expressed reason for further action (to make his infant grandson move), as well as resolution or completion through planning and goal-orientation (finding the father). Thus, the initial feeling creates a concrete reason for formulating a specific goal, and the goal itself is achieved by a pair of elements: the plan followed by a course of action (usually described as a series of repeated events). What makes these stories plausible even when they seem almost excessively bizarre and fantastic (a woman is raped by a bat) is that there are anticipated formulas and fully structured and consistent personalities. Predicaments are resolved by the decisions people make about action. The decisions, in turn, require redefinitions of situations, the careful formulation of plans, or, in the case of a necessity to act very quickly, the nearly instant ability to respond decisively.

All the qualities of intelligence apparent in this scheme—Dyekuku's concrete motivation, his planning, foresight, perseverance, and reasoning by analogy—are passed on to Kwatïngï. In Kwatïngï, however, we see a creative imagination associated with design and craftsmanship, an imagination more complex than Dyekuku's. Kwatïngï is more explicitly characterized by the feelings of *funita* ("loving," "cherishing," "compassionate") and *ifutisu* ("respecting"), an ideal of inner control, dignity, and generosity. These feelings are concretely realized as actions in stories concerning Kwatïngï and several of his grandsons, when he provides discreet but decisive assistance and protection to these youths.

Kwatïngï's greatest masterpieces are the Made Ones, the wives of the Black Jaguar. Fearing for the lives of his real daughters, who themselves refuse to marry the beast, Kwatïngï creates substitutes from various plant materials. The Made Ones pass on to human women the sensuality of human reproductive power, and of meals shared with men, as well as *funita* and *ifutisu*, characteristic of the reciprocity in Kalapalo sexual relations, and which enable families to persist and develop outward, establishing connections with one another. The Kalapalo make clear that these vital tensions—hunger, sexuality, *funita*, and *ifutisu*—are the foundation of interpersonal relationships, for with the creation of the Made Ones human social life begins. While Kwatïngï is not directly present in the action that follows, everything that happens to these daughters on their journey to their Jaguar husband is a consequence of his song spells, which Kwatïngï blows to them while he remains seated in the doorway of his house, quietly observing them all as they journey to the distant settlement.

By creating the first women, Kwatïngï originated human sexual passion, reproductive capacity, and reciprocity between the sexes. Male passion is a consequence of the form the Made Ones were given. Their luxuriant black hair, nut-brown eyes, and white, evenly spaced

Kefesugu and Meki

teeth complement their perfectly modeled, hairless genitals, which are beautified by the bark pubic ornaments that Kwatïngï makes for the daughters as the ultimate preparation for their erotic role. As Kambe's story tells us so clearly, the force of the erotic desire men feel for such women takes precedence over whatever the women might feel for the men. For women, this story implies, what is important is how capable men are as husbands or lovers. This capability is judged far less in terms of the passion men engender, than it is in terms of a man's ability to provide suitable food and to make love in an acceptable manner—that is, as Kalapalo women would like, quickly and painlessly.

During their journey to their future husband Nitsuegï, the Black Jaguar, the Made Ones encounter a variety of creatures who insist on making love to them in exchange for food. While the Egrets and the Falcons are excellent fishermen and pleasing lovers, the women discover that their encounters with these birds are gentle interludes. Other fishermen they encounter are unappealing boors. Armadillo has left his desire home with Mother, Black Vulture and Turkey Vulture serve them rotten food, the two Kingfishers are slobs, wearing scratchy necklaces and ejaculating excessively, Caracara has a hoarse voice, Eel Hawk is a liar, and Crake can't walk properly after relations with one of the women—perhaps he is too weak for lovemaking. Worst of all is the rapist, Weasel. While all of these men (except the Falcons, Egrets, and Maned Wolf, at least in this version) have something offensively wrong with them, the Made Ones are always willing to receive food from them and to reciprocate with sexual favors. From their father Kwatïngï, the Made Ones have learned *ifutisu,* as they show by their controlled and modest courtesy.

Nitsuegï, the Black Jaguar who is husband of the two surviving Made Ones, represents in the extreme the creature the Kalapalo consider most dangerous to human beings. Jaguars are often heard calling on Kalapalo land, their tracks are seen around settlements and along the rivers, and they are not infrequently encountered by people camped at night in the forests or close to water. Needless to say, they were especially frightening when people were armed only with bows and arrows.

In the Beginning, Nitsuegï and his followers—other *ngene,* or land animals who are "furred"—hunted for human flesh, picking off people who huddled miserably for protection in the cleared spaces around phosphorescent termite mounds, the only places in the world where there was any semblance of light. As we learn in the stories of the subsequent exploits of the twins, Nitsuegï's oldest son Taugi gives relief to human beings by providing them with daylight and fire, and happily creates in the furred animals a desire for the flesh of one another rather than for that of human beings.

The twins are born from the union between Itsangitegï, the youngest of the Made Ones, and Nitsuegï. These brothers, especially Taugi, strikingly combine the human attributes passed on to their mother from Dyekuku and Kwatïngï (creative imagination, technological inventiveness, compassion, love, respect) with the violent character of their self-centered, unsympathetic father. The result is creativity and invention that can be extended sympathetically to people, but which can as often be steeped in self-centered violence. The twins' moral sensibilities are ambiguous, or more exactly, they refuse to take responsibility for what they do and seem to feel no guilt. While they act against powerful beings in favor of humanity, from their activities arise many bothersome things (mosquitoes, menstruation, material decay) and all that is dangerous, even dreadful, about human life (hatred between even the closest of kin, witchcraft, the permanence of death).

Returning to the cycle, we come to Taugi's indirect impregnation of the surviving Made One, his "substitute mother" Tanumakalu. As she walks to and from the house carrying manioc balls to be dried outdoors, she crosses over some arrows Taugi has made and deliberately placed in her path. From each of these arrows originates a class of human beings: the Xinguano People, the Christians, and the Fierce People. The Fierce People, unpredictably and unreasoningly violent, help Taugi destroy the original hegemony of furred creatures over human beings. Nitsuegï's followers, the furred animals, are prevented from transforming themselves into human form, given a taste for the flesh of their fellow animals, and dispersed by Taugi. In all ways, they are made less and less powerful, less broadly involved in the world of human concerns, and more narrowly involved with their own kind. In contrast, Taugi directs human beings to their appropriate territories, endowing them with the weapons that will thenceforth stereotype them. Here, in the human sphere, boundaries are created; antagonisms between people replace battles between humans and other more powerful entities. Humanity as it is now constituted begins; humanity is the cumulative result of a pedigree that began with the union between Fishing Bat and Dyekuku's Daughter. Humans are animate and mortal, mobile, creative, and compassionate. They exhibit an intense capacity for eroticism, which not only enables them to reproduce, but which is the source of some of their deepest conflicts. Human beings are verbal and therefore especially deceptive and capable of violent and destructive malevolence.

Kambe

Kwatïngï

Told by Kambe at Aifa. January 1979.

Notes appear on pages 79–81.

"My Children," he said,
   "My Children,"
      to his children,
         to his offspring.
      His offspring were female,   5
         female children.
   Now, I don't remember their names.
      A female child, a female child, a female child . . .
         [holds up four fingers] this many, he had four children.
            His children were female,   10
               Kwatïngï's children.
      He looked like us,
         like us.
      He was human in appearance but a powerful being,
         he was a powerful being.   15
"I'll be going to look for net materials," he said.
   Like this thing here, which we use to kill fish.
      This thing here is what it was.
         Like this thing here.
   "I'll be going to look for net materials, Children," he said. 20
      "All right," they answered.
He began walking on the path,
   far away on the path going toward the Jagamï settlement.
      Ñatasa was Kwatïngï's settlement.
He walked to a distant place,   25
   far, far away.
      To Adyuwatafa.
         It's called Adyuwatafa.
      Isatafa material for nets is found there.
         He took a carrying basket with him.   30
When he got there he cut at it,
   tsuk he cut off the leaves,
      the leaves of *isatafa*,
         the plant's leaves, *tsuk*
            and he rolled them up.   35
   While he was doing that someone was coming toward him,
      a Jaguar was coming toward him while furred animals were
      calling,
         furred animals were calling to each other,
         furred animals were calling to each other.

Then their leader found him, 40
   Nitsuegï found him.
      The Jaguar found him,
        another kind, a huge jaguar found him.
         Kwatïngï was still *tsuk* cutting off the leaves.
While he stood there the Jaguar was moving toward him. 45
   The others began to come toward him,
      they were sneaking up on him.
They had almost reached him while he was so engaged!
   They sneaked up a bit further,
      and ran up to him. 50
There they were, watching him.
   Furred animals were watching him,
      the followers were watching him.
        Keeping themselves hidden deep in the forest, they had
        surrounded him.
        His basket was still empty, 55
         still not filled up with net materials,
           with the *isatafa* leaves he was gathering.
Finally the Jaguar arrived.
   "Here, here, here," Nitsuegï went.
      "Here, here, here now," his followers answered. 60
        "Here, here, here," went the one who had called to them.
With his long feathered arrow Kwatïngï set his bow,
   with his long feathered arrow he set his bow.
      Ndïkï, he aimed at the furred animals.
Creeping up on Kwatïngï the other went, Nitsuegï went, 65
   creeping up behind a large tree.
Kwatïngï stood there aiming his bow.
   He had twisted some poor stuff like this for a bow cord,*
      in order to shoot his arrow at the Jaguar to kill him.
   "My young relative," Kwatïngï went, 70
      "My young relative, back there are some ill-favored women
      I've found,*
        offspring of mine whom I've found."
He had some children,
   children of his who were women,
      he was thinking of those children of his. 75
        Why, to have them be the Jaguar's wives,
         his wives.
"Back there are some ill-favored women I've found, my young
relative," he went,
   "My young relative, it would be nice for you to marry them,"
   he told him,
      "Marry them." 80

"Very well," Nitsuegï answered,
    "Come stand here," he said. *Bok.*
His bow was *madyafi* the black bow.*
    Madyafi.
Kwatïngï climbed onto it *bok,*   85
    booh! and the owner shot him away,
        Nitsuegï shot him away.
Very late in the afternoon,
    while the sun was still in the sky,
        he shot him away to his settlement,   90
            to Ñatasa.
Kwatïngï landed right outside his settlement,
    not too far away.
Keh! He came weeping,
    he came weeping,   95
        to where his children sat waiting for him.
Since it was dusk by now, they must have been resting outside.
    His children were waiting for him.
Then from where they sat they greeted him.
    He didn't answer.   100
    "Should they go?
    I don't know!"
He looked at them.
    Because Nitsuegï had shot him away he had just appeared
    there like that.
"Since he wants them, they should probably go . . . No, let him
remain as he is.   105
    All his followers are furred animals."
He arrived beside his daughters.
    "Wherever were you, dear Father?" his children went,
        the women said.
        "Wherever were you, dear Father?"   110
Then they came up to him.
    "Wherever were you, dear Father?"
        "Father," they kept saying.
    "Don't ask me.
    I don't want anything to happen to you, my children,   115
        I will not do it, no."
        "No, you won't," they answered.
He wept while he sat with his children.
    He was worried the Jaguar would crave them if he sent them,
        he would want to eat them.   120
    "He might eat them,
        the powerful being, the Jaguar," he wept.

Finally there were no longer tears in his eyes,
　his weeping had ended.
　　He still sat there.　　　　　　　　　　　　　　125
"Children," he said to them,
　"The truth is I have promised you to your younger brother,
　your younger brother."
"Have you?" they answered,
　"We can't do it," they said.　　　　　　　　　　130
　　"It's too far to travel," they said to him.
His children refused.
　It was so far away!
They would have to travel to Faukugu,
　they would have to travel to Sagifengo.　　　　135
"It's too far to travel," one of them said.
"I can't do that, you must make her go,
　make her go."
"I can't do that, you must make her go,
　make her go."　　　　　　　　　　　　　　140
"I can't do that," another one said,
　"Make her go," about her younger sister.
　"I can't do that."
Then there was their last-born.
　"I can't do that," she repeated.　　　　　　　145
He was thinking hard.
　He was disappointed with them.
　　Because they wanted to make a lie of what he had told that
　　person he spoke of.
"It happened that I promised your younger brother before,
Children.
　Your younger brother," he went.　　　　　　　150
　　"I promised him, Children," he told them.
He was thinking hard.
　"Is there anything I can do?" he asked himself.
　　"I'm disappointed with my children, with my children."
Following that he went to his older brothers,　　155
　he went to what's-his-name,
　he went to Wafusaka,
　　his brother.
Wafusaka the Tarantula,
　he went to the long-fingered one.　　　　　　160
　　He himself.
　　　Wafusaka is his name.
There is also another one,
　Wafasagï,
　　Wafasagï the younger brother, as well.　　　165

"I should go see Wafusaka."
　　That was his brother.
　　　Kwatïngï's brother.
　　Also Atuta the spinner, the Orb Spider.
　　　The one who spins his net extending far away on the trees,　170
　　　　the spider who does that.
　　　　　He himself.
　　Also Ngafangi the honey maker, the Black Bee.
　　Also that other one, Adyua the Fishing Bat.
"Our children refuse us, they're lazy.　175
　　They're lazy, they won't go," he said.
　　　"To our nephew, Nitsuegï."
　　　　He told the others about the Jaguar.
　　"They're lazy.
　　　'Opuh! It's too far to travel.'　180
　　　I just told them, 'Go to him,' to our nephew, but they
　　　　refused me."
Then they all went to cut down some trees.
　　He took his axe and went away.
　　　He picked it up and went away.　185
He cut down a *wagu* tree,
　　it was a big *wagu* tree.
　　　Tuk! Tuk! It fell down.
　　　　He tied this one up.
　　Then he cut down another one.
　　　He wanted to cut an *iku* tree down to make a body.*　190
　　　　This was another kind.
When that was done,
　　he divided one in half.
　　He divided it, *mbisuk.*
　　　And then he modeled legs, thighs, and he made arms.　195
And once again he divided a tree he had cut down.
From the two pieces,
　　the two pieces,
　　　once again he made bodies from the two pieces of the *iku*
　　　tree.
　　　　This was a young one and there was still another one.　200
He worked on the *iku,*
　　he split that one.
　　　Teh, she was perfect when he made her!
He put on this kind of thing, ears.
　　Teh, they were beautiful!　205
　　Teh, they were perfect when he made them!
　　　They were magnificent when he made them.

Then he put on their teeth,
  teh, of beautiful dark quartz.*
  "Smile."
  Their teeth were black.
  "That's ugly."
Then *katugua* the mangabeira.
  The seed of that tree.
  Then they became *teh*, beautiful.
    When he had finished they were beautiful.
    Then it was this way, look at me.
    That was finished.
"I've got to do something about their lack of hair."
Next, he took *nakafugu*, fiber of the false-burity to make their
  long hair.
Then he put that on, *nakafugu*, the white kind.
  It wasn't any good.
  Teh, it was too white when he did that.
  "Let it be," he went.
  He took it off, *biuk*.
    "I've got to do something," he kept thinking about it.
Well, he went away to Kugekuegï, tiny women who live
underwater,
    underwater.*
    He went underwater to get women's hair.
    He sent Afosoko the Black Water Bug.
      Because he was different from us,
        he was able to go get it for his brother.
        Kwatïngï made him go get it,
          he made him go to the Little People.
      Then Water Bug gave the women's hair to him.
"All right now,"
  he put it on.
Teh, it was beautiful, straight like mine, what he put on, look.
Again, he did the same with the curly kind.
  Teh, he gave some of the curly kind to one of them.
And once again, the curly kind.
The second one had this kind of hair, the younger sister who
  was made of *iku*.
The younger sister's hair was also created.
  She—look—the older twin had the straight kind like this,
  look.
The other one had curls,
  the curling kind of hair.
And so they were finished.
  Teh, they had become beautiful.

210

215

220

225

230

235

240

245

Then he cut some pieces of *tsangakafi*, the large bamboo.*
    "I'll go see your younger brother right away, Children," he said.   250
    "I'll go see your younger brother.
        I want him to make love to you."
He went away to get him.
    He came to get Idyali the Tapir.
He came inside his house.   255
    "Well, Uncle.
        Linger here awhile," Tapir said to him.
            "Very well," Kwatïngï answered.
"Now, I've come to sit down with you, my child," he told him.
"What for?" Tapir went,   260
    "What for?" he asked.
"I have children for you to see."
    He wanted Tapir to lie down with his children.
"All right," Tapir answered,
    "That will be done."   265
        He wanted to try to penetrate their vulvas.
"I'm returning now," Tapir said,
    "How nice!"
        The procured one went with Kwatïngï to pierce them.
        Teh! "Oh, yes!" he said.   270
Then at dusk, it was already dusk and the sun had set,
    the house door was shut *mbuk*.
In the darkness on the far side of the house their hammocks
had been hung apart from the others,
    just like your own.*
        Side by side together.   275
            The younger and the older were both there.
After they lay down he entered.
    He entered the house now that they were lying in their
    hammocks.
    He was inside the house.
He spread her legs.   280
He entered her while she held onto his penis.
He cracked her open and she died.
Once again with the one beside her,
    he lay down that way again,
        and when he tried to spread her legs . . .   285
        she died.
Once again, he did the same to the next one,
    the younger one.
Again, he tried to make love to the younger sister, the one who
had been made of *iku* wood.

"They're still too loose, the way I tied them together with agave
    cord." 290
Then *ngiu*, the youngest sister died after Tapir tried to pierce her.
    So these other two died.
      There were none left.
Once again the next day.
  But this time he did it with *wegufi* wood.* 295
    To do that he went to cut down some trees once again.
    He was going to cut down another kind as well.
  Then *fata*, the white kind called *fata*.
    He cut down one *fata* tree and then another one.
    However, this time he made sure to make even more of them
    than he had before. 300
    Next he shaped their thighs, he then shaped all the parts of
    their bodies.
The next day he worked on them until they were finished.
  Teh, once again he created them beautifully.
    Then he put on their teeth.
    Then again. This time however one had dark skin. 305
      Her body was made that way, that one.
  She herself is Itsangitsegï, who is still in the sky.
  Tanumakalu her younger sister is her twin.
    Tanumakalu is the name of the person to whom we go when
    we die.
      Only one. 310
  Then he went again,
    but this time the tying material was not like before.
  Before he tied them up with agave cord,
    he tied up their muscles.
      So they would be able to keep bearing offspring. 315
  Now he tied them up as tight as he could.
    He redid them correctly, not like before.
He went to Tifigu the Philodendrons,
    Tifigu.
      He came inside their house. 320
  "Uncle, linger here awhile."
  "Very well," Kwatïngï answered,
    "I have come to speak to you all now, Children," he said to
    them,
      "I've come to you."
  "All right," they answered, 325
    Why do you come this way to us?"
  "So you can tie my children together,
    so you can tie my children together."

"All right," they went,
    "Since we've always known how to do that." 330
Then he did it for Kwatïngï.
    "You must go, my young relative," Kwatïngï said to Tapir,
        so Tapir went there.
Then in the late afternoon,
    as it was becoming dark once more he went to lie down with
    them. 335
        Where again they had hung their hammocks apart from the
        others.
    He came to them, *pok*,
        he lay down together with one of them and she was
        completed.
    Lying down together he did to one what he had done before
    with his penis,
        he made love to her. 340
After he was finished, he came to the next one,
    to the younger sister.
        To make love once again,
           and he pierced her.
Then, the one who had been carved from *fata* wood, 345
    and then again her younger sister.
        They lay down together.
           Once again he made love to her and he pierced her.
           The youngest one was secure.
              That was all. 350
"Since it's wrong for people to still be without pubic ornaments,
    I'll make it so they will always wear pubic ornaments."
He went to Kagafïgï the Lianas,
    he went to the forest.
Then, "I'll go to your younger brothers," he said. 355
    So he went away,
        "I'm going to go to your younger brothers."
Tikiii, he entered the house,
    he entered the house.
    "Children," he said, 360
        "As you see, I am indeed here to ask you something, I am."
    "Very well," they answered,
        "Why have you come to see us, Uncle?" they asked.
    "I've come to have you be with my children.
    I want you to be their pubic ornaments." 365
    "You do, do you?" the Lianas went.
        "Listen a moment," they answered.

"Listen a moment. Our brothers aren't the ones.
    They won't do it. They don't want to go back with our
    parent."
        "Very well."   370
"Uncle," one of the Lianas said to him,
    "It can't be us, no.
        Beware that your sons will wrestle poorly,
            that they will wrestle poorly."
Kwatïngï said to him, "Very well.   375
As you see, I came to you just so you could say that to me.
    Stay here, my son," he said to Liana,
        "Stay here."
"Go to that other person,
    to your niece Agëfïgïtisï the Spiny-Leafed.   380
        "Go to your niece, she herself is the one you should go
        to."
            "Very well," he answered.
Once again he went away.
        Once again he arrived at a house.
"Well, Uncle, stay here," they went.   385
"Very well," he answered.
    "As you see, I have come here to ask you something,
    Children."
"What?" they asked him,
    "Why do you come to us with all these cousins of mine?"
"Since you have asked, I will tell you, my child.   390
    I want to have you be on your descendants."
"Very well," she agreed.
    And she brought some bark to him.
"Very well," she said, "Very well.
    Do as you wish, Uncle," she said.   395
"So we shall be. We will be placed on your children.
    We want pubic ornaments to be on the children.
Now go once again, this time to your younger male relatives.
    Go to the creek in the forest where the Uafagu Trees live."
        Well, again he went.   400
When he finished traveling, *tikiii,* he came once more to a house.
    "Here is our parent," he went.
    "I am indeed here, my child."
    "What do you want?" the Tree asked him,
        "What is it that brings you to see us?"   405

"I want you to be on your sisters."
"Listen to this," he said to his brother, "Listen to this."
     "That will be done.
          That's how we will always be," I'm told they said to each
          other.
"Since their daughters can bathe, go to your nephews."   410
     He was talking about the Wagitsuegï Trees.
Then Kwatïngï went on again.
     Again he came inside a house, *tikiii*.
"Here is our parent," someone said to him.
"As you see, I am here, my child."   415
"Very well," I'm told they answered.
     "Why have you come to us, Uncle?"
"I want you to be on your sisters."
"Very well," they replied,
     "That will be done.   420
          That's how we will always be for your children," they
          answered.
"So that their pubic ornaments can be made, go to your
nephews.
     Their women can always be found on the shore of the river."
Again he went away.
     Then he came into a house once again,   425
          it was he himself,
               Kwatïngï began to enter a house.
                    He who had been making everything began to enter a
                    house.
                    He who had been making everything.
"I have indeed come to you, my children," he went.   430
     He had indeed come to the Ungatafanga Trees.
"Here is our parent," they said to each other.
"As you see, I am here, my children," he said to them.
"Yes you are. Very well," I'm told they went.
     "Very well."   435
          "Why do you come to see us, Uncle?" they asked,
               "Why?"
"I want you to be on your sisters."
"Very well, that will be done," they said.
     "If they are worn when your children go to bathe, they will
     become soggy,   440
          the pubic ornaments will become soggy.
               It happens if they do that," they told him.
                    "When your children are bathing they will take them
                    off." (They were telling him about themselves.)

When that was done, "Go to your nephews," they said,
   "To Tate the Burity Palm,   445
      to Burity Palm."
         He went once again to Tate.
"As you see, I am here, my children," he said. "Me."
"Why are you here this time?"
"I want you to be on your sisters."   450
"All right," they said,
   "That will be done."
   That was all,
      they were the last.
Afterward, they became what women wear,   455
   they became our pubic ornaments.
That other person, the chested one made something.
   Fitsifitsi the Swift.
What was on his chest was copied by someone else as a design
for the pubic ornaments.
Kuaguku the White-chested one,   460
   Kuaguku the Swallow-tailed Kite.
      She herself did it.
         "Go ahead now." Kite put Swift's chest design on the
         pubic ornaments.
When it was ready,
   "Here it is," Swallow-tailed Kite said to Kwatïngï.   465
      "Here it is."
She gave them to Kwatïngï.
   To be our pubic ornaments. *Teh,* he had created their
   beautiful pubic ornaments, they had come into being.
      Then, I'm told, at dusk Kwatïngï sent them to the women.
Then, "To their husband,   470
To the Jaguar,
To him himself,
To the Immense One,
      Far away, to Faukugu!"
While they slept, that was said about their going to the Jaguar's
settlement, to his settlement.   475
That was Udukututu the Screech Owl perched high above
them.
At dusk it came up here to the rooftop.
   It perched there.
        "*Udukuututu, udukuututu!*"
         That was how it was sending them away.   480

"Why, listen, my child!" Kwatïngï said,
"Father, what does that one up there keep saying to you?"
    his daughter asked,
        she asked.
            That Made One asked.   485
                "The Made One" is her name.
Itsangitsegu spoke:
    "What did it just tell us?"
"Since you asked me, my child, I will tell you. It is
commanding you to leave.
    It wants you to go to your younger brother."   490
"Well, but all this time it's been trying to get us to leave, has it?"
his child said.
        "All this time it's been trying to get us to leave, has it?"
            "Why, the furred animal has sent it off from his plaza,"
            I'm told he said.
                And so the Screech Owl flew away.

The next day,   495
    "Go, children, go now."
So they took down their hammocks,
    they rolled up their palm-slat seats and they went away to
    marry,*
        his children went away.
Two had been made of *wẽgufi*,   500
    two had been made of *fata*.
They and their younger sisters.
They all went away together to marry,
    to become his wives,
        to become Nitsuegï's wives,   505
            the Jaguar's wives.
"You will arrive right at the place where your younger brother
stays,
    you will arrive at Dyakufenu's place."
        Armadillo's place.
            He is Ikwagutafa, the Armadillo,   510
                He is Armadillo.
                Armadillo's name is Dyakufenu.
What Kwatïngï meant was "You will arrive at Dyakufenu's
place."
    "He stays at his fishing place,
        seated by his fish traps," as the Made Ones went away.   515
Their father was seated in the doorway.
    He will stay there while they travel.
        While he was seated here, they traveled on.

Since he is a powerful being,
   Kwatïngï is a powerful being,   520
   He is a powerful being.
They came to Armadillo's place.
   Fire, fire started to burn there.
     Armadillo had caught some fish.
He looked around.   525
   Teh, they were so pretty, truly beautiful!
"Sisters," he went,
   "Where are you going?"
"We have to go marry the headman."
"Yes," he went,   530
   "You must go, you must go."
So they all sat down.
   "Sisters," he went,
     "Let's all eat for a while, let's all eat for a while.
      Here."   535
   He took something off the fire, *bok*.
     They quickly ate up the fish.
     They were eating what he had given them.
When the sun was here they finished.
   "We'll have to leave now," they said.   540
"All right, Sisters," he went,
   "I think you should give me your payment now,
     give it to me."
     He wanted to make love to one of them.
"All right," they said.   545
"She over there goes, your older sister," he went,
   "I want her."
     So they went away.
But nothing happened,
   he had no erection.   550
     His erection was still in the house.*
"Do it if you want to!"
   But nothing happened.
"Sisters," he said,
   "My erection must still be in the house.   555
   I'll go see right away," he said.
"Go ahead if you wish,
   go look right away."
     Pu pu pu he trotted away to find his erection.
"Let him remain as he is," they said,   560
   and they left.

His mother was seated in the doorway.
   "Mother," he went,
      "I've come for my erection.
         My female cousins are here." 565
         "All right," she said.
He put his erection on and went back.
   "Sisters," he went,
      "I've arrived . . . Sisters?"
They were already far away when he said that, 570
   they were far away.
They had left when that happened.
   They left while he was becoming aroused.
Then *bok*, he slapped his penis.
As they went on smoke kept rising from somewhere. 575
   This time it was a Feathery One,
      seated by the place where he fished.
Isagiku the Black Vulture, the small vulture.
   That's his name, Isagiku.
      He'd been smoking fish. 580
   "Sisters," he said,
      "Where are you going? Where are you all going?"
   "To marry the leader,
      we're going to marry."
   "Very well," he said, 585
      "You must certainly go. Go, go," he went.
Ugh! Rotten, his fish catch smelled rotten.
   "Sisters," he said,
      "I'd like you to have some of this food."
   "All right," they said. 590
Then *buk* to one,
   and to another one.
It was disgusting, rotten food.
When they were all finished,
   "Sisters, give me payment right now, lest you prove unworthy. 595
   This one," he signaled to a sister.
They went away and he was making love to her.
   The bamboo tube inside her vulva cut him.
      The bamboo tube cut him.
         Their father had put it inside their vulvas, 600
            anticipating the Birds' lovemaking.
   So they went away.
Then *tikiii*,
   they came to another person.
      Again something was smoking. 605

Seated by his fishing spot this time was the Bald One,
   Dyuwafula the Turkey Vulture,
     the larger vulture,
      the larger one.
"I suppose this person here is our younger brother
Dyuwafula."   610
"Sisters," he went,
  "Where are you all going?" he asked.
"Well, we're going to marry the leader."
"Good, you must go."
His fish catch was smelling so fishy,   615
   they could hardly eat it.
When they were done,
  "Give me payment."
   "All right," they said.
"I want her, I want this sister."   620
   He made love to a younger sister.
    When he was finished,
     they went on.
They came to a Bird again.
  Seated by his fishing spot this time was Ugisa the Great Egret,   625
   the White One.
    Buh, his fish catch was huge!
"Sisters, where were you going, where?"
"We're going to marry the leader."
"Very well, you must go," he said.   630
   "Have something to eat," he said.
    "All right."
This time the fish he offered them tasted very good,
   they weren't rotten at all.
    So they all ate.   635
When they were done,
  "We must be going," they told him.
   "We must be going."
    "All right," he answered.
"Sisters," he said,   640
  "First, give me payment.
   Give this sister here.
    We'll return very soon, I assure you."
     "All right," they said.
"I want her, I want this sister."   645
   He made love to her.

After he had finished, they went on.
   They could tell it was Tete, the handsome Orange-breasted
   Falcon.
   Falcon was seated by his fish traps this time, it is said.
      Falcon was. 650
         The red one.
   The younger sister spoke up:
      "There's a young man we can make love to."
   "All right," the others said.
   "Our younger brother should lie down with me, with me," 655
      their older sister said.
         The older sister who was made of *wẽgufi* wood.
The fish he had caught were delicious *kwatagi.*
   "Sisters," he said.
   "Yes?" 660
   "Where are you all going?"
   "We're going to marry the leader."
   "Yes," he said,
      "Go there," I'm told he said.
   "Let's eat now," he said. 665
      Bok, he gave them a lot of roasted fish!
When they were done,
   "Sisters," he said,
      "Give me payment.
         Give this sister, here," 670
            that was the oldest sister he was speaking about.
   About Itsangitsegu.
      She herself was the one he made love to,
         and they went on.
Someone else was there. 675
   Tete the Sparrow Hawk,
      the tiny falcon.
      the very small one.
   The small one waited there.
      He was handsome. 680
         Fish, as before.
   "Where are you going, Sisters, where?"
   "To Nitsuegï, to marry the leader."
   "That's good, you must go.
      Let's eat now." 685
         He gave them the grilled fish,
            and they ate the fish.

When the sun was here they finished.
 "Go now," he said to them.
 "First give me payment," he said,   690
 "I want her, this sister."
  "All right."
He made love to her,
 and they went on.
Where smoke kept rising, Ituga the Amazon Kingfisher sat beside 695
his fish grill.
 When they came to where he was,
  he hid his necklace from them.
   He turned it around to the back of his neck.
    Thus it stayed that way.
The fish he had caught were *safundu, bah* a great many of them! 700
 "Sisters, where are you going, where?"
 "To marry the leader, the Jaguar."
 "Very well, you must go.
  Please eat now," he said.
 "All right," so they ate.   705
 "Sisters," he went,
  "Give me payment right now.
  I want her, I want this sister."
He made love to her.
He ejaculated hard.   710
He ejaculated.
She flicked his semen at him,
 onto Amazon Kingfisher,
  tak tak tak like that.
Amazon Kingfisher became splattered with his own semen. 715
His necklace was still on the other side of his neck.
 I mean it remained turned around.
What I mean to say is, next they went to the place where his
younger brother stayed.
 Tuitui the Green Kingfisher was there, the small kingfisher.
  Tuitui.   720
Bah! there were so many fish there!
 That's what they wanted to eat.
When they had finished eating,
 "We must be going now."
 "Go now if you wish," he said.   725
So when the sun was here,
 "Sisters," he said,
  "Give me payment now," he said.

"I want her,
     I want this sister." 730
     "All right."
So he made love to her.
She threw his semen at him,
     and he too became splattered here on his neck.
          Then they went away. 735
Next Fakagï the Snowy Egret,
     the white heron.
          His name is Taguwagafi,
               that's his name.
     "Here we are, Younger Brother." 740
     "Very well, where are you going, Sisters?"
     "We're going to marry the leader, to marry."
     "Good, you must go there.
          Please eat now."
               So they were eating his fish. 745
When they were done,
     "Sisters," he went,
          "Give me payment now.
               I want her, this sister."
     "All right," they said, 750
          so he made love to her,
               and they went away.
They were coming toward the place where Akutsagï the Red-
throated Caracara stayed.
     As they began to come toward him he looked up at them.
     They greeted him. 755
     He cleared his throat and he spoke because he wanted them
     to eat.
     He was alone by himself.
          Akutsagï the hoarse one.
He was seated beside his fishing spot.
     "Let's eat now," he told them, 760
          so they all ate.
     "We're going now," they said.
          "All right," he answered.
     "Sisters," he said,
          "Now give me payment. 765
               I want her, this sister."
     "All right," they said,
          so he made love to her,
               and they left.

Then they came to Kuatata the Eel Hawk's place.   770
    Eels were the things he had caught, eels.
  "Sisters," he said,
    "Where are you going, where?"
  "To marry the leader," they answered.
  "Very well," he went,   775
    "You must go," he went.
  "Sisters, I have no fish to give you."
    But he was deceiving them,
      even as they sat eating the water creatures.
  "Give me my payment now.   780
    I want that one, that sister."
      "All right."
      He made love to her.
Isogoko the Maned Wolf was starting to chop his firewood.
  Bah, he had a huge catch of *itofake!**   785
  "Sisters," he went,
    "Where are you going?"
  "We're going to marry the leader," they said.
  "You must go, go," he said.
  Bok, he gave them some grilled fish,   790
    and they ate the fish.
      The *itofake* were delicious.
  "We're going now," they said.
    "All right."
  Then he made love to the youngest of all the sisters,   795
    and they went on.
Tuk, Akutsu the Tayra was starting to chop into a tree.
  He was chopping out a nest full of honey.
  "Sisters," he went,
    "Where are you going?"   800
  "To marry the leader, to marry," they said.
  "Go there, you must go there," he said.
  "*Fuh*, eat this honey," he said, blowing a spell on them.
    How good it was, yum!
      The honey was delicious.   805
  "Drink it, drink it," he went,
    blowing a spell on them.
  "*Toho! Toho!*" they choked on it.
  Tetsu tetsu, their feet rubbed together,
    as they became unconscious.   810
Then he began to take each one of them,
    until he had made love to them all.

They got up after a while, they all woke up.
"Give me my payment."
"No, you've already had it." 815
They all knew what he had done to them,
    so they went on.
Then when they had gone very far, they came to the very last one.
They pulled out the bamboo tubes *tsuk,* from their vulvas,
    those things that had been inside their vulvas, 820
      and threw them away.
    When they had awakened,
      there certainly was so much bird semen inside.
        There certainly was a lot of bird semen inside the tubes
        of bamboo.
    Henceforth their vulvas became like everyone's, 825
      became as they continue to be now.
There was smoke starting up again.
Teh, it was handsome Enënama the Crake.
    "Our Younger Brother should touch me this time."
      Teh, she was beautiful! 830
    "Sisters," Crake went,
      "Where are you going, where?"
    "To marry the leader," they answered.
    "You must go, go," he said.
    "Let's eat now," 835
      he gave them fish and they ate the fish.
    "Sisters," he said,
      "Give me payment.
        I want that one, that sister."
          "All right," they said. 840
    "Give me payment.
      I want that one, that sister."
        "All right," they answered,
          "Take her."
He made love to her. 845
    "How nice!" he told her.
After that he tried and tried to get up *beh beh beh beh, beh beh
beh beh.*
But their insides had weakened him.
He tottered *beh beh beh* as he stood up.
She blew a spell, 850
    she blew a spell.
"Stay that way, stay that way," she said.
    Beh beh beh beh, beh beh beh beh, really tottering!

They left after she had done that to him.
They went away. 855
They went a long, long way.
He back there had been the very last.
When the sun was here,
there were some burity palms growing,
burity palms. 860
"Older Sister," one of them said,
"Let's see what's over there.
Let's see.
Let's see our belts.
I want to cut it down for us, 865
because all of our younger brothers want to make love
to us."
"All right, go ahead if you wish."
Their father was still watching them as he had been before,
seated in his doorway.
He watched them, 870
Kwatïngï did.
As she crept up,
puh, puh, puh,
as she crept up the trunk of the burity palm,
tsuk, she cut it off. *Tsuk, tooh, tsuk,* the burity shoot landed
upright. 875
Tsiuk, uuh,
it stuck out from among the water plants.
The burity shoot stuck out.
She began to come down to pick it up.
She was right above the burity, 880
about to pick it up . . . when the burity *tsiuk, mboruk!*
It speared her, it did.
It split open her insides,
it did,
and she died. 885
The burity shoot still pierced her.
"She will remain as she is," her father declared, "She will
remain as she is."
Then they buried her there at that same place where she had
died,
and they went on.
The sun was here.
They had gone a long way toward Faukugu in order to marry the
leader.
That was why they were going,
to marry him.

They were thirsty.
　　They were looking for a place where they could drink
　　something to quench their thirst.　　　　　　　　　　895
　　They saw some water flowing in a creek.
　　"Old Sister," one of them said.
　　"What?"
　　"I'm thirsty, Older Sister," she said,
　　　　"So I'll drink some of this water right now."　　900
　　"No, let it be," the other told her,
　　　　"I'm sure it's bitter water.
　　You mustn't do that.
　　　　I don't think you should kill your thirst with it.
　　I don't think it's for drinking.　　　　　　　　　905
　　　　Stay thirsty a while longer."
　　"No, I'm thirsty, I'm thirsty.
　　　　Even so I'll drink it, even so."
　　"Wait, you can drink on the other side."
　　"No, I can't wait,　　　　　　　　　　　　　910
　　　　I'm too dry to forget my thirst," she answered.
　　"You'll be poisoned."
　　"Even so, I'll drink it."
　　"If you want to drink, go ahead." Her sister spoke angrily to
　　her.
The younger sister came to the water's edge to drink.　　915
　　She scooped it up in her hands and drank.
　　And she died,
　　　　because she was poisoned by the bitterness.
　　　　　"She will remain the way she is."
　　There were only two left, they say.　　　　　　　920
　　The ones who had been made from *fata* were the two who
　　died.
　　　　The two halves who had been made of *wegufi*,
　　　　those two were still alive.
So then they went on once again.
　　The sun was here in the western sky as they approached
　　Faukugu.　　　　　　　　　　　　　　　　925
　　　　They were approaching his settlement, the Jaguar's
　　　　settlement.
　　　　They came to a place just above the water's edge and they
　　　　stopped there.
　　　Next someone else came that way to that very same place,
　　　　　a wife came that way.
　　　　　　The wife of a large cat came to get water.　　930

On her head she carried a water gourd, a water gourd.
　　Fagagi the Sariema was the wife, Sariema.
　　　　She herself, the one who whistles this way [a low,
　　　　extended whistle],
　　　　　　she was the wife.
　　　　　　　　The ugly wife,   935
　　　　　　　　　　the ugly one.
　　　　　　　　Her son was Kogokogoti the Black Ibis,
　　　　　　　　　　her son.
Next *tom*, she dunked her hair in the water.
　　Sariema's hair, her hair wasn't very long.   940
　　　　She dunked her hair in the water and took it out.
She smoothed down her hair.
And looked at her calves that were bound with cotton.
　　Her calves were skinny,
　　　　Sariema had very skinny calves,   945
　　　　　　Sariema's calves.
　　　　　　　　She still bound her calves with cotton like a maiden,
　　　　　　　　her calves.
"My calves were becoming heavy because I've bound them
well,
　　　　not like Kanatsu's calves.   950
　　　　　　I've seen them. Kanatsu's calves aren't nearly as nice as
　　　　　　mine."
　　　　　　　　She had been speaking about the calves of that other
　　　　　　　　person.
She smoothed down her hair,
　　her hair that couldn't grow out very long.
The others were just above her,   955
　　the Made Ones were just above her.
One of them pulled off the edge of her fingernail, *itsik!*
She pulled off the edge of her fingernail and threw it,
　　she threw it at Sariema.
"Who just did that? I'll hit her, hit her."   960
　　Sariema jerked her head around this way and that, even
　　though it had something on it.
Next her water bottle *tauk* began to topple over as she looked
around.
　　Tauk to the other side again, the gourd bottle tipped and
　　once again . . .
　　　　mbisuk her water bottle fell and broke.
　　　　　　Buh! all her water spilled out.   965
"Maah! Nitsuegï is bound to be angry with me! The way he
always is."

She marched huffily away as sariemas do.
　　She went away, still angry.
　　　　Without that thing she had brought.
　　　　　She no longer had her water bottle. 970
The sun was still visible in the sky, low on the horizon.
　　Their father was still seated in his doorway, watching them.
　　　"Their younger brother must come there.
　　　　The one who knows about them, there.
　　　　　He'll be there. 975
　　　　　　The unadorned one will certainly be there."
　　　　　　　(Afua the Puma,
　　　　　　　　Puma, his cousin,
　　　　　　　　Jaguar's cousin.)
　　"The one who knows about them will be there. 980
　　　His cousin will come there. The unadorned one."
I'm told Sariema had gone right away, to tell the Jaguar.
　　She came and went into his house, *tikiii.*
　　　"Leader," she said to their husband. Sariema spoke.
　　　　"Leader, your brides must have just arrived, your brides. 985
　　　　　My water bottle just broke."
　　"All right," he answered,
　　　"Are you sure?"
　　　　"Yes."
The other one left and went to the water's edge. 990
　　The big cat went,
　　the powerful being went.
　　　To the water's edge.
　　"Sisters," he told them,
　　　"You are my brides, my people. 995
　　　　You are my brides."
　　"Come on, surely he's the very one," the younger sister said.
　　　"Surely he's the very one."
　　"This person isn't our cousin.
　　　This person isn't he. 1000
　　　　No, he's not."
　　"No, that's him."
　　"No, it's his cousin!"
　　"Now, you certainly are my brides, Sisters.
　　　You certainly are my brides!" 1005
　　　　The cousin had come to marry them.
　　　　　Puma had come to marry them pretending to be their
　　　　　younger brother.
　　　　　I don't know why the other one didn't try to follow
　　　　　him.

"Listen," Sariema had said.
　　"Leader," she said,   1010
　　　　"Go look at your brides. Your brides are ready to be
　　　　housed."
"All right," he said,
　　but their cousin Puma went to them instead.
"Sisters," he said,
　　"You're my brides," he said.   1015
As he began to come toward the two women,
　　"Don't go!" Even so her younger sister went with him.
　　　　So they all came back together.
　　　　　　When the sun had just set.
　　　　　　　　They all came back together to his house.   1020
　　　　　　　　　　To the doorway.
"But where's his house? The leader's house?"
Teh, that person's house was very beautiful.
But Puma's was poorly made.
His house was covered with palm leaves.   1025
　　It was a poorly thatched house with holes in the roof.
　　　　They had gone to the wrong place.
"Look," she said,
　　"This isn't the right house."
So they stayed there and they slept,   1030
　　they slept, they slept,
　　　　they slept.

"Children, Children, Children, Children," Nitsuegï called to his
people,
　　"Let's prepare to go hunting."
　　　　The furred animals were preparing to go hunting again. 1035
Then he pierced two tucum palm nuts for his arrows,*
　　the leader's arrows.
Then he said, "Cousin, I expect we'll go hunting very soon,"
　　to his cousin Puma, who was keeping his brides,
　　　　who was keeping his wives.   1040
"Tomorrow, let's go hunting, tomorrow," he said to his
followers.
"All right, that's fine with us," his followers said.
Then they all slept.

The next day at dawn,
"Let's go, let's go, let's go," he called them out to the plaza.   1045
"Let's go, let's go, Children.
I want us to go hunting right now.
Come along now,"
so they all went away,
every one of them.   1050
Nitsuegï had a small *fikuanga* shell from underwater,*
the kind we use to cut open piqui fruit.
"Cousin, I'm going to relieve myself a moment," he said.
"All right, go if you wish," Puma answered.
He stood ready, waiting for him,   1055
and the followers also waited for him there on the path.
Nitsuegï relieved himself and after that—there—with the
oyster shell . . .
tsiuk, he cut himself.
Tsiuk, his blood flowed out when he cut himself.
And so following that *tsik tsik* he hobbled back.   1060
"Well, Cousin," he went,
"See for yourself how badly I've hurt myself just now.
Look at this, I've been wounded by a piece of wood.
Phew, this has really done it."
Giuk, he had really done that to himself.   1065
Tsik, tsik, he came slowly hobbling back.
"Friend, I can't continue this way. See for yourself how badly
I've hurt myself," he told him.
"You go with our people," he told him.
"Go with my relatives, I have to go back," he told the others.*
"Go back," Puma said,   1070
his cousin told him,
"Go back."
"All right," Nitsuegï answered.
Tsik tsik he staggered back.
He went by way of a private path,   1075
toward the house,
his cousin's house.
He shot the whistling arrows *piaaa*
right into the doorway.
Two. P*iaaa!*   1080
That's just how it sounded.
And once again, *piaaa . . . tik!*
They landed in front of the Made Ones,
those who had come to marry him,
those who had come to be his wives.   1085
"Arrows!" they said to each other.

Bou bou the youngest one picked one up and then the other sister
did the same.
    Then they walked over *ti ti ti* to be his wives.
        They went inside his house where he awaited them.
            They were met by Nitsuegï in the doorway of his beautiful
            house.   1090
By dusk when the sun was here,
    the others arrived,
        the others were all coming back.
            Bah haa, they had so much game!
His mother,   1095
    his mother Kafisatiga,
        she was Puma's mother.
His mother was weeping,
    his mother.
        "Wa, wa, wa," as she went outside.   1100
She looked strange, she had cut off all her hair.
Nitsuegï had wanted her to die as if from an evil presence.
"It must happen to you," so she had lost all the strength in her
neck.
        "Wa, wa, wa," as she went on.
        She was dying from the evil presence.   1105
"Bring back my son's wives, bring back my son's wives!" she
kept telling him,
        she said.
            One of the women glanced behind her and right away
            Puma's mother went insane.
Then after the hunters arrived they ate the meat in the plaza.
    So when he was finished Puma's mother came to him.   1110
        "Dear child," she went,
            "Dear child," to Puma.
        "Your older brother has just taken my children away.
        "They themselves went to marry your nephew."
        "All right, let them be that way."   1115
Then, "Did he really do it, was he making love to you before?"
Nitsuegï asked.
        "No," they said.
            "That's the truth," they said,
                "Is that true?" he answered.
    "Did he really do it,   1120
        did he lie down on top of you before,
            lie down on top of you?"
        "Yes," they answered.
    "Then it did happen, it did happen."

"All right," he went away to get some stomach cleansing
medium. 1125
Then with the stomach cleansing medicine,
"Wu wu wu,"
"Eh, eh, eh,"
well, they forced up Puma's semen.
That became a fish we like to eat, one that lives in the grassland
ponds. 1130
They're his semen,
Puma's semen.
Kalapalo say, "Puma's child."
They finished.
The medicine was all used up. 1135
Tsï tsï tsï tsï it all dripped away.
Then they stayed there and they made love again to Nitsuegï,
he kept making love to them.
He made love,
he made love, 1140
so finally one sister became pregnant.
Something was inside her stomach.
Inside her stomach was something.
His mother came to her son,
to sweep the house. 1145
She came, and while she was sweeping the house,
she kept farting.
The pregnant one was there,
Itsangitsegu's stomach was almost ready to give birth.
Her younger sister was Tanumakalu, 1150
her younger sister.
They were still co-wives,
co-wives.
But anyway, Itsangitsegu was making agave string,
agave string, 1155
while her mother-in-law *pisuk, pisuk, pisuk,*
swept her son's house.
Then her mother-in-law came closer to her just as she spat out a
bit of agave.
"Pitsuh!" she suddenly went,
"Pitsuh!" 1160
"Hey, why did you start to spit at me, you fool?"
She addressed her daughter-in-law most rudely.

Then her mother-in-law tore off a fingernail *tsiuk,* and threw it
toh.
    Ubom! Itsangitsegu fell down,
      she was dying.   1165
        Tsiuk, her mother-in-law had slit her neck.
He was planting his corn.
    In the manioc fields. Her husband was in his manioc fields
    with her younger sister,
      with Tanumakalu.
    Tikitik, he felt a twitch along his thigh.   1170
    "Hurry up, let's go back. Your younger sister is no longer alive."
    Lying by her seat here in the doorway
      she was nearly decapitated.
    She was nearly dead.
      Itsangitsegu was nearly dead.   1175
      After that her body was taken up to the sky.

Listen.
Then he took her to the top of Alidyu's house,
    that of Whirlwind.
    So she would be killed by its deadly odor,   1180
      there in the dwelling place of that being.
Following that *puh*
    while she lay there nearly dead, they say,
      she gave birth to them.
        She gave birth,   1185
          while she lay there nearly dead.
    First Sun emerged,
      he came into existence.
        Sun.
    Their father was just about to make some arrows,   1190
      he was just about to make some arrows.
    Sun was born with a tail just like his father.
    Tsaka, his father sliced it off
      with a large oyster shell,
        and he threw it away.   1195
          What was left is this, the tip of our spine.
    Moon came next, so there were two of them.
    Then Nitsuegï threw her on top of the house,
      so that Whirlwind's deadly odor would kill her.
    Her sons stayed behind,   1200
      Sun and Moon.

Their grandmothers presented themselves in order to cradle
them, and sing to them.
The first was Akā the Banded Tinamous,
    Akā.
    Tikii, she came inside the house.   1205
"Granny," Nitsuegï said,
    "Why have you just come to us now, why?" he asked.
"I'm here, as you see, because I want to cradle our
grandchildren."
"You have, have you?" he answered.
But they knew how to do it,   1210
    the Banded Tinamous themselves,
    Pïnoso the Great Tinamous,
        and Iseu the Brazilian Tinamous who followed her.
        Bah, a crowd of them came into the house!
        Those people presented themselves there.   1215
Boh, they picked up the older brother.
    Boh, his younger brother as well.
    They all sang to him.
    However, I don't want to sing that one.
Eke the Snakes wanted to hold them also.   1220
    The Snakes wanted to hold them.
    I'll sing this other one,
        that of the Snakes, the Snakes.
[sings] "He will search for food, he will search for food."
Afaga the Tree Frogs also cradled them.   1225
    "*Au au*," that's their call.
Next Tsafudyaka the Striped Heron (Oops! I forgot my wife's
mother's name!).*
    Striped Heron cradled the younger brother again:
[sings] "He will be *amunau*, he will be the leader.*
    Tsaudyaka, Tsaudyaka.   1230
    He will become the leader, he will become the leader.
    Tsaudyaka, Tsaudyaka.
    He will become *kapitaū*."*
Next that of Tufokugeu' the Parauques:
    "He made love in the middle of the path   1235
    Tufokugeu' Tufokugeu'!"
        I think they said something like that,
        that was what they said.
            "That's enough of that," he told them.
Then on the path some others came.   1240
    Then Tafitse the Blue and Yellow Macaw came, "*Nga! Nga!*"

[sings] "He won't wake up . . ."
 "Let it be, go away!" their father said,
  so they went away,
   still going, "*Nga!*" 1245
 Kuguagi the Turkey Vulture,
  the one who waits for dead game:
[sings] "Kuguagi, uwanagi
  uwa a a, uwa a a"
   that was how she did it and kept on: 1250
 "This time it's the rotten one Kuguagi, uwanagi
  uwa a a, uwa a a."
   That was all.
Very soon after they were about as tall as this, like four- or five-year-
olds.
 They were growing, 1255
  and growing.
 Now, their mother was still alive on top of Alidyu's house.
  Alidyu is the name of Whirlwind.
  Alidyu is the name of that being.
 They lived there and they grew up. 1260
  Very quickly.
  The older brother and the younger brother were this tall,
   still small.
    So they were there.
When they were this big, about like seven- or eight-year-olds, Sun
came beside the entrance to the house. 1265
 "Father," he said,
  "Make some arrows for me right away.
   Some arrows to hunt lizards."
 "All right." Their father made four of them.
  For hunting lizards. 1270
 They didn't have any names at all,
  but they were already wandering around by themselves.
 Then they asked their substitute mother for some manioc
 bread.
  They always ate manioc bread.
 Then they met Isogoko the Maned Wolf. 1275
  Maned Wolf found them.
 "Grandchildren," he said,
  Maned Wolf spoke.
 "What are you doing here?"
 "We're trying to hunt lizards," they answered. 1280
 "All right, that's what you should be doing," he said.
 "What are your names?" he asked,
  "What does your father call you?"

"There aren't any," they answered.
"Very well. Both of you will have my names.   1285
    May all my names stay with you."
"All right," they said,
    "Who is this one?"
"You will be Maned Wolf."
    "Very well."   1290
"And you will be Twisted Path."
    "Very well."
        The younger brother was Twisted Path.
"Go ahead, say 'Maned Wolf' and 'Twisted Path'."
"Maned Wolf." "Twisted Path."   1295
    "What?"
"Didn't I tell you? Listen to what your names will be like."
    Those were Maned Wolf's names.
Then they went to bathe.
    "Maned Wolf's namesake, go bathe."   1300
Their father was there.
    He heard them.
"Who gave you those names?" their father said.
They went away again to shoot some more lizards,
    while their father stayed behind.   1305
Next they returned to their house.
Their names were Maned Wolf
    and Twisted Path.
They found Giti the Sun,
    they found Sun,   1310
    the large-chested one,
    Taki the Grasshopper.
It was the large-chested one whom they found.
    Here, this part of him was chested.
"Grandchildren, what are your names?" he asked them.   1315
"Maned Wolf."
    "Twisted Path."
"Those are ugly, let me try out my own names on you."
"What are they?" they asked.
    "What are they?"   1320
"You will be Giti, 'Sun', and you will be Ngune, 'Moon'."
    "All right."
"Go ahead, say 'Giti'," he said.
"Giti."
    "What?" Sun answered.   1325
"Ngune."
    "What?"

"Now listen. That's what your names must be.
  Your names will always be that way.
    You have new names now. 1330
    You may use them."
     They weren't very tall as yet.
Then once again their substitute mother gave them manioc bread.
  She carried it under her arms to her children.
Their substitute mother spoke: 1335
  "Children," she said,
   "Go scratch up the peanuts that your grandmother planted."
  "Where are they? Where?"
  "Way over there, far from here."
Their mother had finished making manioc bread for them, 1340
  a small one,
   so they went away.
  They were digging up the peanuts.
   There were so many of them!
Ĩtifi the Red-Winged Tinamous was the owner. 1345
  She was the person whose things we have now.
Their manioc bread was finished,
  and there was still a large pile of peanuts
   when the Red-Winged Tinamous came.
  Bah! they came, 1350
   the Red-Winged Tinamous came.
    Now, after the two had scratched up all their peanuts,
    three Red-Wing Tinamous came sneaking up on them.
  "Maah! What's this I see?
   Someone's beginning to scratch up our peanuts.
   They must be having trouble finding food, aren't they?* 1355
    Those who always say 'Mother' to that substitute
    mother of theirs have pulled up all our peanuts."
  "What happened to us?
   Let's run over to that grandmother of ours over there."
   "All right," Moon answered.
Tuh, they ran over to her. 1360
  "Well, it's my darling grandchildren!
   It's my darling grandchildren!"
    She embraced them.
     "My darling grandchildren are here!"
  "Granny," Sun went, 1365
   "What did we hear you say to us just now?"
  "Did I just say something to you, Grandchildren? What?"
  "No, Grandmother. You said something about some
grandchildren of yours, and their mother,
  You spoke of their mother just now."

"What could I have said?   1370
    'They must be my darling grandchildren,
        who are scratching up my peanuts,
            my grandchildren.'
            That's what I said about you."
"No, Grandmother," he told her.   1375
    "Be careful.
        That's not what we heard you say about us at all, Granny."
        This was the very first time they felt anger.
"'Let them have trouble finding food.
    Those who are pulling up all my peanuts,' you told us.   1380
'They're the ones who always say "Mommy" to their substitute
mother.
    Let them have trouble finding food.' That's what you just
    said.
        Yes, Granny."
"Yes, Grandchildren.
    Since you ask I will tell you.   1385
No, she is not your mother, no.
    It was your grandmother who decapitated your mother.
        It was Kafisatiga."
"Is it really true?"
"Yes, indeed. It's your substitute mother whom you're
accustomed to calling 'Mother'. She's your substitute mother." 1390
    "I see."
"Your father has taken your grandmother to Flat Breasts and
surrounded her with wasps.
    He surrounded her with wild pineapples.
        He surrounded her with snakes.
            He surrounded her with all kinds of wild things,   1395
                and with spiders.
He barricaded your grandmother far from here,
    he barricaded his mother there.
        He barricaded your grandmother.
            He barricaded your grandmother far away."   1400
                "I see."
"Your father has brought your mother to the top of the house of
Whirlwind.
    That's where he brought your mother."
        "Oh," they went,
            "Very well."   1405
"What's to be done with our grandmother, Older Brother?"
"Our grandmother will remain as she is now.
    Our grandmother will remain as she is now."

Then they picked up the little basket she used for carrying
peanuts
    and *ta ta ta ta* shook her until her neck was stretched out. 1410
    "Well, go far away forever, go away.
      Go away to the Mortals' clearings."
        Listen to her call.
          She still walks around there.*
Having not yet seen their real mother, 1415
    they came crying "Oi oi oi."
Their mother was kneading manioc mash.
    She was kneading manioc mash.
The sun was here when they arrived in the doorway,
    a doorway like this one here. 1420
      The doorway.
    Weeping, they came toward her.
      They came toward the place where their mother was,
        on top of Whirlwind's house.
        Itsangitsegu—she who had been put there— 1425
        their mother had been hidden long ago.
  "Nefuku, look at what our parent did.*
    Look at what our parent did!
      Our grandmother certainly knew what she was talking
      about."
        "Yes!"
Their real mother was emaciated. 1430
    It had been a long time since her head had been almost cut
    from her body.
      Their father was ashamed of this,
      he was.
They began to mourn when they saw their mother, 1435
    they were crying when they saw their mother.
      That's what happened when they saw their mother.
      That's what happened.
Their substitute mother was squeezing manioc mash inside the
doorway.
    She was carrying balls of coarse manioc mash, like these
    here, 1440
      out to the drying rack.
    She put them down outside,
      pika pika pika, like that.
    She was carrying them outside to put them on the drying
    rack.

She kept going, 1445
    their mother was carrying them on her arm.
        On the drying rack *pïka pïka pïka,*
            she put them down.
Then "Achu, achu," one of them blew his nose.
    So, she looked outside. 1450
        They were crying.
    "Come inside now, both of you must come inside."
    "Mother," Sun went,
        "Is it true that you were never our real mother?"
She started with fright. 1455
    "You weren't our mother,
        our mother is no longer alive.
            It was our grandmother who decapitated our mother."
    "Yes, my child," she went,
        "A long time ago your mother was murdered here by your
        grandmother. 1460
            Your father carried your mother away to the top of
            someone's house.
                He put her on top of the house of Whirlwind."
                Their mother wept.
    "At the same time your father took your grandmother away to
    Flat Breasts."
They were so sad! 1465
    They were all weeping.
Their father sat in the doorway, making some hunting arrows.
    "Leader," she said,
        "Here come our children, they're crying.
        We are done for, 1470
            we are done for, Leader.
            We are done for.
        Our children will surely kill us,
            our children will kill us."
Soon after they came inside. 1475
    Sun carried his peanuts wrapped in some leaves.
    His younger brother also had some wrapped up.
    Peanuts.
        Peanuts belonging to her,
            to Red-Winged Tinamous. 1480
                She had taught them,
                now they knew.

Sun sniffled as they approached.
His mother was putting the balls of manioc mash on the drying
rack,
    pokï pokï pokï,   1485
        when they lay down on their sides with their backs to her,
        this way.
            They fell asleep.
"We're done for, Leader.
    We are done for," she told her husband.
        They kept on sleeping soundly.   1490
Soon after they woke up.
    "They've just awakened," the mother said,
        "They've just awakened."
"You've met your grandmother, haven't you?" she said.
    "Yes," they answered.   1495
        "As you can tell we met Granny."
"Leader," Sun said.
    "Leader, why didn't you ever let us know about what you
    did?"
And so finally he berated their father.
    And so finally he reproached him for having done what he
    did.   1500
"Leader, why didn't you ever tell us about what happened?" *
"About what?"
"The truth about Mother.
    It was Granny who just taught us about her.
    It was Granny who just taught us about what you kept
    hidden from us,   1505
        so we wouldn't hear about it.
            What you kept hidden from us.
While we were digging up her peanuts she saw us.
'What's this I see? Someone's beginning to scratch up our
peanuts,' that's what we heard her say to us.
'They must be having trouble finding food, aren't they?
"Mother," they said to their substitute mother,' that's what
she said.   1510
This is what you've kept hidden from us."
"What your grandmother told you is a lie. Your grandmother
was lying to you."
"We want to see her, Leader.
    We want to see Mother.
        Because it's true, you are still keeping her alive."   1515
Their father was frightened.
    He was becoming very frightened because they wanted to
    see her.

They stayed there.
   Moh oh, their noses were huge,*
      their noses.   1520
"Let's go look for our grandmother, Older Brother.
   Let's begin looking.
   In the past our parent was mercilessly murdered by our
   grandmother.
      By our grandmother."
They went searching for her with their hook,*   1525
   they searched for her *giduk!*
Finally, it landed on her house.
   "Well, here she is!"
Sun then went to get Kaka the Laughing Hawk to devour her
spiders.
   While Tapir trampled down the spiny pineapple plants,   1530
      tsau tsau tsau tsau.
Tikii, they came into her house,
   they were inside her house.
   "Come on, Older Brother."
      "Come on," he went,   1535
         "Come on."
They came,
   they were this high,
      still very small.
He had put stones here in this place.   1540
   Stones are inside our knees,
      this thing here, our kneecap.
         Upïk, on the other side as well.
They also put them in the middle of their feet.
   Well, they were very heavy indeed!   1545
They began to go away after that.
   She saw them.
      Ti ti ti they began to walk away very slowly.
   "So, my little grandchildren are here!
      Why are my dear little grandchildren here?   1550
         My little grandchildren are here."
They went on each side of her.
   They came to meet her.
   Suddenly they grew tall.
   "What do my dear little grandchildren want? What is it?"   1555
Inside the house *tigi tigi tigi* she playfully shook them.
   Eh eh eh.
As she shook Sun the rocks pressed into her body.
   She put him down.
      He had made himself short again.   1560

She rubbed her neck.
"I want to sing," she said to them.
"I was the one who decapitated your mother," she sang.
The younger brother was the angriest,
 Moon was. 1565
Tigi tigi tigi.
 As she shook him harder he suddenly grew up,
  tigi tigi tigi.
Nduku she fell down.
Well, *tututu* bats flew about! 1570
Having become frightened, the two brothers went behind a
large tree.
When they did that *tututu* her butterflies flew around trying to
slice off their heads.*
Aulukuma looked around the side of the tree,
 just a little.
Tuu, indyuuik, part of his nose was sliced off! 1575
Because of that there's this space on our noses.
 Taugi's nose is still very big, the way it was then,
  still with the space filled in.
After that happened it was over.
"Well, go get fire, Older Brother," Moon said. 1580
 "We have to burn up our grandmother while she's like this."
As they went away,
 they went away,
  a wasp stung his older brother,
   his older brother *tsik!* on his eyelid. 1585
"Mother," Moon said,
 "I've come for some fire.
  Older Brother has just been stung.
  He wants to use it to burn wasps."
"Leader," she said, 1590
 "I'm sure our child met his grandmother just now.
  I'm sure that happened to him just now."
So finally they burned her up once and for all.
Pu pu, her butterflies flew away.
Tuh! Suddenly she exploded. 1595
"Too bad you were like that," Moon said,
 "Long ago you mercilessly murdered my mother."
"All right now, go get our grandfather."
 They wanted to bring down their mother from the housetop.
That person is at Natasa, 1600
 far away around Jagamï.
  He is at Natasa.
   On the other side of Kwatakago.

They came there.
They came toward him, I'm told, 1605
they came to him.
Those who were their grandfathers,
Atuta the Spiders,
they themselves were their grandfathers.
They themselves were the ones who had made their
mother. 1610
The Atuta are this small.
They're striped.
All of them came.
Their older brother as well.
(However, I shouldn't name our grandfather because my
father-in-law has his name.) Go ahead, say it, Kofoño.
("Yanama. 1615
Yanama did that,
Yanama.")
Their older brother,
their older brother.
An oyster shell had opened. 1620
He wasn't held in a womb like human beings.
His mother is Fikuanga the Oyster.
She is his mother,
Oyster.
Teh, how beautiful he is! 1625
His nails are unblemished.
There's nothing wrong with him,
nothing.
His nose, *teh,* how perfect! Name him again, Old Woman
("Yanama.
Yanama is his name, 1630
Yanama.")
He himself came,
and all of the others.
They all brought her down,
brought her down, 1635
they brought the twins' mother down.
"This is for me to do right now.
I'll bring her down to you.
I want to bring her down,"
the older brother went to get her. 1640
He held her in his arms.
That was how he brought down their mother.
Iih! she was so thin!
their little mother.

That was the condition she was in. They all waited up there
   while he held her. 1645
      "This is the worst thing that could have happened."
        "That's certainly so."
   How they wept!
The others were coming down with her from the housetop.
   This is how they did it. 1650
   "Pass her down to your younger brother," they said,
      "Pass her down to Aulukuma."
        Then he himself was bringing her down.
   Next she was passed down to their older brother,
      to Yanama. 1655
        He wanted to carry her down.
   Then the first one reached for her again.
      Ti ti the older brother went again,
        Taugi went again.
          Down to the ground. 1660
   Next their grandfather Kwatïngï was doing the same thing this
time.
   (His other name is Kwamïtini.
      Kwatïngï and Kwamïtini. You can use either name.)*
   He himself was bringing her down here.
      Once again he was carrying her toward the ground. 1665
        He passed her down to the older brother.
          Once again.
             One after another they carried her down until she
             was brought inside the front door.
When they had finished bringing her down from the housetop,
   they laid her down. 1670
      Bok, they laid her down.
        She was lying down.
   She had become very thin.
      She hadn't drunk anything at all,
        nor had she eaten manioc bread. 1675
They all expected to leave, I'm told.
   They walked around outside for a while,
      and they returned *tikii.*
   "Mother," they went,
      "Mm," their mother answered. 1680
   "You're still alive, aren't you?"
   "Mm," she murmured.
      Very softly.
   "Mother."
      "Yes?" 1685

"You're still alive, aren't you?"
　She was trying to speak to them but she was too weak.
"Aulukuma," he said,
　"Aulukuma," he said.
"Our parent will remain as she is,   1690
　our parent will remain as she is, as she is."
　　"All right," Moon answered.
Her hammock strings had been made from cotton thread.
　Her hammock strings.
Tsiuk, Taugi pulled off a few.   1695
Then he cut them up and he put some beeswax on the tips,
puka puka puka.
Then he spung the waxed strings *dïïï.*
　More beeswax.
He put those things on the ground beneath her.
　He put them both beneath her.   1700
They waited for something to happen.
"Ajah! How weak I am!"
Taugi sat beside her.
"Glance beneath you, beneath you."
　"All right," she said.   1705
"Look at this thing down here."
How emaciated she had become!
　She had been up there for a long time.
She glanced beneath her,
　and then she died.   1710
She was stricken,
　their mother was stricken. The life of Sun's mother was
　extinguished by an evil presence.
This thing is a snake,
　a snake.
This kind I'm speaking of is red,   1715
　and there's another one that's black.
He had painted it,
　striped it with beeswax.
　　Here was beeswax,
　　　here was beeswax, like that.   1720
That thing is an evil presence.
　It became an evil presence for the Kalapalo.
When it runs along a path, Kalapalo die. Afterward.
　Up to now it's been that way.
Taugi had stricken their mother, so she died then once and for all,   1725
　she died.
They were mourning her, "Mother, Mother, Mother!" they
　wailed.

All of them were mourning her.
    Even their father.
"All right, Grandfather, you go," they said,   1730
    "Go tell him what happened."
He came to that distant place to tell Kwatïngï what had
happened.
    He went to her father.
        That was Isogoko the Maned Wolf.
"When you arrive, tell him right away."   1735
    "All right," he answered, and he went on.
He went to that place I spoke of earlier,
    to Natasa.
"Waaa!" he did that in the bush, around the settlement.
    "Waa!"   1740
"I think I understand what happened to her," the other said.
Her father spoke,
    Kwatïngï spoke.
"I think I understand what happened to her,"
    as the other returned.   1745
Maned Wolf was frightened by what had happened,
    he was frightened because they wanted to club him.
        Thus he ran,
             he had gone to tell about it.
Because he had told them what had happened,   1750
    her relatives were angry with them.
    His followers wanted to kill them.*
They wanted to kill the furred animals, they wanted to kill the
furred animals.
    They wanted to kill all the furred animals.
Her fathers' companions who had brought her mother down from
Whirlwind's house.   1755
    They were all weeping.
"Leader," he said, "I warned you about this before.
    I told you about it.
        This is just how I said it was."
             They had been taught all about it before by Red-
             Winged Tinamous,   1760
                their grandmother.
"Leader," Taugi went,
    "I want some arrows for shooting lizards."
        "All right."
Then Nitsuegï was making this kind of thing for him,   1765
    bows.
        He was making arrows as well, bamboo arrows.
    Taugi wanted them for the Fierce People.

After they were made he gathered them up.
    He gathered them up, 1770
      he gathered them up.
    Their bows had also been made.
    A great many bows for the Fierce People had been made.
When that was done,
    Taugi cut off a small piece of arrow cane. 1775
    These were to become Tafugi the Minnows.
      Minnows are fierce people.
      They're like this,
        very short people.
        Tafugi are skilled at shooting their bows. 1780
    He wanted a great pile of arrows,
      and pieces of arrow cane,
      and jointed bamboo arrows.
While Taugi began to put the feathers on his arrows, their mother
(following her usual practice),
    their mother was kneading manioc mash. 1785
    Taugi began to fasten feathers to his arrows.
    Their mother prepared to carry her balls of manioc mash
    outside.
Moki, he put some arrows on the ground for her to walk over.
    Their mother crossed over them when she returned.
    She crossed over the arrows. 1790
    "Mother," he said,
    "Right now you're pregnant, Mother.
      You've just been made pregnant now."
    She hadn't made love to anyone,
      he just made it happen, 1795
      Taugi made it happen to her,
        he wanted to impregnate her that way.
    Unknown to her,
      it suddenly happened.
      Yes. 1800
    She didn't realize what had happened.
    He made it happen when she walked over the arrows.
Then she came back.
    "He must have tricked us,"
      so she came inside, 1805
    "He must have tricked us."
      Her womb had become filled with her future offspring.
      Those who were going to kill his followers.

"Go ahead, Mother."
    She went out behind the house and gave birth.   1810
    She gave birth to Angikogo the Fierce People.
       A whole lot of them!
"Go ahead now," Taugi said to the wood shavings left over from
his arrow making.
    Pupu. Pupu the Great Horned Owl.
    His wood shavings had turned into those beings.   1815
  At dusk it flew away.
    Taugi wanted to kill the followers,
      he wanted to kill his father's followers.
And so at dusk,
    Great Horned Owl began to call out: 1820
      "Puu puu puu puu."
    "I understand what you're saying," he told it.
    Great Horned Owl flew above the settlement,
      while a crowd of Nitsuegï's followers appeared.
       Great Horned Owl had gone the way owls do to tell
       Nitsuegï.   1825
         He came back to the house,
         to the house.
Then just before sunrise, this continued with Kugukaga the Small
Dove.
    "Go ahead, you go there," he said to Dove.
    "I understand what you're saying,"   1830
      That was how Taugi told Nitsuegï.
      Dove told him about it.
Taugi had just terrified him because he realized his followers
were going to kill him,
    were going to kill him.
       His own son was going to kill his father's followers,   1835
       all his furred animals.
"All right, you go now," he told Kusauka the Couvier's Toucan.
    It plucked at the housetop, *tsok tsok tsok.*
    "Hihohaha,"
      it called out three times and then it flew away.   1840
  Wind came,
  wind came,
      that was because Taugi had just brought the Fierce People
      their arrows.
       Nitsuegï knew it was the black vulture's wing feathering
       that caused the wind.

Early in the morning Taugi had brought arrows to those
people and was instructing them. 1845
Couvier's Toucan had said,
"Their Grandfather, he's teaching them about arrows."*
Once again, just before sunrise Taugi said,
"Go ahead, you go."
Someone else approached. 1850
Fitsagu the Cuckoo came.
It came to instruct Nitsuegï.
"*Ho ho ho,*" it went.
"He's going to exterminate us all. I understand what's
being said."
Very early, at dawn, 1855
Ui the Tiniest Owl.
It was made from a very small bow shaving,
it was.
It told Nitsuegï about what was happening.
It told him. 1860
Buk, it came to the top of the house in order to tell him,
and then it went away.
At dawn they were shouting with rage.
So many of them were doing that!
They besieged Nitsuegï, 1865
they were surrounding him.
The Fierce People were doing that.
He was surrounded.
They cut off all escape.
Here to one side was the younger brother. 1870
On the other side was the older brother.
The Fierce People had encircled their father.
They began to kill his followers.
They began to kill them,
the Fierce People were killing them. 1875
They killed every one of the furred animals.
Their father tried to flee to one side.
"Father," Taugi went,
"Stay right here!"
The older brother was standing on that side. 1880
So Nitsuegï fled to the other side where the younger brother
stood.
Aulukuma put him on his bow and shot him high up into the
sky.
He stayed there forever after that.

"Where is he, where is he, where is he?"
　　All of Nitsuegï's followers, *mbisuk,*　　　　　　　　　1885
　　　　they were dead.
　　　　　The Fierce People had killed them all.
　Only one fled,
　　　Akugi the Agouti.
　　Since he scurried between the legs of the others he was able
　　to flee them.　　　　　　　　　　　　　　　　　　　1890
　　　He scurried away as agoutis do.
　　There was only one true escaper.
　　　He didn't die the way the others had died.
Then Taugi endowed them all with life.
　　Furred animals, as exist now.　　　　　　　　　　　　1895
　He endowed them with life,
　　furred animals as exist now,
　　　with their blood.
　Their human images,
　　the ones that belonged to them,　　　　　　　　　　　1900
　　that had covered them,
　　　Those things remained behind forever.
　　　　Their human bodies.
　Aulukuma had already shot their father away,
　　their father.　　　　　　　　　　　　　　　　　　　1905
　On the other side was the older brother.
　　The Fierce People weren't able to catch him for that reason,
　　no.
Their mother then gave birth,
　　she was all ready.　　　　　　　　　　　　　　　　　1910
　Pain came and she gave birth.
　　"I'm giving birth right now," she told Taugi,
　　Tanumakalu said.
　　　Hence all those of us here came into existence.
　Her name is Tanumakalu,　　　　　　　　　　　　　　1915
　　her name.
　　　But her companion Itsangitsegï,
　　　　she was Taugi and Aulukuma's real mother.
　　　　　Itsangitsegï.
　　　The one Kafisatiga decapitated.　　　　　　　　　　1920
　　　　As for her, her womb's contents were Taugi and his
　　　　brother.
When Tanumakalu was giving birth the others came out as
newborn infants,
　　males.

They looked just like those of us here.
Their small bows were strung tightly in their hands. 1925
Taugi cradled them in his arms.
Then once again they were coming,
    her womb's contents kept coming out.
There were even more of them.
    She had walked over three arrows. 1930
The hatted ones,
    the Christians' ancestors came into being.
        They were to be the Christians' ancestors.
            We had all come out.
They began to grow. 1935
    Mbutsik, they shot up until they were fully grown.
    They were wearing hats,
        they wore this kind of thing, shirts,
            and shoes as well.
Their shooters were carbines which they picked up. 1940
They became adults,
    those who had been in her womb.
        They kept growing.
As she kept suckling them,
    and they grew. 1945
        They were almost fully grown.
They all grew to be the same size.
    They were tall, they were fully grown.
        They had become adults.
Those were the older brothers. 1950
The Christians were placed far away from here.
    They were placed,
        the Christians were placed far away.
    "Go away," I'm told he said to them.
        "People will remain here." 1955
            I mean we people, such as exist now.
    We remain living here,
        as we do now.
            All of us remain here in our settlements.
Land was also given to those other people. 1960
    They went to a distant place.
    "Go far away," he told them,
        "Go far away to your possessions."
            He sent them away.
Christians' possessions. 1965
    Things like this here,
        they became abundant.

Even more new things like this were created by him.
　　Such as knives.
　　Such as axes. 1970
　　Such as scissors.
　　　　Such as brush cutters.
　　　　Such as cane cutters.
　　　　All kinds of things.
　　　　The object used for looking at oneself. 1975
　　　　　"Go far away," he said.
He also gave out possessions to us.
　　Such as shell belts to acquire,
　　　　which still exist.
　　Such as shell collars to acquire, 1980
　　　　which still exist.
　　The large land snail which is still worked, as you've seen.
　　That's all.
　　Gourds.
"You'll always be poor, you people. 1985
　　Whatever you want to acquire, you'll go ask for it.
　　Your possessions will be used for trading.
　　　　You'll give your possessions to someone like this.
　　They are to be used for trading.
　　　　You'll give your possessions away." 1990
　　Their older brother said this,
　　　　Taugi spoke.
　　　　　Sun spoke.
　　　　　　That was what he told them.
　　"All right," they agreed, 1995
　　　　as they went away.
They went away after that,
　　　　carrying their possessions.
　　We people,
　　　　those like us took the gourds. 2000
　　Taugi's possessions are also gourds.
　　Taugi's settlement is at Faukugu, far far away!
　　　　In the direction of the Culiseu River.
　　　　　Far, far away!
　　I myself once saw his settlement. 2005
　　　　My people have never seen it.
　　　　　I alone saw it once.
　　My people here are still ripening.
　　　　Their penises are still black,
　　　　　they're merely children. 2010
　　However I'm much older.
　　You yourself are still the same as they.

Look at all my people,
　　think of who my children are.
Once I was a child,　　　　　　　　　　　　　　2015
　　now I've grown old.
They went away,
　　and then they appeared there.
　　　　They stayed there.
They began to marry.　　　　　　　　　　　　　2020
　　They reproduced.
The Christians grew numerous.
At this place, at that place,
　　they went all over.
　　　　They went all over.　　　　　　　　　　2025
They multiplied,
　　they multiplied,
　　　　while they settled in many places.
　　　　The Christians settled all over.
We are still here.　　　　　　　　　　　　　　2030
　　Those who are like us are still here.
We are settled on our land, which Taugi set aside as ours.
We stay right here because he set aside this place as ours.
But you people must keep to your own land,
　　the land of the Christians, I mean,　　　　　2035
　　　　which he set aside for you,
　　　　which Taugi set aside for you.
Even newer things were invented,
　　you people made airplanes.
You people invent new things.　　　　　　　　2040
　　This thing here . . .
　　　　the tape recorder was made that way.

It's over. It's finally ended.

Notes to "Kwatïngï"
lines
68　　Kambe indicated a piece of crudely made cord hanging nearby, of a
　　　type that can be made on the spur of the moment from some in-
　　　completely processed materials.
71　　"some ill-favored women I've found . . .": a self-deprecating remark
　　　that is usually made by Kalapalo men when they offer daughters
　　　in marriage. (See also "Taugi Gets Fire from King Vulture," lines
　　　270; 330.)
83　　*madyafi:* a bow made from a dense, black hardwood that is now the
　　　specialty of the Tupi-speaking Kamaiura settlement.
185–190　*wagu, iku:* rather common trees whose wood splits easily.

209	Quartz nodules, used to make arrowheads, was gathered in the past on a certain sand bank in the southern region of Kalapalo territory.
227	The "hair" given by these powerful beings was actually several species of water plants.
249	This bamboo was used to line the women's vaginas and to arouse Tapir and, later, their other lovers. Some Kalapalo men make an aphrodisiac irritant from it.
274	"just like your own": a reference to my hammock, which at the time was slung by my own hearth in Kambe's house.
295	*wegufi:* an unidentified species of extremely dense hardwood with a distinctly red heartwood, from which memorial posts are now made during the *egitsu* ceremony that commemorates dead leaders. The Kalapalo call this species the "leader" of the trees.
498	"palm-slat seats": a type of seat used by women.
550–551	Because Itsangitsegï, the oldest sister, had blown a spell onto his penis.
785	*itofake* or *wagiti* (in Portuguese, *matrinxão*): a common, highly desired fish belonging to the Brycon genus.
1036	These whistling arrows are made from the pierced nuts of the tucum palm (*Astrocaryum tucuma*).
1051	*fikuanga:* a large bivalve whose shells are used for cutting purposes.
1069	Twitches on various parts of the body are interpreted as messages about the person's relatives.
1227	Kambe is suddenly embarrassed as he remembers that he has been using the name of one of his long-dead mothers-in-law, in violation of Kalapalo expectations about how people should talk about relatives by marriage.
1229	*amunau:* word for "leader" in Mehinaku, an Arawak-speaking settlement.
1233	*kapitaū:* from the Portuguese *capitão,* a title given by outsiders to Xingu leaders, called *anetau* in Kalapalo.
1355	The Tinamous imply that had the boys' real mother been alive they wouldn't be hungry.
1414	The red-wing tinamous bird typically lives in the scrub found around Xingu settlements.
1427	"Nefuku" is another name for "Moon."
1497–1501	Taugi addresses his father by the title "Leader," rather than as "Father," indicating his deep estrangement.
1519	Huge noses without bridges are characteristic of powerful beings. Here, as elsewhere in the story when he comments on this feature, Kambe is alluding to the beings' nasty character.
1525	Taugi owns a magical hook that he uses to pull distant settlements to him when he wants to visit them, while he remains stationary. As a trickster, his means of travel is the reverse of that of ordinary people, who must walk or canoe to get to their destinations.
1572	The "butterflies" were actually bats.
1661–1663	"Kwamïtini": the name used by Arawak speakers in the Upper Xingu to refer to Kwatïngï. Von den Steinen (1894) reported this name in use by the Carib-speaking Bakairi of the Paranatinga River to the

south of the Upper Xingu Basin. The Bakairi claimed Kwatïngï was buried in that region.

1732–1752 This is the origin of the current Kalapalo association of the maned wolf with death and sorcery. The animal is also connected with distant travel because of its ability to run quickly for exceedingly long distances (see "Taugi and Fiery" for one development of this idea). The zoological name is *Chrysocyon brachyurus*.

When Kwatïngï traveled to Nitsuegï's settlement to weep for his daughter, he originated the practice of publicly mourning a dead relative at the place of death. Kwatïngï was accompanied by his co-evals Sataka ? the hook-billed kite (*Chandrohierax uncintus uncintus*), Ikwagutafa the Six-banded Armadillo (*Euphractus* species), and Aguga the Giant Armadillo (*Priodontes*). The calls of these animals, henceforth considered the Masters of Mourning, seem to be dirges. The latter two animals are excellent burrowers, and together with the digger wasp (*tunutunugi*) made the first tunnel-graves for Itsangisegï. Thus originated the practice of burying deceased hereditary leaders in this manner.

1847 "Grandfather" is a respectful term of address for an older person with grandchildren. The respect is engendered by the speaker's relation through marriage to the listener. Here, Toucan addresses Nitsuegï as if they were son-in-law and father-in-law. The "grandchildren" are the Fierce People who have just been created by Taugi, and this seems to imply that Taugi's impregnation of his substitute mother is interpreted as incestuous. Although her impregnation occurs magically by means of arrows, the word for arrow (*fïgéy*) is a pun on the word for penis (*fïgi*).

I have been told the story of Kwatïngï five times, in varying degrees of detail, always by older male dignitaries. Each time, the narrator extended his narrative past the final events, to comment about the relationship between native peoples and Europeans or "Christians." When I first heard the story from Apihū, he concluded by emphasizing the peaceful nature of the people of the Upper Xingu basin, in contrast with the violence of both the Fierce People and the Christians:

"Each (human group) received weapons from Taugi. War clubs to the Fierce People, guns to the Christians, bows and arrows to we people. That is why we people who live here are peaceful, why we don't get angry with other human beings. When we're angry, it's just with our mouths, because we are all brothers, we have all come from one mother, we have *ifutisu* for other human beings."

And here, too, Kambe reflects upon the carelessness with which Europeans fail to heed their territorial mandate from Taugi. At the time Kambe was telling me the story, the Kalapalo and their neighbors were coming to realize how close ranchers and farmers were living to them; it was a time of serious conflicts in the north of the Park between settlers and Indians, whose lands were being deliberately invaded. People were starting to travel to Brasília to complain about the lack of protection from the responsible government agency, FUNAI.

The story "Kwatïngï" is deeply relevant to these concerns for reasons other than the description of how Christians and Indians came into being as distinct peoples. In fact, their appearance, and the potential for conflict between them, is directly related in the story to the fact that they were created by the trickster Taugi. Relations between the Indians and others are complex and ambivalent because Taugi created possibilities for effectively peaceful and mutually beneficial relations, on the one hand, and for violence and hatred between entire categories of people on the other. In other words, it is up to individuals to create whatever conditions will actually effect one or the other kind of possibility; Taugi enabled such conditions to be effective.

The distinctive, noble character of Kwatïngï is neatly contrasted with that of Taugi or other, more human characters who seem to embody all the negative feelings of which people are capable. Kwatïngï's presence is like an island, calming, comforting, and healing, in a sea of turbulent episodes. Typically, in these stories, one of his grandsons undergoes painful or humiliating ordeals that are apparently impossible to accomplish, and which are designed to destroy him. As an anxious and determined grandfather, Kwatïngï concretely expresses his restrained dignity and compassion by helping his relatives and by grieving when he believes they are lost to him.

The story of how Kangangafanga overcomes his older brother Kangangatï is as much about the contrasting feelings Kwatïngï has for these brothers as it is about their own bitter rivalry. The trials of the younger brother are successfully resolved with the help of Kwatïngï, who repeatedly explains to his grandson how to survive the ordeals his obsessive, vengeful older brother devises for him. In other stories, about his grandsons Yanama and Akwakanga, Kwatïngï dresses the beautiful youths in the repulsive disguise of running sores, in order to trap their various relatives in guilty displays of hateful envy and erotic selfishness.

Muluku

Kangangafanga

Told by Muluku at Aifa. November 2, 1979.

Notes appear on pages 107–109.

Listen.
   This is what Kangangatï did to him.
Kangangafanga spoke:
   "This thing here is like Ukwaka's vulva,
      that's like this thing. 5
         That's like the flower of *afusagu* bushes," he said.*
His older brother heard him.
   "I see, you have seduced her.
      Out of envy for me you have done this,
         very well," he said. 10
Following that,
   "Well, Ukwaka," he said.
   (That's her name Ukwaka, Kangangatï's wife.)
   "Ukwaka," he said,
   "Send the father of our children-to-be to capture *takugugu*, a
      puffbird.* 15
      Make him go capture a puffbird,
         to capture my pet.
         There are some to be found," he said.
   "Very well," she said.
She came to him. 20
   "Well, Kangangafanga," she said,
   "I came to you in order to send you to capture a pet for your
   older brother," she said.
      "A puffbird's child.
         There are some to be found at a certain place.
   'I've made a mark on the trail,' he told me." 25
   "Very well," the other said,
      "I'm going right away," so she left.
"Well, Grandson," he said,
      Kwatïngï spoke.
   "What did the mother of our non-existent children say? What?* 30
   I don't speak to my grandson."
   "Well, I'm leaving to capture your grandson's pet."
   "I don't speak to your older brother," Kwatïngï said.
      "That is certain death," he continued,
         "That's how your older brother will kill you." 35

"I see," Kangangafanga said.
"This time you must take those of my flesh with you, my
flesh," Kwatïngï continued,*
        "Go with those of my flesh," he said.
        Faka, the Burity Palm shoots.*
    "Go with your Grandfathers."   40
        "Very well," Kangangafanga answered.
Then when the sun was at its height,
    "My grandfathers," Kangangafanga said,
        "To capture your grandson's pet," he said.
            "Very well," they answered.   45
They came,
    and then they all went away to that place.
When they came to that place the snakes that were there bit
into the spongy palm shoots,
        the snakes coiled around them.
            They were rattlesnakes.   50
        Next *bïk!*
            Kangangafanga grabbed one.
Then,
    "Kangangatï," he told him,
        "Here is your pet."   55
    "All right," his older brother answered.
        "Bring it here to me."
Well, he brought him a rattlesnake!
    "This isn't a proper pet," Ukwaka said, his wife said.
        "There's nothing good about this pet of his."   60
            Kangangatï beat it,
                he beat the snake to death.
Then after he did that he pulled out the snake's teeth,
    the snake's teeth were pulled out by him.
"Well, Ukwaka," he told her,   65
    "Send for the father of our children-to-be right away.
    Because I want to scrape him," he said.*
        "I want to be his scraper."
        "All right," she said.
Then she came to him.   70
    "Well, Kangangafanga," she told him,
        "He wants to be your scraper, so go to him right now!
        He wants to be your scraper."
            "All right," he replied.

"Well, what did she just tell you?   75
What did the mother of our children-to-be just say?" Kwatïngï
asked.
    "It's just that your grandson wants to scrape me, your
grandson."
    "He does, does he?" he replied,
        "That is certain death.
    Why did you have to speak that way about your older brother's
    wife before? Why?   80
        Your older brother is always doing this.
    He will kill you.
        Your older brother knows how to kill you.
This time you must take your grandfathers with you," Kwatïngï
continued,
        "Those of my flesh."   85
    Fegita Palm and *Katsëgë* Tree,*
        those are the names of Kangangafanga's grandfathers.
"Go now," Kwatïngï said.
    "Your older brother wants to kill you with the snake," he told
    him, as the other went away.
"Come here right now, I want to scrape you all over."   90
    Tsiu tsiu tsiu, all over.
Then it was finished.
    "That's all," Kangangatï said.
    So Kangangafanga left.
Then he removed the pieces of plants from his body *kï kï kï kï . . .*
tsik!   95
    He threw them away.
    "Now, go someplace far from here!" he said.
Then *tsiu tsiu tsiu*, his grandfather scraped him.
    That time Kwatïngï did that with his own bloodletting
    instrument.
        When he was finished, Kangangafanga had become beautiful
        once again.   100

Following that,
    "Well, Ukwaka," Kangangatï told her,
        "Send the father of our children-to-be to get my *wegufi* log,
        my *wegufi* log."*
            "All right," she replied.   105
    She arrived.
    "Well, Kangangafanga," she said,
        "I've come to you in order to send you for your older brother's
        wëgufi log."

"All right," he answered.
"I'll go there again without delay." 110
"Well, Grandson," he went, Kwatïngï said.
"What did the mother of our children-to-be say, what?
I don't speak to my grandson."
"Why, I'm leaving to get his *wēgufi* log."
"You will die that way," Kwatïngï told him. 115
"Your older brother wants your bones to be crushed."
"I see."
"This time take those of my flesh with you," he said.
They were Nguke the Termites.
"All right." 120
Then when the sun was here,
"Come along to get your grandson's *wegufi* log."
"All right,"
and they all left, *titititi*.
The Termites blew a spell, 125
they blew a spell onto the log and it grew lighter.
It was no longer as heavy as it was.
Then Kangangafanga arrived outside the house of his older
brother.
"Well, Kangangatï," he said,
"Here is your *wēgufi* log." 130
"All right, bring it inside.
Bring it inside and put it down in the entrance."
Then he came inside with the *wēgufi* log and *bom*, tossed it
down.
It didn't feel heavy to him at all,
because of what the Termites had done to it. 135
"Well, how was he able to do that?"

Following that Kangangatï said,
"Well, Ukwaka, Ukwaka.
Send the father of our children . . . Do, make him go get *kaifa*,
some tucum nuts."*
"All right," she answered, 140
and she left.
"Well, Kangangafanga, go collect your older brother's tucum nuts,
your older brother's tucum nuts."
"All right," he replied,
"I'll certainly go." 145
Then,
"Grandson, what did the mother of your children-to-be just
say? What?

He deceives us, I don't speak to my grandson."
"I see.
I'm going to collect your grandson's tucum nuts."   150
"I see," he answered.
"Now, you will certainly be done for! You'll be done for,"
he said.
"There are monsters there who will eat you."
"I see," the other said.
"You must go with your grandfathers.   155
This time take those of my flesh with you."
(Those are Atuta the Spiders,*
and Igu the Squirrels.
Those two are Kwatïngï's brothers.
Both of them.)   160
Next Kangangafanga traveled.
He walked on *ti ti ti* to the lake of the Kamaiura.
There it was,
the Kamaiura Lake.
He went to it.   165
In the middle of the lake were the tucum palms,
and the monsters as well.
Many of them.
Afterward the others came.
The Spiders were spinning webs across the water.   170
The Squirrels went on top of them to get the tucum nuts
and returned safely.
Then at dusk Kangangafanga arrived home.
"Alas my grandson, alas my grandson," Kwatïngï was saying.
"Grandfather, open the door for me. Grandfather, open the
door for me."
"Why, who are you beating on my door?   175
Why, you can't be my grandson!"
"Grandfather," he said.
"It's really me."
"My grandson is right here!"

The next day before dawn Kangangafanga went to bathe and they
heard him pounding the water.*   180
"There he is, he who was your daughter's burden, your
daughter's burden."*
Then again *tuk! tuk! tuk!*, he pounded the water.
"Listen, Kangangafanga is bathing," Ukwaka said.
"The monsters finished eating him a long time ago as they
always do.

The monsters finished eating him a long time ago as they
always do." 185
"I'm going to see who is over there."*
She went away.
"You're here, aren't you?" she said.
"Yes, I'm certainly here."
"Kangangatï," she said. 190
"Look, Kangangafanga has arrived, look."
"Those with dangerous power should have destroyed him, why
didn't they?
What shall I do now?" he said.
"What is the best thing for me to do?"
Then, "Here are your tucum nuts, here are your tucum nuts." 195
"All right.
Well, bring them here to me.
I sent you because it was hard for me to do."
"All right."
"What can I do now?" Kangangatï said. 200
"Ukwaka, send the father of our children-to-be to get my belts.
Make him go to Aikaku.
For my shell belts."*
"All right," she went.
"As you wish, I'll speak to him right away," his wife said. 205
Ti ti ti she left.
Ti ti ti she arrived beside him.
"Kangangafanga," she told him,
"Go to Aikaku for your older brother's shell belts."
"All right," he replied, 210
"I certainly will go."
"Well, Grandson," Kwatïngï said.
"Grandson, what did the mother of our children-to-be say to you
this time? What?
I don't speak to my grandson."
"I'm going to get your grandson's belts, his shell belts. 215
At Aikaku."
"But we don't go there.
That is your certain death.
The Aikaku monsters will be sure to kill you,
The Aikaku. 220
That's not a place we go to.
Go with your grandfathers,
this time you will take your grandfathers with you.
My flesh will accompany you."
"All right," he answered. 225

The next day long before dawn,
"Let's all go."
They all left *ti ti ti ti,*
ti ti ti ti and entered the path to the Aikaku settlement.
They were near Aueti.   230
"Stay here," he said to his grandfathers.
Leg Cramps, Leg Prickles, Slips on Mud, Ifogogu the small
stick that catches on our toenails, Isatë the hooked vine that
catches onto our hair.
Five of his grandfathers.
"Stay here, you must stay to watch."
Then he arrived.   235
"Koh koh koh!" the Aikaku cried out.
"Someone who causes hunger who causes hunger who
causes hunger is here," they said.
"Who are you?" they said.
"Why, someone who causes hunger is here!" they said.
"We plan to eat you."   240
"Why, he must be Kangangafanga."
"Why, we'll soon start to eat him."
They all took hold of him.
He was held by his wrists and brought to the plaza.
"Stay here."   245
"This part of him here is mine!" one of them said, as he placed a
belt around his waist.
"This part here must be mine!" another said.
"This part."
"This part."
He was covered all over with their shell belts.   250
There were even some around his brow,
and all over his body.
"That's enough," the Aikaku said.
"Listen to what I say, dear grandfathers.
Let's wait some more because I want to sing for you, I'll sing for
you," Kangangafanga said.   255
"However when I am finished you can eat me right away,
here in your plaza."
"All right!" they answered,
"That's all right with us," they told him.
"Soon our grandson will be destroyed," the Aikaku said.   260
Then they began to dance,
they were dancing around the plaza.
"Look, you'll be destroyed."
"When he's finished singing we'll all eat him, when he's finished."

Being the last one in line he ran to the path.   265
    Well, he ran away, he ran away!
    As he ran,
        "Look, he's running away!"
    They ran out from the plaza,
        all the Aikaku ran.   270
    Burudu burudu, as they passed by the house circle they began
    to fall down,
        the Aikaku began to fall down.
    The first one *bum,*
        the next one *bum.*
    It was Leg Cramps,   275
        it was Slips on Mud,
        it was The Stick that Trips Us,
            it was Hooked Vine.
    Kangangafanga was running as hard as he could!
        How he ran after that!   280
    He went around them and in that way they missed him.
        Oh! He ran hard that time!
    "Now, let him be," the Aikaku said.
        "He's really gone, that one," they said.
            "He didn't let us catch him even though we tried hard.   285
            Well, he's gone,"
                as the others went away.

Then they arrived at dusk.
    "Alas, my grandson!"
        "Grandfather, open the door for me!"   290
    "Why, who are you?" he said.
        "Why, you're not like my grandson.
            You've just been making fun of me, haven't you?"
    "No, Grandfather, it's me," he replied.
    "Yes, I do think my grandson is here . . . no, he's no longer
    alive," the other said.   295
        "No, he's no longer alive.
            That's not a place we go to,
                that's not a place we go to."

The next day before dawn *tuk tuk tuk,*
        someone was bathing.   300
    "Well Kangangatï," she told him,
        Ukwaka said.
    "Kangangatï, listen.
        Your younger brother is bathing."

"The Aikaku finished eating him a long time ago, as I expected
them to.
A long time ago."
"I'll go see,"
as she went away to the water's edge.
Ti ti ti she arrived at the water's edge.
"So you are here," she told him.
"Yes, I am here."
"Very well," she replied.
Well, she came back.
"Say, Kangangatï," she said,
"Go look for yourself,
your brother has already arrived."
"I was sure he'd be destroyed by their dangerous
power. What happened?" he said to himself.
At dawn Kangangafanga brought the shell belts to him.
"Kangangatï," he told him,
"Here are your belts."
"All right," the other answered.
"I thought he would be destroyed. Why wasn't he?
He must have his own dangerous power, he must have his own
dangerous power.
Is there anything I can do to kill him?" he said.
"Well, Ukwaka, send the father of our nonexistent children
to get some shaman's rattles.
Make him go to Eke the Snakes.
I want my shaman's rattles."
"All right," she answered.
Then *tikii* she arrived in the doorway of his house.
"Well, Kangangafanga, go to the Snakes to get your older
brother's rattles."
"All right," he answered,
"I will certainly be going."
"Grandson," Kwatïngï said,
"What was it your older brother's wife just said? What?
I don't speak to my grandson," he said.
"I'm going to the Snakes to get your grandson's rattles."
"You're done for if you do that," he told him.
"Why, those grandfathers of yours will eat you.
Why, we never go to that place, I tell you.
We never go there."
"I see," the other replied.

305

310

315

320

325

330

335

340

"You must take your grandfathers with you this time without
fail,
    your grandfathers."
        "Very well."   345
            (Grasshoppers who are called Rattle Speakers, that
            time it was the Rattle Speakers.)
    "You must take your grandfathers with you this time,
        go with your grandfathers."
            "Very well," he replied.

At the very beginning of the next day they left, *tititi*.   350
    So, they arrived at the Snakes' settlement.
    Then they were there,
        just outside the house circle.
            That's where they all waited.
One of the Snakes was shaking a rattle at its grandchild inside the
house.   355
    Kangangafanga beckoned to it,
        and the Snake came to him.
    "Well, why are you here?" the Snake said.
    "I came to get this, to get some of your rattles."
    "All right," she said,   360
        "Take this one, I'll make another one."
    "All right," he said,
        Kangangafanga said.
Then she brought him another one.
    "Go get another one!   365
    Soon someone else will come to you.
    You must say, 'The rattle no longer works because it shattered
    when my child dropped it.'"
    "All right," the Snake said,
        "My poor little child has broken its toy."
    "Yes, that's right," Kangangafanga replied.   370
Then she came to the others.
    "My dear child's toy no longer works."
    "All right, here's another one."
        They gave her one.
    The Snake brought it to Kangangafanga.   375
        And another one.
            Kangangafanga now had three.
"That's enough," he went,
        "I'm leaving now."

He walked away, *ti ti ti ti ti ti.*
He entered the visitor's path,
"I want to try them out right here,
I want to try them out right here."
"All right," his companions the Grasshoppers answered.
Tsuk!   385
The owners heard,
the Snakes heard,
the Snakes.
"Hey! Who's touching our things?
Quickly, let's go look!"   390
They ran off in different directions—Ekefugutinïgï the Blackened
Snakes did that—to get their rattles back.
Tsik tsik tsik tsik,
it was the Rattle Speakers,
the Grasshoppers.
"Here, here, here!"   395
The Snakes surrounded them.
"Well! These people are doing that, Rattle Speakers.
Rattle Speakers are the ones who are doing that."
They left them alone.
"Let them be, they're the ones who are doing that," they said.   400
They went away,
They finally did go away!
Then the others arrived home.
After that Kangangafanga brought the rattles to his brother.
"Kangangatï," he said,   405
"Here are your rattles."
"All right!" he said.
"Because it was difficult for me to go I was the one to send
you there, because it was difficult for me."
"Very well," he said.
"Now Ukwaka," Kangangatï said,   410
"Send the father of our children-to-be to get tobacco leaves,*
tobacco leaves, to get its leaves.
Send the father of our children-to-be to get tobacco leaves.
Make him go to Atuguakuegï the Whirlwind
on the other side of the sky."   415
"All right," she said, so she left.
"Now Kangangafanga," she said,
"Your older brother just sent me to you to make you get
tobacco leaves, he wants you to go."
"All right," he answered,
"Why, I will certainly go."   420

"What did the mother of our children-to-be just say?"
Kwatïngï asked.
"Oh, I don't speak to my grandson!"
"I am going to Whirlwind to get your grandson's tobacco
leaves for him."
"I see," he said,
"You're sure to be destroyed if you do that.   425
Why, your older brother will use them to kill you."
"Very well."
"You must take your grandfathers with you, your
grandfathers."
They were Kwosose the Moths.*

Then very early while it was still dark he left.   430
"Grandfather, I'm going right now for that thing."
"Go then."
He left for that same place, *titititi*.
"My grandfathers, go ahead. You will all go with your
grandson. Take his place."
Then they all went away together.   435
Next he began to pick the tobacco leaves.
Then he picked those that had been placed in the very middle
of the house.
In the very middle he picked the tobacco leaves.
At the place of Whirlwind.
The owner was listening.   440
It was late at night when he began to pick it.
At night.
They were picking the tobacco leaves.
"Who is that picking your tobacco leaves?"
They came and saw the Moths.   445
"It's only these creatures here who are doing that, let them be."
"All right," Kangangafanga said. "That's enough," he went,
"Let's go now," he told them.
They all arrived home.

"Alas, my grandson," Kwatïngï was saying.   450
"Alas, my grandson," he said.
"Grandfather, open the door for me!"
"Why, who is that just starting to make fun of me?
There is only one grandson of mine," he answered.
"Grandfather, it's really me!"   455
"Why, my grandson is no longer alive!" he said.
"Grandfather, I really have come back to you!"
"Very well," he replied.

"I wasn't killed. Not at all."
"Because we don't go there your grandfathers don't speak to
them.
    We don't go there.
        Why, they aren't human."
After Kangangafanga arrived, the next day he brought his older
brother the tobacco leaves.
    "Kangangatï, here are the tobacco leaves."
    "Do bring them to me!
        I sent you because it was difficult for me,
            because it was difficult for me!"
            "Very well," he answered.
    "He is still safe because of his dangerous power.
        Is there anything I can do?" Kangangatï said.
            Is there anything I can do?"
"Ukwaka," he said.
    "Send the father of our children-to-be to get the thunder
knife.*
        Make him go to Storm to get the thunder knife,
            I want his thunder knife so badly!"
    "All right," she replied.
        "As you wish, I am going right away," and she left.
    "Well, Kangangafanga, I've come to you because now your older
brother is sending you away. Your older brother is doing this."
    "All right."
    "Your older brother wants you to go to Storm to get the thunder
knife."
        "All right," he answered,
            "I'll certainly go," he said.
"Grandson," Kwatïngï said,
    "What did the mother of our children-to-be just say?
        I don't speak with my grandson."
    "I'm going to get the thunder knife,
        I'm going to Storm to get the thunder knife for your
        grandson."
"I see.
    Now you're done for.
    We don't visit those beings you're talking about, those beings.
        We don't go there.
            It is death," he told him.
    "Your older brother won't stop trying to kill you," Kwatïngï was
saying.
        "Very well," Kangangafanga said.

460

465

470

475

480

485

490

"You must be sure to take your grandfathers with you this time,
your grandfathers.   495
        I mean those of my flesh.
            Tuluma the Large Woodpecker, Itu the Smaller
            Woodpecker, Agapawa the Curved-Bill Creeper, Itsïka the
            Least Woodpecker.*
That is how you must go this time, taking them with you.
        You will take your grandfathers with you.
Then you will speak to your grandfather.   500
        He is my flesh.
        'Grandfather,' that is how you will address him.
        'My flesh really gossips about you,' you must be sure to say to
your grandfather.
        'My flesh really gossips about you.
        'My grandfather seems to slander you when he speaks to his
grandchildren's mother.' You must be sure to say that to your
grandfather.
You will go to the center of the plaza, your grandfather will be
escorting you to the plaza.   505
        'Grandfather, listen carefully to what I say to you,' you will say.
            'Our grandfather seems to lie about you all the time to your
            grandson's mother.
            Your flesh really gossips with her, Grandfather.'
                You must be sure to speak that way to your grandfather!"
                "All right."   510
"While that is happening, your other grandfathers must take
the form of woodpeckers and fly inside to steal his possessions.
        Have the others do that."
        "All right," Kangangafanga answered, and he left.
"Let's go, my dear grandfathers," he told them.
So he walked away, *ti ti ti.*   515
        He arrived at the settlement of Storm.
Far across the sky.
        "Grandfather," he said,
            "As you see, I have really come to you, I have come to you."
        "Very well, it really does seem as if my grandson has come here.   520
            It really does seem to be my cherished grandson.
Well, Grandson," he said.
        "Why have you come to see me, why?"
        "There's no particular reason why I've just come to see you this
time. I've just come to see you."
        "All right," Storm answered.   525
        "Come sit by me."

He went to get a wooden seat for his grandson to sit on in the
plaza.
"Grandfathers, while he's doing this, you go get it!"
"All right!" they answered.
"Well, Grandfather, your grandson's grandfather certainly speaks
of your flesh!
530
He seems to lie to his grandson's mother all the time.
Your flesh gossips about you.
Your flesh speaks of you."*
How Storm laughed at him!
His grandfather was laughing,
535
Storm was laughing.
He questioned Kangangafanga about what Kwatïngï said,
he questioned him.
"Ha ha, what does he say, Grandson?"
"Your flesh gossips about you.
540
He seems to lie to your grandson's mother,
to your grandchildren's mother.
Your flesh gossips about you.
Your flesh talks about you."
"I see!" Storm said.
545
Oh, he laughed so hard!
"Ah ha ha!"
He went off to the side away from Kangangafanga.
Storm went rolling around on the ground.
While he was doing that the others approached as they had
planned.
550
Big Woodpecker, Little Woodpecker, Curved-Bill Creeper,
Least Woodpecker.
To get the thunder knife.
They were bringing it to Kangangafanga at the far end of the
entrance path.
"Grandfather," he said, "I must go now."
"Go then.
555
You really gossip yourself, you: 'Your flesh gossips about
you.'"
He couldn't stop laughing!
While the others were doing as planned he was left there,
still smiling as he had been doing before.
Then he came back, he was arriving at his house.
560
He came inside, Storm came inside.
He kept the thunder knives lined up on the house rafters,
high on the top of the house.
He looked at them.
They were no longer in place.
565

He became enraged,
  Thunder was enraged,
    so he hacked at his own house posts.
  "You certainly lied to me, didn't you?
    Why, it was you who was lying to me!" 570
Then Kangangafanga arrived home.
  "Alas, my grandson," Kwatïngï was saying,
    "Alas, my grandson," he cried out.
  "Now Grandfather. Open the door for me!"
  "Who is making fun of me? 575
    My grandson is no longer alive."
      "I am really here, Grandfather."
The next day he brought it to his older brother.
  "Well, Kangangatï," he said.
    "Here is your thunder knife." 580
  "All right," he said, "Do bring it to me.
    Because it was a difficult place for me to go to I was the one
    to send you, to the place that is difficult for me.
      Do bring it to me!
        Your powerful spells have kept you alive.
          (Is there anything I can do?)" 585
"Well, Ukwaka!" he said.
  "Send the father of our nonexistent children to collect my pet.
    Make him to go to the children of *kutsu*, the ornate hawk-
    eagle."*
  "Where?"
    "Just beyond the manioc fields." 590
      "All right," she answered.
Tikii, she came inside the house.
  "Why are you here?"
  "Your older brother wants you to find a pet, to get the ornate
  hawk-eagle's child.
    There's a nest just beyond the manioc fields," she said. 595
  "All right, I will go without fail, I will go there," he said.
  "'Make him go with me without fail.'
    You must say that to him," that's what Kangangatï told me to
    tell you," she said to him.
      "All right."
Then *ti ti ti* he walked over to Kwatïngï. 600
  "Grandson, what did the mother of our children-to-be just say?
    I don't speak with my grandson."
  "I'm going to get your grandson's pet,
    to get the ornate hawk-eagle's child."

"I see.   605
    That is certain death, death.
        You will starve," he said to him.
            "You will starve," he told him,
                Kwatïngï said.
"You must take your grandfathers with you, your grandfathers.   610
    Some of my flesh are Umbe the Mice.
        This time take those grandfathers of yours with you."
            "All right," he said.
"This time, kill some of your grandfathers."
            "All right," he said.   615
Then he killed some.
    He put them in a small basket.
"Kangangatï, come on, let's go.
    Let's go collecting near the manioc fields.
        I'm afraid of collecting, I'm afraid."   620
"All right," he said,
    "Let's go," he said.
        Ti ti ti the two brothers walked away.
            Ti ti ti ti.
"That's it up there," Kangangatï said.   625
    "Just as you wish, I'm going right up."
Kangangafanga went climbing up, *tsïgï tsïgï tsïgï.*
He was way on top of the *fingi* tree.
    "Well, is it there?" Kangangatï asked.
"There's nothing here.   630
    There doesn't seem to be anything like it here.
        It's just a tree, just a tree."
"Go farther up, lie down on the branches,
    go farther up lying on the branches."
"There's nothing here!   635
    There's nothing here."
"You don't see anything?"
    "Nothing."
"Very well, so be it."
Then Kangangatï slapped the tree *tuki tuki tuki!*   640
    Far up high! Onto the sky, very far above!
"You can stay there.
    Starve, since you did that, starve.
        You just couldn't stop cheating me before, you kept doing
        that.
            It might have been another person who kept doing that
            before, but it was you and you alone who could never
            stop!"   645

There in that same place Kangangafanga cried and cried.
    He was way on top of the tree.
    He picked off some bromeliad plants that were also on the tree,*
    and *kidi*, sat down way on top.
        There he remained, weeping.   650
Then he slept, he slept, he slept,
    he slept ten days on top.
        He was really starving to death!

Then Kuguagi the Vulture came.*
    "Well! Grandson, what are you doing here?   655
    Was it really your older brother who made this tree grow so
    high?"
    "Yes," he answered.
        "Look at this and think about me, I'm going to starve."
    "Yes, you will," she answered.
    "Look, would you please be able to rescue me, to rescue me?"   660
    "Yes, I will," she said.
    "Wait a short while longer, I want to get your grandmother,
    your grandmother.
        My own canoe is just a small one, just a small one."
        "Very well," so she went away to another vulture.
  "We should go get that grandson of ours who is over there," she
said.   665
        "All right," the other Vulture said.
    So, they came once more,
        the Vultures came.
        This time there was a large one as well.
  "Well, your grandson is starving to death."   670
    "Well, your older brother despised you, your older brother
    despised you!"
    "Yes, look at this and think about me," he answered.
        "All right," she said.
    "Now look!
        We should try these things we eat right away.   675
        We should try these things we eat."
    "All right," the other said.
    "I want to nibble on them right now."
    So she ate them,
        she ate the mice.   680
When that was done,
    "Let's go, let's go carry away our grandson, our grandson."
    "Get on here."

They carried him away.
   They went away, 685
      they went far away onto the other side of the sky!
         To Tolofïtï, the Place of Many Birds.
They all arrived.
   "All right now."
He was concealed, 690
   he became housed in a seclusion chamber.
"Let's get our grandson's medicinal drink," the Vultures said.
   "Our grandson's medicinal drink."
      "All right," the other said.
That was *tafatagi.** 695
   "Go ahead, drink this.
      Very soon you will be lively again, soon," the Vultures said.
Then he used the medicine, *tsu tsu tsu.*
   He cleansed his stomach.
After a short time he became fat, 700
   he became fat.
      He remained with his rescuers.
Then a Bird Woman spoke.
   "Well, who could that be in the house next door?
      Who is staying in the rotten-smelling people's house?" 705
         (Those people were known as "the rotten-smelling ones.")
   "Someone is over there.
      Who's that person over there?
         Am I right that there's someone being secluded now?"
   "Go ahead and look." 710
      "I'll go see," the Bird Woman said.
She saw his shell collar gleaming inside the house.
   "Well, who are you?"
   "I'm sure it's me."
      "All right," she said. 715
Then he made love to her.
When he finished another one came inside,
   then another Bird Woman came to him.
He was pulling out their tails, *tugu!**
   All of them came to him. 720
Then the Vultures brought fish to him for his food.
   The Vultures brought fish that had been killed by fish poison
   vines.
There were no furred animals,
   because he never ate furred animal flesh.*
      Just one kind of food—fish—was Kangangafanga's food. 725

"All right, now we must bring our grandson outside."
   Because he had pulled out the tails of all of the Bird Women.
      "All right, now we must bring our grandson outside.
         Why is it that those who prepare our food have had their
         tails pulled out? Why?" the Birds were saying to one
         another.   730
   The Vultures had been listening.
      "Well, let's bring our grandson outside."
"Come here."
   His hair was painted,
      his hair was painted, *pok pok pok pok.*   735
         His arms were wrapped with cotton cord,
            he put on earrings, knee wrappings, everything,
            all of his ornaments.
When the sun was here, at its height,
   they began to dance,   740
      the Vultures began to dance.
   That was *fugagi,*
      the Birds' dance that we perform,
      the Birds' song.
   They were dancing,   745
      they danced *fugagi.*
         The Vultures danced.

The next day they came to him.
   The Vultures came bringing things to him *tooh* when they arrived.
      "Do stay here with us, Grandson," they said.   750
      "Look, you can enjoy hunting our food with your
      grandmothers, our food."
      "All right, let's go far from here and look for something."
   They flew off *toooh* right then.
      A tapir was walking about.
      Kangangafanga shot it for the Vulture's food.   755
         It died.
      "Go away now," the Vultures told him.
         He went away.
   "Alas, my grandson," Kwatïngï was saying.
      "Alas, my grandson."   760
   "Well, Grandfather, open the door for me."
      "Why, who just started to joke with me? Who?
         Why, there was only one grandson of mine, go away from me!
            Why are you all joking with me?"

"Grandfather, it's really me!" 765
"Could my grandson be here, after all?"
"Grandfather, I have really come to you again."
    "Very well," he answered.

At the very beginning of the next day before dawn Kangangafanga
went to bathe.
    "Kangangatï," Ukawaka said, 770
    "Listen for once. Your younger brother is bathing.
        It seems to be your younger brother," she told him.
    "He starved a long time ago."
    "All right," she replied.
        "I'm going to see, to see him." 775
"Well, you have come here again."
    "Yes."
"Kangangatï," she said,
    "This time, look. Your younger brother has returned."
"Again his dangerous power has kept him from being destroyed. 780
    What am I to do?" he said,
        "What am I to do?"
"Well, Ukwaka. Send the father of our children-to-be for my food,
make him go for us.
    Make him go hunting."
    "All right," she said, 785
        "As you wish, I'm going to tell him."
At the beginning of the day some pieces of wood were there,
    pieces of wood.
        Pieces of wood were there at the beginning of the day.
The pieces of wood were ready to be made into a swamp deer. 790
Kangangatï was going to try out the swamp deer,
    made from the *uwagati* tree.
He made the antlers from another kind of wood,
    very hard and sharp.
        Then it was all ready. 795
"This is how he will die.
    Because you were the one to cheat me, because you were
    the one."
It was all ready.
"The next day we will all go. Well, the next day we will all be
going.*
The next day we will all be going." 800
Then Kangangatï was going.
    "Come along everyone, let's go," he said.
        "Let's all go, let's all go, let's all go."
            All of the people left.

"Grandson," Kwatïngï said, 805
"What did the mother of my children-to-be just say, what?
I don't speak to my grandson," he went.
"We are all going to hunt for your grandson."
"Are you?" he said,
"That is your certain death. 810
If you do, your older brother is going to kill you.
What did you say to your older brother before? What?
You must be sure to go inside that thing first.
Your older brother will remain just exactly as he is, since
your older brother always behaves as he does.
Your older brother will remain just exactly as he is now,"
Kwatïngï said. 815
"All right."
"As I said, you will be going inside of it first."
They had gone on.
By then they had come to the old gardens.
Kangangatï was there, beside the figure, 820
beside the figure,
beside the image of the swamp deer,
the image of the swamp deer.
"Here, here, here!" he called.
"Here, I've found it!" 825
He was the very first one to approach, to come toward his
younger brother.
Puk, as he approached, his brother went inside,
inside the container.
"Let's go to it!" the people said.
Then Kangangatï was next to it, 830
iitiki he was standing right in front of it.
"Watch out!" the others said.
Kangangafanga stood waiting for him.
It killed his brother,
the swamp deer was killing him *tsuk!* 835
The antlers of the deer pierced him right here, in his
chest.
Kangangafanga had intended to kill his older brother,
and he killed his older brother.

By then it was over.
It was over, Kangangatï died. 840
Kangangafanga then carried him far away to a certain place in the
grasslands.
He carried his older brother there after he had finally died,
he carried his older brother away.

Next, *tutututu* he crossed over a small creek *tuk* to the other side.
Then *tu tu tu tu* he carried him far out into the middle of the lake,   845
   far out in the middle of Lake Kafïdyaga.
      That's its very name.
   There is a lake there.
      The deer is in the middle of the lake, stuck in the mud.
Kangangatï had finally died.   850
   "So, stay here," Kangangafanga said.
   "You should have done this before with someone else.
      Someone else.
         See, you were the one to die this way," as he came back.
Then he arrived home.   855
   "Well, Grandfather, once and for all your grandson is no longer
   alive."
   "Very well," Kwatïngï said.
   "So he will remain, your older brother," Kwatïngï declared.
   "So he will remain, because your older brother really
      wanted to do that to you," Kwatïngï declared.
      "So he will remain."   860

Notes to "Kangangafanga"
lines

6   *afusagu: Clitoria* species. As the botanical name suggests, the flower
         of this bush is thought to resemble the human vulva.

15   "father of our children-to-be": one of several terms referring to a
         listener's relative by marriage, who is also a close relative of the
         speaker. These terms allow the speaker to show respect due such a
         person by avoiding the referent's name; this is a respectful reserve
         that would not exist if the speaker and referent were friendly. The
         form used here is employed when the referent is childless. Note the
         contrast between Kangangatï's manner of referring to his brother,
         and Ukwaka's use of Kangangafanga's name as well as the more in-
         formal kinship term, "your younger brother."

15   puffbird: a member of the family *Bucconidae*, probably *Notharchus
         macrorhynchus,* the white-necked puffbird. Some Kalapalo say these
         voluble birds are easily tamed and make nice pets.

30   "mother of our non-existent children": again, this expression pre-
         serves a sense of high family decorum on the part of the grandfather,
         in contrast to Kangangatï, with whom Kwatïngï "does not speak."

37   "those of my flesh," that is, Kwatïngï's own relatives.

39   Burity palm shoots have a spongy, durable texture. When the snakes
         bite into them, their teeth are held fast.

67   "scraping" (*fifi-*): a medical technique involving mild bloodletting.
         The instrument is a triangular piece of gourd in which dogfish teeth
         are embedded.

86	The spathes of the *fegita* palm and the bark of the *katsëgë* tree (both common plants of the *cerrado*) bear deeply ridged sulci. The Kalapalo believe these ridges were created by the bloodletting tool set with snake's teeth that was used to scrape Kangangafanga.
103–104	*wëgufi:* an unidentified hardwood, extremely dense and heavy. A tree common in the high forests.
139	*kaifa:* the tucum palm (*Astrocaryum tucuma*), whose small round fruit are used to make arrowheads.
157	*atuta* spiders: a small insect (orb spider?) that spins glistening webs. At sunrise in the *cerrado*, the webs can be seen extending from the highest tree branches all the way to the ground.
180	"pounding the water": as young Kalapalo men do when they bathe before dawn.
181	"he who was your daughter's burden": a reference to a daughter of Kwatïngï—the mother of Kangangatï and Kangangafanga—when she carried the younger brother about as an infant.
186	Ukwaka makes her relationship to Kangangafanga clear by meeting him at the water's edge, as lovers (*adyo*) are accustomed to do.
203	shell belts: valuable ornaments made by the Kalapalo from shells of the *iñu* land snail.
411	This is how human beings acquired tobacco.
429	*kwosose:* very large commensal moths whose fluttering can sometimes be heard at night.
473	thunder knife: visible only to shamans. Kwatagi, who said he had seen it in a dream, described it to me as a kind of sword, in the middle of which is a large eye.
497	*tuluma: Drycopus lineates* (?); *itu: Celeus sp.; agapawa: Campylorhampus procurvoides,* not a woodpecker but a member of the *Dendrocolaptidae* family, which the Kalapalo group with *Picidae; itsïka:* unidentified *Picidae.* The woodpeckers' tails were torn and burned when they stole the necklaces, and remain ragged in appearance to this day.
531–33	Kangangafanga implies that Storm's love affairs are the subject of his family's gossip. Here, there is irony in the fact that Kangangafanga's travels are motivated by his ardor for Ukwaka.
588	*kutsu:* an extremely large eagle (*Spizaetus ornatus,* the ornate hawk-eagle). For the Kalapalo, these birds are an important source of feathers for arrows and ornaments. They are sometimes captured as fledglings and raised inside cages.
648	Large bromeliads grow in the crooks of trees. Kangangafanga pulls some of them off so he can have a place to sit.
654	*kuguagi:* general term for vultures.
695	*tafatagi:* a medicine made from wild plants used to "cleanse" the stomach. The Kalapalo give it to boys to fatten them up during puberty seclusion.
719	"their tails": Kangangafanga takes these feathers to bring back to his settlement. Metaphorically, taking these ornaments indicates he has sexual relations with them. The tails represent the curved burity palm straws women wear between their buttocks as dancing orna-

ments. When they are worn, the cord that binds them to a woman's belt impedes intercourse.

724   "he never ate furred animal flesh": just as Kalapalo currently avoid such food. (See Basso, 1973, Chapter 2.)

799   This line is spoken, as if Kangangati were a hereditary leader (*anetu*). If he were such a leader, his fratricidal behavior would be all the more horrible.

The serial imagery of the story "Kangangafanga" offers itself readily to structural analysis. The repeated ordeals, which ultimately total nine, represent a logical progression. Kangangatï sends Kangangafanga farther and farther away from his settlement, to increasingly more dangerous places, to acquire increasingly more valuable and powerful objects. The particular techniques for survival offered by Kangangafanga's helpers form pairs of contrasting semantic operators. Each pair refers to a distinctive form of agentive power that turns the ordeal to the hero's advantage. See Table 2.1.

Table 2.1. Contrasting Semantic Operators

Ordeal	Item Sought	Place	Danger	Helpers	Semantic Operator
1.	puffbirds	near a path	snakes	burity shoots	sponginess, light weight (safely carried)
2.	wegufi log	nearby forest	crushing weight	termites	heavy, dense (not easily carried)
3.	tucum nuts	distant lake	lake monsters	spiders/ squirrels	equilibrium (acrobatic strength)
4.	shell belts	powerful beings on land	cannibal monsters	bodily disequilibria	disequilibrium
5.	rattles	powerful beings underground	snakes	grasshoppers	music
6.	tobacco	powerful beings in sky	Whirlwind	moths	noise
7.	thunder knife	powerful beings on Other Side of sky	Storm	woodpeckers	extractors, "nibblers" (dexterous eaters)
8.	eagle fledglings	dead tree in manioc field	own brother (starvation)	dead mice (vultures)	"tearers" of rotten flesh

The eighth ordeal brings Kangangafanga close to home. This time his own brother, rather than a distant monster, tries to kill him by starving him amidst plenty.

On the ninth and last occasion, which is cumulatively the most obnoxious, Kangangafanga finally is told by Kwatïngï to kill his older brother:

9.	game	close to the settlement	own brother (model of swamp deer)	self	human intelligence (deception)

Stories About the Twins Taugi and Aulukuma

We saw at the end of "Kwatïngï" a shift in emphasis from struggles between humanity and powerful beings to conflicts between people themselves. And stories about Kwatïngï's grandsons describe such conflicts among the most ancient Dawn People. There is much missing, though, at the conclusion of the long "Kwatïngï" epic, an absence of favorable conditions that would allow people to experience the world more fully, free from the fear of jaguars, able to engage in satisfying discoveries and to create pleasurable inventions. In other stories, Taugi changes that: he causes the Jaguar to eat animal flesh, he later acquires fire and light, water, and erections, and he rids the world of the Fiery Monsters. These are the changes in the world that the Kalapalo believe led to its present physical character.

First, King Vulture is tricked into giving up fire and light, but in his turn he sends his ugly daughters, the Ani Women, to be the wives of the twins, Taugi and Aulukuma. Underscoring certain female needs, these women discover peculiar discomforts in their new home: there is no water to draw for cooking or bathing, and their husbands can make love only with their fingers. They know where the things they need can be had, and tease the brothers into setting off in search of them. (Taugi pridefully insists on going, while Aulukuma is worriedly cautious.) In all these stories, Taugi becomes a successful trickster hero. The destructiveness and unforeseen consequences of his deceptive actions, however, seem inevitable adjuncts to his particular kind of creative imagination.

Nitsuegï's Food
Told by Muluku at Aifa. February 11, 1979.

Listen.
Then Taugi spoke.
  "Well, Leader," he went.
    "Have your followers make your arrows right now," Taugi said.
  "All right," he answered,   5
    Nitsuegï said.
  "Do it right now," the other said.
  "Children," Nitsuegï said,
    "Make your arrows right now,
      your arrows."   10
        "All right," they answered.
  "Our grandson has just ordered me to do that."
  "All right, that will be fine with us," they said.

The next day they made arrows,
    they made arrows.   15
Buh! his followers were all furred animals,
    furred animals.
All his followers,
    Nitsuegï's followers.
      Furred animal followers.   20

They finished making those things with which they had been
occupied.
  Then they all feathered the arrows in the plaza,
    his followers did,
      Nitsuegï's arrows.
  "Aulukuma," Taugi said,   25
    "Aulukuma.
  Keep looking at our parent.
  Let's think about him.
  That's our flesh our parent eats,
    our flesh.   30
  Look.
    Even now they are just like us.
      They have our hands,
        they have our eyes,
        everything.   35
  This time let's think about our parent.
    Because he eats our flesh.
      Our parent consumes it.
      Our flesh is being exterminated."

It was still very early at the very Beginning.   40
    We were still living around termite mound clearings,
        termite mound clearings.
    That was what Taugi was speaking about.
Because he wanted to do something about it Taugi began to think.
    In order to do something about it.   45
    "Well, let's do it right now!" he said.
    "Let's go kill the leader's food right now."
    "All right, come over here!"
    "What's the perfect way for us to do it, Aulukuma,
        what?   50
    I've got it!
    We'll shoot some food for our parent."
        "All right!" the other said.
Outside the doorway someone had fallen asleep,
    Asakuegï the Swamp Deer had fallen asleep.   55
    "Let's shoot this one's body,
        this one's body.
        She will remain as she is."
Ahtsuk! something pierced her ear.
    He killed her,   60
        Taugi did.
        He killed Swamp Deer.
            Tsuk, with a burity palm leaf rib.
            So she died.
Then they both carried her and put her down inside the doorway.   65
    "Let's cook her, we'll cook her."
Next *tsïka tsïka tsïka* Taugi butchered her,
    he removed her guts.
When that was finished,
    buk, he put the meat inside a large cooking pot.   70
    Their father was in the plaza.
    Kulukulukulukulu.

Then *tikii*, their father entered the house.
    "Children," he said.
    "What are you doing?" he said.   75
    "Nothing," they answered.
        "Nothing."
    "What's that you're doing to your grandmother,
        what?
    You must never kill your grandmothers,   80
        your grandmothers.
            All the people around here are your grandmothers."

So they stayed there.
    Then it was boiling.
        Kuluk.   85
When it was finished,
    they stirred it *pupupupu.*
When that was finished,
    they put salt in it.
When that was finished,   90
    they put toasted piqui kernels in it.
        He mixed it all in,
            Taugi did.
        He put salt in it,
        he put toasted piqui kernels in it,   95
        he put hot peppers in it,
        and it was ready.
"What have you been doing with your grandmother just now?"
their father said.
        "What?
        That is your grandmother you shot for no reason,   100
        your grandmother."

Then Nitsuegï sniffed at the food,
        he sniffed it,
        he sniffed it,
            so Taugi spoke about it.   105
"Well, Leader," he said.
    "Here is your food," he said.
"No, I can't eat your grandmother.
    That's your grandmother there."
"Never mind that," Taugi said.   110
    "Keep listening to what I say, Leader," he said.
"I want this to be your only food, your food.
    This is so you don't kill our flesh,
        don't.
    This is what I want your food to be,   115
        so try it this time.
        Try it this time as I'm suggesting to you."
"Very well," he said and he nibbled on it.
    The fragrance of it made him desire it,
        so he ate some of the meat.   120
        It was really tasty so he ate some of the meat.
"Well, Leader," Taugi said.
    "Leader, bring it out to your followers,
        to your followers.
        Have your followers eat it."   125

So then he brought it outside,
  Nitsuegï did.
After that his followers ate it up.
  "This must be your only food,
    your food.   130
  This is so you won't kill our flesh,
    don't," Taugi told them.
  "Our flesh is being exterminated by you," he went.
    "You're exterminating our flesh.
  This will become your food," Taugi declared.   135
    "This is what you will always eat," Taugi declared.

It's over. That's all.

Fiery

Told by Muluku at Aifa. February 2, 1979.
Notes appear on page 123.

Taugi went to get his manioc starch.
> Taugi went for it because he wanted to use it to memorialize his
> mother.*
> He came away from Mogena,
>> from Mogena.
>>> To Sagifengu from Mogena.
There Fiery rested,
> Fiery did.
> Taugi caused his genipapa leaves to drop,
>> his genipapa leaves to drop.
>>> (He travels as wind, you see.)
Now because that kept happening Fiery began to burn,
> because of that.
>> After that happened Taugi went on.
"Let's wait here," he went.
> "Let's wait here," Fiery said.
>> "Let's all stay here."
Now Taugi was carrying the manioc starch across to "Where
Dogfish Are Divided,"
> "Where Dogfish Are Divided." *
>> That's where Fiery waited,
>>> where he waited.
Then Taugi approached.
> "Here he comes," Fiery said.
>> "He's finally coming!" he said.
> "When Taugi comes will I speak to him," he went.
>> "When Taugi comes I'll speak to him."
Then the other came toward him with his manioc starch silo on
his back.
Then Fiery encircled him and surrounded him,
> Fiery encircled him.
>> He encircled Taugi.
>>> Everything kept burning after that, kept burning.
"Well, Taugi," he went,
> "Taugi," Aulukuma said.
> "Who's doing that over there? Who?"
> "Look, that's some apparition, that's some apparition," Taugi
said.

5

10

15

20

25

30

"No," his brother answered,   35
    "What I see does look just like fire, I see something fiery."
"No, I'm wrong," Taugi said,
    "No, it really does seem to be our grandfather."
But now as he said that everything kept burning.
    "We're done for now, Aulukuma," Taugi said.   40
        "We're done for," he said.
            "What are we to do?" as he put down his manioc starch.
The fire rose up high,
        it rose up as Fiery came closer.
            It was all around them!   45
    They beat it out except one patch.
        They beat it out until only a little patch was still burning.
            While it was like that they ran and Taugi and Aulukuma
            passed through it.
Next five Kawagitaū Burity Mats ran through and they kept
blowing spells as Taugi came,
            toward Agifanugu.*   50
    When they were almost there Aulukuma began to pant,
        Aulukuma was panting.
            By then they had just made it across when he started to
            do that.
    "Taugi," he said,
        "Taugi, I'm really exhausted," he said.   55
    "Very well," the other replied.
        "Be this way, be this way," he said.
    "But you know you're always the one to be killed," Taugi said,
        "You'll have to stay here for a while."
He encircled him with a small pond.   60
    He was in the water,
        in the water.
    The other ran on,
        Taugi ran on.
"Here, here, here!" he went, Fiery said.   65
    "Here, here, here!"
Tïï Aulukuma went inside a *kugipisi* seed.
    Tï tï tï he closed himself up.
"Here, here, here!" Fiery said,
    as he burned toward Aulukuma.   70
Tuk! Aulukuma exploded right away,
    he exploded,
        and he died.
"Hurry, let's go, Taugi won't be speaking to him any longer.
    Taugi won't be speaking to *him* any longer."   75

Taugi had placed some giant *anetufe* there,*
    this was giant *anetufe,*
        but he went around it,
            Fiery went around it.
Then Taugi came to Kagupe.   80
    Whirlpools were there,
        whirlpools.
    Bok, when Taugi came there Tikutakeugï the Oysters were
    there,
        so he dove underwater.
"Here, here, here!" he said,   85
    Fiery said.
        "Here, here, here, here!"
    Tuk, well, the water began to dry up.
Because of that the water was divided,*
    and it went downstream so there was no longer any more
    water there.   90
        He went inside one of those things I just mentioned,
            inside Oyster, *bok!*
"Dear Grandfather, you must watch out and blow a spell on me.
    You must watch out and blow a spell on me," Taugi said.
    "My grandchild is right here, my beloved is here," Oyster
    answered.   95
        The water had already died.
Then Fiery did nothing more.
    They had burned up everything.
    Mbisuk, nothing was left,
        there was nothing more to burn.   100
        Nothing.
    "All right," he said,
        "What are we to do?" Fiery said.
        Nothing was there.
"Let's pick this up and carry it to a rock, let's pick it up,"   105
    Fiery was speaking about Oyster.
"Let's pick this up," he said.
    "I want to smash this Oyster down on a rock,
        so we must pick it up."
"Oh, look, dear Grandfather!" Taugi said.   110
    "Look, blow a spell on me, while I do the same as hard as
    I can,
        the same."
        "All right," Oyster replied.

Then as one of the others carried Oyster,
    "I'm going to make it possible for you to be destroyed by
    human beings," Fiery said. 115
        "I want all of you to be destroyed by human beings.
        "I want human beings to destroy you."
It took all of them to carry it.
"Look, we're doing it!"
Tïk mbuuh! 120
    Water shot out,
        water shot out while Fiery was carrying it.
"My arms are tired from doing that,
    my arms have become tired."
"Let me do it," another one said to him. 125
Next that one himself carried it farther on.
    Puk'mbuuuh! Nothing happened.
Once again, another one *puk!*
    The same thing happened again,
        and once again *puk'mbuuuh!* 130
Once again *puk'mbuuuh!*
    It was the last one.
"I want all you people to die," Taugi said.
He was telling them that as they carried Oyster.
    Tuk'mbuuh! the water shot out as before, 135
    the water shot out.
There were five brothers,
    the Fiery Brothers.
        Five of them.
"Do let him be," they said. 140
    "Let him be."
        "Let's go, let him be."
"He almost died, he almost died," as they all went away,
    Fiery went away.
        Then he slept two days, 145
        Taugi slept.

"Granny," he told her,
    Taugi said.
    "I'll go see your grandson right now,
        I'll go see your grandson," he said to her. 150
        I'll go see him,"
            so he walked away, *tï tï tï*.

Aulukuma had died by the edge of the Agifanugu Creek,
  he had died.
"Alas, my dear little brother has died.   155
Look at yourself.
  I don't know why you always die this way."
Taugi articulated all his bones together,
  he articulated them together.
When he had finished he saw that the finger that goes here
between the thumb and forefinger was still missing.*   160
"Where could this one be?
Here is this one, here is this one, here is this one, here is this
one, here is this one."
  The one that goes here between the thumb and forefinger
  was still missing.
    This finger that was once on our hands had been
    swallowed
      by Isogoko, a Maned Wolf.   165
"Where must I go to look?
  To their settlement, to the Maned Wolves!"
    He meant the home of the Maned Wolves.
"Kaw kaw kaw, Taugi, Taugi, Taugi," the Maned Wolves went,
  Taugi Taugi Taugi Taugi!"   170
"Why are you here?" they asked him.
"I've come to see you," he told them.
  "To see you.
    I want you to teach me about what you know.
      That's why I've come, Grandfathers," he told them.   175
        "Your knowledge," he said.
"Very well," they answered.
"Come over here to me right now," Taugi said.
"There's something you should do," he said.
  "I want to see you all race,   180
  I want to see you race," he said.
    "All right," they said.
"Your knowledge of it."
  "All right," they answered.
"Go ahead, go on."   185
  "All right," and one of them began to run.
Tutututu he ran around the plaza in front of the house circle.
As he was going Taugi tickled his stomach and he vomited,
  the Maned Wolf vomited.
"Well, let it be," he told him,   190
  "That's enough," Taugi said.

Another one of them again, then another one, then another
one, then another one, then another one,
     well, every one of them.
          All of them ran as fast as they could.
"Could it be that one of our relatives has been left out?"   195
"There isn't anyone else."
"Where's that other fellow?" Taugi asked.
     "Go after him right away!" he told them.
     "All right," the Maned Wolves answered.
"Where were you?"   200
"I was roaming around far from here," he answered.
          "That was what I was doing, I was doing that.
               I've been roaming around,
                    I've been roaming around," he said.
                         "I must have eaten the remains of some powerful
                         being, because I'm a little sick."   205
     "Bring him over here," Taugi said,
          "He's the one!"
"Go ahead," he said,
     "Go ahead, go on now," Taugi said.
Well, the Maned Wolf ran off *tu tu tu* going in front of the houses.   210
Taugi tickled his stomach.
Tï tï tï tï tï tï tï tï tï he vomited what was left of Aulukuma's
finger.
"Let it be.
     You were the one to do that to your grandchild, the dead
     one.
Go far away from here," he said.   215
     "Furred animals don't have settlements.
          Furred animals don't have settlements like you do," Taugi
          said.
               Then they all ran away.
When that was done he came back. Taugi carried it back,
     the finger that goes here.   220
          The one the Maned Wolf had swallowed.
               He finished returning,
                    and he arrived.
He put it on *gïï duk,*
     but it couldn't be fixed.   225
          The one from here that was missing.
               It was long ago that such a thing was achieved,
                    our hands, everyone's.

So they both came back then.
Aulukuma had become well again,   230
he had become a person.
Next they arrived,
after they went back to their own settlement,
Taugi and his companion had gone there.
"Aulukuma," he told him, Taugi said,   235
"We must see our grandfathers right away."
Then they went on farther,
to Fiery's settlement.
They took along Ñafïgï when they went there,
they took along Ñafïgï.   240
They approached Fiery's plaza,
and then they went away.
Once again as they approached she followed them.
And once again they went away.
That was how they all went.   245
Fiery's people were terrified from seeing them all,
Taugi and his companions.
They all went on once more,
and as they arrived here in the plaza,
"Koh! Taugi, Taugi, Taugi,"   250
as they came toward Fiery's settlement.
"What are you here for?" they asked.
"I came to you all, to you all."
"Very well," they said.
"Why have you come to us, dear Grandfather, why have you
done that?"   255
"Listen to what I say, Grandfathers," Taugi told them.
"Leave this place, this place."
"We will," they answered.
"Disappear," he said.
"Disappear beneath the water, disappear."   260
"We will," they answered,
So then they all went away,
Fiery went beneath the water.
They went beneath the water.
"Mortals will travel about in this place," Taugi declared.   265
"Mortals would be afraid of all of you.
They would have to watch out for you when they walked
around here.
So remain invisible, hide yourselves," Taugi said.
And so they hid themselves,
Fiery hid themselves.   270

It was over.

Fiery had tried to burn up Taugi.

Notes to "Fiery"

lines

1–2   Taugi was actually carrying an entire silo of manioc, which was to be used to make food for the guests at his memorial ceremony.

18   "Where Dogfish Are Divided": a place along the Culuene River where people stop to roast fish for lunch. Dogfish are commonly caught nearby.

49   Accompanying Taugi were woven burity mats, which are used to dry manioc starch. He had enabled them to move as human beings.

50   Agifanugu: grasslands to the south and west of the Culuene. In this story, Taugi is traveling the entire length of the Upper Xingu Basin from his own settlement at the confluence of the Xingu headwaters (mogena) toward his mother's burial place, Sagifengu, the settlement of Nitsuegï. I have not been able to identify this site of Sagifengu, but Kalapalo tell me it is located in the far southerly region of the Upper Xingu Basin, in the former territory of the Dyagamï people, close relatives of the Kalapalo.

76   *anetufe:* a deadly, poisonous plant the Kalapalo use to kill dogs.

89   "the water was divided": a place where there are now rapids.

160   Hence there is now a space between our thumbs and forefingers.

To Get Fire

Told by Muluku at Aifa. February 8, 1979.

Notes appear on page 134.

There still wasn't any fire, either.
  A reeking decay,
    he was going to lure them with stench,
      because before in the Beginning there was still no fire, it
      is told.
        None.   5
  Then he went traveling.
    Taugi went traveling in his canoe.
    Taugi went paddling *pu pu pu pu.*
    Taugi had made his canoe from earth.
      Pu pu pu pu.   10
        Taugi had made his canoe from earth.
  Formerly our canoes,
    the Dawn People's canoes were made from earth,
    from earth.
      They were made from the earth of anthills,   15
      the earth of anthills.
Some others came also,
  Ducks were coming, they were Birds.
    Ducks were coming.
  Their canoe, however, was made from *wagi* bark.*   20
  "Well, Grandfathers," Taugi said,
    "Where are you all going? Where?
    Where are you all going?"
  "Nowhere special," they said.
    "Nowhere special."   25
  "That's some canoe there."
  "Do look at how we travel.
    Look at how we travel.
    Peh, we cut out a piece of *wagi* bark."
      That was the Ducks' canoe.   30
  "Yes," he answered.
    He looked at his own canoe.
      His own canoe was nothing.
        Taugi had made his canoe from earth.
Following that they traveled on.   35
  Then when their canoes came near to each other,
  "Grandfathers, let's trade our canoes."
    "All right."

"I want your canoe for my own, your canoe."
    "All right," they said.   40
They gave him their canoe and went away in his while he
remained in theirs.
This canoe of theirs kept him dry,
    but as for the canoe in which the Ducks rode,
        well, it sank.
    "Now, so they will remain!   45
    Stay just the way you are, stay just the way you are," Taugi
    declared.
        Their canoe then became as it is now.
        "They will remain as they are," he said.
        They went on *pu pu pu pu pu* downstream.
Next Taugi met Afangi the Chigger.   50
    "Where are you going?" Taugi asked.
    "Why, I'm going to a place where there are lots of big-nosed
    people."
    "Very well, and I'm going to a place where there are lots of
moon-faced people."
    Taugi went on.
Then he met Kusu the Bare-faced Currasows.   55
    "What are all of you doing?"
    "We're making hats."
    "Let me have one, I want one of your hats."
    "No, this thing isn't for someone like you."
Then Taugi grabbed it and crammed it down on that Currasow's
head.   60
    Because of that the bare-faced currasows' hats are like that.
    "Why, so they will remain."
        He went on.
Next Taugi encountered Fekïgï the Small Caimans.*
    They were making manioc scraping boards.   65
    "I want one of those boards for myself."
    "No, this thing isn't for someone like you."
    "Well, they will remain the way they are."
He slammed the board on that Caiman's tail.
    "Why, they will remain the way they are."   70
        That was all.

Then a swamp deer.
    He made a swamp deer from *itali* wood.*
    Taugi made something that smelled rotten.
    It's called *kanasï*, the decoy.   75
        A large one that he himself named.

When it was ready, "You should do something," he said.
    It wasn't yet rotten while he was engaged in making it.
"You should go ahead and rot now."
    So the swamp deer rotted. 80
"Grandfather," he went.
    Taugi spoke to Agua the Blowfly.
    "Go ahead, tell the others," he said,
    "Tell the others right now."
"All right," Blowfly answered, "All right." 85
" 'I came to tell about your leader's food,' you must say to them."
    "All right," he said.
" 'It doesn't look like the trickster to me,' you will take care to say.
When they will ask you about it, don't agree with them.
    'No, no,' you must say. 'No, I'm sure that's our leader's food,' 90
    you will take care to say that."
        "All right," he answered,
        Blowfly answered.
Then, well, he went away,
    he went away to the Place of Many Birds 95
        across on the other side of the sky.
    "Why are you here?" they asked him.
        "Why are you here?"
He told them in his own language, *"Mm mm mm mm."*
    He told them in his own language but they didn't understand
    him at all. 100
    He didn't use the Birds' own language.
"Go ahead, you do it," their leaders told someone,
    and so a messenger went to get Kwi the Yellow-rumped
    Cacique,
        Kwi.*
    "Do go right away. 105
    You must listen to someone's speech and interpret for us."
        "All right," he answered.
Then he came to Blowfly.
    "Well, why are you here?" Cacique said,
        "Why are you here? Why?" 110
    "I had to come tell you about your leader's food.
    There's some food for your leader," Blowfly answered.
        "There's some food for your leader," Blowfly answered.
        "There is some, there is.
    Listen further. 115
        Nor does it seem to be our death, no."
        "No," the other answered.

"All right, go look."
    Fefulugi the Dung Beetle arrived.
        Buh! there was the hulk of swamp deer. 120
He went to examine it,
    the huge thing still lying where Taugi put it,
As he went toward it he saw nothing.
    In and out of the anus he went,
        and inside the mouth, but he saw nothing, 125
        so he went away.
"Is it all right?" they asked,
    "Is it all right?"
"I don't know. Yes, it seems to be so," he answered.
    "Yes, it seems to be so," he went, 130
        "As you say, that's probably your leader's food."
        "Very well," the Birds said.
"All right, now you go look, go ahead."
    Fisi the Yellow-headed Caracara,
        that Bird. 135
"Go ahead." They wanted him to see.
    He saw nothing.
Following that he arrived home.
    "Is it all right?" they asked.
    "I don't know. 140
    I didn't see anything there at all, I didn't see anything there."
"All right, you all go."
    "All right, tomorrow we'll all go see."

The next day they came there once again.
    This time when the Birds came, 145
    all the Birds came.
        To eat it, *tsu tsu tsu.*
And the next day,
and the next day,
        and the next day. 150
    Isagiku the Black Vultures,
    Juwafula the Turkey Vultures, Fisi the Yellow-headed
Caracaras,
        and Ugufu the King Vultures as well.
Great King Vulture himself hadn't yet come.
    But all the other Birds had, 155
    all the different households.
The next day,
and the next day,
and the next day.
        They didn't stop. 160

Taugi was there underneath a toenail.
He was right there,
   underneath the deer's toenail.
The Birds kept bringing some of it back,
   kept bringing some of it back. 165
      The Birds were bringing some of it back.
   The decoy was really rotten by then!
"Go ahead," she went,
  "Your little son does keep begging me for some of the swamp
deer, your son.
Go tomorrow," his wife told him, 170
  "Go tomorrow."
    "Because you never leave here your child does feel hungry."
"Well, I agree. I'll go tomorrow," he said,
  "Tomorrow.
    That's probably food for a leader so tomorrow we'll
    all go." 175
  Well, so many of them came then,
   the sky was torn open.
"Aulukuma," Taugi said,
  "Look, our grandfather is coming!"
Because Taugi did all that, Great King Vulture's coming made it be
the way it is now. 180
  When Great King Vulture came, it became the way it is now.
  Teh when he arrived, the beautiful daylight appeared.
   The daylight,
    that had been located very high up in the sky.
     Very high up in the sky. 185
"I should do something," he said,
  and he looked at it.
  He had two heads,
   two,
    Great King Vulture's heads. 190
"I should do something," Great King Vulture said.
  Finally he ate what had been left there,
   he ate some of it.
  He carried home some of the food he had found,
   he kept carrying some of the food he had found home. 195
    He was no longer afraid to eat it.
  Since Taugi had blown a spell on him,
   it tasted delicious to him.
   It was delicious.
"It's time something happened," he said, 200
  "He doesn't think there's anyone here at all."

And so Taugi grabbed him by his feet.
"Look, Grandfather, you never saw me did you?" he said to
him.
Huh! Suddenly all the followers flew away!
He really did hold onto their leader!
Buh! they all went away while he held onto Great King
Vulture.
"I'm not killing you, Grandfather," Taugi told him.
"You won't die while I do this."
So, they came to his house,
and Taugi tied up Great King Vulture.
The others all arrived,
they all arrived,
the Birds all arrived home.
"Our leader is no longer alive," they told each other.
They missed him terribly.
Then they slept, they slept, many days passed.

So, the people came to see his son.
"Go look for your father," they said to him,
"Your father."
Well, he came.
He was Afukugu the Swallow-Wing,
that was who his son was.
Swallow-Wing was King Vulture's son.
He had two other children,
women.
Swallow-Wing was a man.
He arrived.
"Father, are you all right?" he said.
"Yes," he answered, "Everything about me is still all right," he
said,
"Still all right."
"Grandson," he said,
"Why did you want to capture me like this, is there a reason?
You captured me," he told Taugi,
"What for?"
"Yes," he answered.
"I captured you because of what you own.
For what you own."
"I do have something there.
There is something."

205

210

215

220

225

230

235

So he told his son,   240
    "This was done only because of what we own. That's why our
    grandson captured us."
    "I see," he answered.
    "Now, you must bring it here right away, bring it here.
    You must bring it right here."
Swallow-Wing then went to tell the others.   245
    He went away.
    He arrived.
    "The one who captured him wants fire.
    The one who tied up our dear father wants fire.
        He did that because he wants fire.   250
            Let's go free our dear father," Swallow-Wing told the
            others.
    "Very well," they answered.
    "Take it then,"
        and they gave him fire.
            They gave him fire so that he could bring it to Great
            King Vulture.   255
    "Here it is, here it is," Swallow-Wing said.
    "Well, Grandson," King Vulture said,
        "Here.
        Now you can make fire.
    Here, make fire.
        With this make your fire.
            You must arrange some dead wood for lighting."   260
They will be the first to collect firewood.
    "You must get your firewood and you will be the first to
    arrange it for lighting."
        No one had gone for bark yet.*   265
    "We will? All right," Taugi answered.
    "All right now," he said.
    King Vulture blew on it and the fire grew up.

"Well, Grandson," King Vulture said,
    "As you may have guessed, there are unfortunately some ill-
    favored women whom I've found, there are."   270
    "Have you really? Very well," Taugi said.
        "Very well," he replied.
    "Well, even though I don't have to, I should leave. I'd like
    to leave."
    "Do you really? Go as you wish, go then.
        You must certainly go. Go to the ill-favored women whom
        you've found. Very well."   275

Then Taugi untied the dried palm fronds that bound his ankles.
He tied a string from his hammock cord to King Vulture's ankle,
        so that later he could find the Place of Many Birds,
            King Vulture's own settlement.
The other went away,   280
        he went after Taugi did that,
            he went away,
                he went away.
"When your fire goes out, Grandson," he called to him,*
        "When your fire goes out,   285
            when your fire is completely extinguished you will look for it
            inside arrow cane,
                inside arrow cane you will certainly find it."
Because of that,
        that one has it.
"Also you will look for it inside the urucu plant,   290
        inside urucu."
            "Very well," he replied.
Because of that,
        that one has it.
"Also you will look for it inside arrow cane,   295
        most certainly you will look for it there."
            "Very well," he said.
Because of that,
        that one has it.
"Also you will look for it inside *olite* wood, you will look for it
there."   300
            "Very well," Taugi said.
"Also you will look for it inside gourds, you will look for it there."
            "Very well," he said.
                That was all.
Following that, Great King Vulture went,   305
        he went away.
The others had already replaced him with another leader,
        with the bald one.
            This was Black Vulture.
They had plucked out his hair,*   310
        kiu kiu kiu.
Their leader was replaced.
After that was done King Vulture arrived.
        "Our parent is still alive!"
            Once again the Birds rejoiced.   315

Then Taugi went,
    Taugi went.
    "Aulukuma," he told him.
        "Aulukuma, let's go see our grandfather,
            Our grandfather went up to the sky, so high and far
            away!"   320
They went there too, up to the sky.
    They followed the path of the hammock string.
    They arrived.
At the very end of the day,
    "Kaau kaau," as the two brothers arrived the Birds cheered.   325
    "Oh, Taugi Taugi Taugi," they all said.
    "I should do something," King Vulture said to himself.
    "Why are you here?"
    "As you see, we have come to you, unworthy as we are, for the
    ill-favored women whom you've found.
        That's why we have come to you, Grandfather."   330
    "Yes," he answered,
        "You have, have you?
            Go ahead, you can take them away with you now.
                It was only because I was afraid of you that I told you
                about them."
    "Very well," they answered.   335
So they married,
    they joined together.
    The older sister joined Taugi and the younger sister joined his
    younger brother,
        they became their wives,
            those who were King Vulture's daughters.   340
Then they slept, they slept,
    after they slept three nights they came back.

"I am leaving right now.
    I am leaving right now with your grandson and I want to leave
    you behind."
    "Are you?" Great King Vulture said,   345
        "Very well," he agreed.
    "Well, it does look as if you should take your sisters away with
    you,
        your sisters."
        They brought them back.
    "Take them with you," Vulture told them,   350
    King Vulture said.
    "Take your *tuafi* with you.*
        Those."

He gave his daughters many, many *tuafi*.
"Any time you bring them outside way down there, 355
    if you open them just a crack, the early morning dawn will
    appear," he said to his daughters, King Vulture said to his
    daughters.
"Then more dawn, just a little,
    then even more dawn, just a little,
        then dawn becoming beautiful."
If that should be done, it's morning for us, 360
    our morning.
"Well, go now."
Following that they came and they were arriving home,
    they were all arriving home.
Following that as they came on the entrance path Taugi did
something unfair to Aulukuma, he cuckolded Aulukuma
unfairly. 365
As they were all arriving home,
    he went on ahead with both of their wives,
        Taugi did that,
            it was Taugi.
"Go ahead," he said to them. 370
    Now, as they all arrived home,
        Aulukuma felt bad about that.
            Aulukuma felt bad because his brother had stolen his
            wife.

Then before dawn at the beginning of the day one of the women
took her *tuafi* outside,
        Great King Vulture's daughter did that. 375
            Just opened it slightly.
    Then true dawn appeared there.
        Teh that was beautiful!
After she had caused that to happen,
    our dawn became as it is now. 380
        As it is now.
    When the Ani Women take their *tuafi* outside,
        and they are walking around with them opened up.
She made the night come.
    And it became dark. 385
    "No," Taugi said,
        "Do to the darkness what you just did."
        "All right," she said.

That was accomplished.
Ever since that happened our dawn has been as it is now. 390
    Over and again darkness becomes dawn,
        over and again.
        It never ends,
        no.
Formerly there was no sun until that happened. 395
    Nothing.
His decoy kept reeking.
Until Taugi made it happen,
    we human beings were always without fire.
        That's all. 400

Notes to "To Get Fire"
lines

20   *wagi* bark, that is, of the tree called *jatobà* in Brazil. Formerly, canoes in the Upper Xingu Basin were made from fire-shaped pieces of the thick bark from this tree; these have been replaced by dugouts.

64   *fekïgï:* kind of small caiman.

73   *itali:* a rotten-smelling wood. Men use the pungent resin to paint their bodies, especially before wrestling.

103–4   *Kwi:* A bird known for its deft mimicry of other species. In Kalapalo stories, it is often called upon to translate insect languages. (See "Taugi and the Chiggers.")

265   Women now collect bark from burned trees that have fallen in the fields, to use as firewood.

284   King Vulture begins to list the sources of fire; these are materials from which the Kalapalo still occasionally make fire drills, or use as tinder.

310   "plucked out his hair": a rite for replacing a leader. Formerly, men in the Upper Xingu Basin wore tonsures.

352   *tuafi:* mats woven by women from burity leaf ribs and cotton or agave thread. In this case, they are a well-made kind used by men for storing valuable feather ornaments.

To Get Erections

Told by Muluku at Aifa. June 6, 1979.
Notes appear on page 138.

Listen.
Ani Women.*
   Those who were Aulukuma's wives were Ani Women.
     Taugi had many different wives.
       Many were Taugi's wives.   5
   He used to make love to them with his fingers.
     Taugi made love to his wives that way,
       Taugi did.
         That was how he made love to his wives.

Because he was doing that to them the Ani Women were saying,   10
   "Well, even though Taugi is a powerful being he always does that
poorly.
     Only with these things of his,
       he makes love with his fingers,
         with his fingers."
The Ani Women were saying,   15
   "Why, Ufiti Lizard has always had erections,*
     Lizard has them.
       Even though Taugi is a powerful being he always does that
       poorly."
Taugi was listening to them.
   "Well, what did you just say about me?   20
     What did you just say?
     What did you all just say about me,
       you who prepare my food,
         you who prepare my food?
   Where is he?" he said,   25
     "Where is he?"
"Kïtsikïtsikïtsikïtsi . . . he is far from here," the Ani Women
said,*
     "He is far from here.
       Ufiti Lizard has them,
         he has always had erections."   30
            "Very well," Taugi said.

Then the next day Taugi went there to get one.
   "Let's go, Aulukuma."
   He threw his hook onto the house of the other,
     kuruck!   35

Then he sang a spell:
"*Keri wata, Keri wata*
Kami wata, Kami wata." *
Which means:
"Comes to Sun, comes to Sun   40
Comes to Moon, comes to Moon."
Then he pulled on it,
so that it came close to him,
Kuk kuk Lizard's house came close to him.
Then they were arriving there.   45
"*Kaw kaw kaw*," Lizards' people shouted.
"Why, there's Taugi!" they said.
They were arriving,
and they arrived at his house.
Tikii, they came inside the house.   50
Bah, there were erections hanging from all the rafters,
bouncing *puh, puh, puh.*
Lizard's wife was there all alone making love to them.
Puh puh puh.
Lizard had gone to his manioc garden.   55
His wife was there by herself making love to the erections.
"Well, Aulukuma, look at our grandmother.
This is a good thing we have come for."
"Grandmother, we have come to you."
"Grandchildren, I see you have come here. Why have you done
so?"   60
"We must have these things for ourselves."
"I see."

Then Lizard arrived from his manioc fields.
"Well, Taugi," he said,
"Why are you here?"   65
"Well, Grandfather," Taugi replied,
"As you see, we have come to you, to you."
"Well, what for?"
"We came to get erections,
to get erections."   70
"Why, you're both right, my Grandchildren.
You're both right.
We do indeed have what you want in this place," he said,
Lizard told them.

There they were all lined up,   75
    hanging from the rafters,
        puh puh puh.
            They were all lined up.
            Bah! so many of them,
                moving, moving *puh puh puh.*   80

"Grandfather, I want this one here," Taugi was telling him about a
very big one.
    "No, Grandson, that one isn't for you."
    "Be careful, Grandfather, don't be stingy!"
    "Look, take this one here."
        Lizard gave him one from nearer the end of the line.   85
Taugi took it away,
    and *pok* he put it on his penis,
        Taugi did.

Then he arrived home beside his wives,
        Taugi arrived home.   90
            Bah haa he had so many wives!
    He suddenly had an erection as he arrived,
        he had an erection as he arrived.
            "Taugi has arrived."
Right away he went to make love to his wives,   95
    he went to make love to all his wives.
Again the next day,
again the next day,
again the next day,
    for a long time he stayed there making love to his wives,   100
    Taugi did.
        At first he had made love to his wives with his fingers.
        "Ajah! Taugi!" it was too much for them.
        They were all exhausted because he never stopped making
        love.
He himself became thin,   105
    he had become very thin because he couldn't stop.
        He couldn't stop making love.

Then he took it away,
        Taugi did,
            to the owner,   110
            to Lizard.
                He took it away.

"Well, Grandfather. Here I am.
 I've had to return to you.
 I can't stop this thing."   1▌
     He gave it back to Lizard.
Then Lizard gave Taugi one from wa-ay at the far end of the line,
     a much smaller one.
 "Take this one," Lizard said.
 "All right," he answered.   12
When he was ready,
     he began to arrive home,
     and he arrived home.
Then at night he made love once,
     and it stopped.   12
Then he slept,
          he slept,
     and made love again,
               once.
And so it continued to be as it was then.   13
     Taugi returned to Lizard that very strong one he had gone
     to get.

Listen.
Taugi had just used his penis on his wives for the first time.

Notes to "To Get Erections"
lines
2   Ani Women: the daughters of King Vulture. The smooth-billed ani,
           Crotophaga ani, a bird with dull brownish-black feathers, is com-
           monly seen around old fields.
16   *ufiti:* a very large lizard of the Tupinambis group, often reaching over
           a meter in length. Lizards are associated by the Kalapalo with penile
           erections because of their *hemipenes* or "double penises." The *ufiti*
           hemipenis is sometimes used as a male aphrodisiac.
27   "kïtsikïtsikïtsikïtsi . . .": an expression spoken in a somewhat shrill
           voice while the speaker rotates a pointed index finger around his or
           her head, until the proper direction of a place asked about is remem-
           bered, located, and finally indicated.
37–8   This song spell is apparently in Arawak, a language spoken by the
           neighboring Mehinaku.

It is hard to imagine the Upper Xingu Basin without water. Six major tributaries flow northward to converge ultimately in the Xingu River, one of the major tributaries of the Amazon. These streams are sluggish, with meandering and braided patterns, and their periodic fluctuations in level and changes of channel form swamps and levees. These characteristics strongly influence the environmental configurations of this complex ecological zone.

During times of high water, a traveler can pass by canoe from a large river into channels that open up into the flooded forests. Pushing through vines and over submerged logs, occasionally throwing in a line for piranha and other small fish that live on falling fruits and seeds, the traveler comes to oxbow lakes filled with tucunare and other large carnivorous fish. Beyond, one finds embayments and swamps that have their own distinctive species and extraordinary tropical birds. If the water is high enough, it is sometimes possible to travel by canoe to one of a number of large, shallow lakes—created as a consequence of things Taugi did. These are filled with stingrays and otters, bordered by extensive groves of burity palm, so useful in providing thatching, fiber, and food to the people of this region. The constant presence of water dominates Kalapalo reality, and much of their life has taken shape according to its ebb and flow.

People fish, gather turtle eggs, and hunt the turtles themselves throughout the drier times of year. For a long time, these were the most obvious activities that distinguished the Kalapalo and their neighbors from other indigenous peoples of the *cerrado*, particularly the speakers of Ge languages, who valued hunting far above fishing.

The Kalapalo are fastidious people, bathing several times a day and always seeming to be washing their clothes, their shell and bead jewelry, and their well-used pots and pans. One of the important domestic duties of women and girls is to maintain a constant supply of fresh water in the house. There is a nearly steady movement of people on their way to or from the local source of water: bathers, water carriers, groups of children going to fish or catch butterflies, and lovers discreetly following.

But water also flows into Kalalpalo thinking in ways that are more subtle and poetic, which connect the world of humanity with other worlds. The story of Sagangguegï describes one of these worlds, that of the "ever-flowing" Sagangguegï, the Lord of Water. Underwater, even today, the Kalapalo say, lives a great variety of powerful beings. In certain places along the Culuene River, people canoe silently past deep pools in which dwell dangerous monsters—giant fish, peccaries, and jaguars—who would tip over a canoe and devour its occupants should they speak in loud voices. Even more important are the Fish People, who bestowed both the *undufe* songs (performed each year)[2] and manioc, the most important element of the Kalapalo diet.

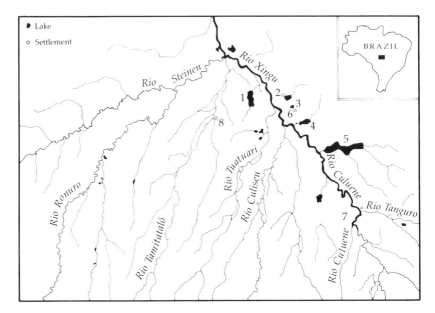

Rivers and Lakes of the Upper Xingu Basin
The Upper Xingu Basin consists of numerous rivers and small creeks flowing northward, eventually forming the Xingu River, a major tributary of the Amazon. The origin of these streams is told in the story "Saganguegi." The Kamaiura Lake (1) was formed when Dove spat water over the land, also described in "Saganguegi." The large lakes to the east of the Culuene River were created after water exploded out of a tree trunk, as told in the story, "Lake Community." Their names are (2) Migiyape, (3) Aifa Ipagu, (4) Anafanga, (5) Tafununu. These lakes are the sites of Carib-speaking communities, including the Kalapalo settlement of Aifa (6). The Kalapalo settlement of Tangugu is located at the confluence of the Tanguru and Culuene rivers (7).

When the rains end, and the constellation Ogo ("Storage Platform"—the Great Square of Pegasus) begins to appear before dawn on the southeastern horizon, people begin to think about making new fields. The Fish People, they say, have already begun making theirs. They see that the waters are covered with thick mist, which is the smoke from fires the Fish People have set to burn off the newly dried slash. Also living in the depths is Mbambangisu, who gave Aulukuma the materials for personal adornment that people still use. Others who dwell there, Zakwikatï, Kwambï, and Pidyu, gave ritual masks and music, contributing to the formation of Kalapalo ritual life as it is now practiced. Still others are the powerful *kagutu* flute and her older, less powerful sister, the smaller *kuluta*.

Sagangguegï

Told by Ulutsi at Aifa. February 8, 1979.

Notes appear on pages 152–153.

Aulukuma's wives, who were Ani Women.
  When they all went to the manioc fields,
    it was there Aulukuma heard a ritual being performed.
      "Kah kah kah," he heard some people utter.
  "What could that be that's caught my ear?"   5
  "We don't know.
    What you just heard were the most deadly of things.
    Dangerous powerful beings like yourself who will kill you,"
    they told him,
      his wives said.
  "Look," they continued,   10
    "That is Sagangguegï.
      They are Sagangguegï's followers.
        They are the ones who are making you listen.
  Taugi doesn't know anything about him,
    nothing.   15
      You don't know much about our powers."
  "Be sure not to tell him.
    I'm worried if you told him he would take me there,"
    Aulukuma said.
      "All right," they answered.
The one of whom they spoke was the Lord of Water.   20
  What the others used to bathe in was only a poor puddle.
    "It's too bad this isn't like the real thing
      where we could go for water.
    What we draw water from is different from that other thing,
      the real kind.   25
    We want to draw real water.
      There's another kind that's real."
        He was the Lord of Water.
Someone else was listening to them.
  When they arrived home Taugi came to where they were.   30
    "Where is Aulukuma?" he asked.
      "Where?"
    "At the manioc fields."
    "All right, I'll wait for him here."
      He stayed there.   35
  "Why isn't there any real water here?
    Real water should be here," the Ani Women whispered to
    each other.

The one who arrived was still there inside their house—
Taugi—
  the one who had arrived waited there.
"Taugi's power is ordinary," they said to each other,
 the Ani Women said.
"Well, what did you just say,
 you who prepare my food,
  you who prepare my food?"
   (That was the Ani Women's name.)
    "Well, what did you just say?"
"Nothing."
"Come on, tell me right now.
 Be careful."
"It really wasn't anything, despite what you think."
"Listen to me:
 'Taugi's power is ordinary,'
  I'm sure you all said that about me just now,
   you were talking about me just now."
"Yes, that's so."
"Come on, tell me.
 Tell me now!"
"Sagangguegï is the Lord of Water."
"Where is he?"
"Kotsikotsikotsi," they pointed in the direction of that place.
 "It's got to be very far from here."
Then at dusk,
 "Aulukuma," he said,
 "Now, I've come here so we can smoke together."
  It was dusk.
  He was smoking tobacco.
"Now, I've come here so we can smoke together."
Then they sat outside smoking tobacco.
 "Well, Aulukuma," he said,
 "Those who prepare my food just said something."
"What?" Aulukuma asked him.
"'Why isn't this thing here like the real water that's somewhere
else?' That's how those who prepare my food spoke just now,"
Taugi said to him.
 "'I've been wanting to bathe in that,' that's just what those
who prepare my food said. 'Taugi's power is ordinary.' That's
just what those who prepare my food said."
"Well, Sagangguegï is the one who has water," Aulukuma told
him.

"All right, we've got to go see him."
"It must be very far from here," he told Taugi.
  Aulukuma was frightened.
"Tomorrow we will have to leave—tomorrow—to see him."
Then the others came by.
"Well, what made you just tell him about the water?"
  Aulukuma said to his wives,
    to the Ani Women, that is.
      The Ani Women.
"What made you do it?
  'You must not tell,' I'm sure I said that to you.
    'Don't tell.'"
    "Yes, you did," they answered.*
The next day Taugi and Aulukuma left to see Sagangguegï.
  They blew out a stream of their tobacco smoke far away,
    and it settled on top of his house.
"It does seem to be there,
  far from here."
Taugi threw his hook onto the house,
  his hook.
He pulled it toward him.
  "Let's go, Aulukuma," and they left.
They arrived.
  As they came toward the entrance path,
    there was water.
  "Look, Aulukuma,
    look at our grandfather!"
The sun was here, in the afternoon.
  "*Kaah, koh koh,*" people did that,
    but they were powerful beings,
      not human beings.
  "Well, Taugi is arriving!
    Taugi, Taugi, Taugi, Taugi, Taugi!"
      He wore his cacique feather headdress.
        "Oh, Taugi, Taugi, Taugi!"
The Dove was there.
  "Well, let's go where our grandfather is."
  "It's really you?" Taugi said.
  "Well, it's really me.
    It's really me, Grandchildren.
      Where are you two going?
        Where?"

"We're going to our grandfather.
    To be with Grandfather."
"Very well, go then."   120
"Come along with us."
    "All right."
Ti ti ti.
    By Sagangguegï,
    "Well, Grandson," he went,   125
        "Why are you here?"
    "Well, we've come here to see you, to see you."
    "All right," he answered.
They came to a large house where there were some containers
of water.
    There was no standing water whatsoever anywhere else.   130
        Not here, not there,
            that's how it had been for a long time.
When their darkness fell,
        they slept.
    Buh! There was so much water lined up.   135
    "Look at our grandfather, Aulukuma.
        You must be very careful so you won't be killed."
        "All right."
            They were there because of that very thing.
The others were beginning to fall asleep.   140
    "We mustn't sleep. We won't sleep."
At dusk he came,
    Sagangguegï came carrying his fish net on his back in the dark.
In the very middle of the night Taugi didn't sleep at all,
        because there were monsters who were going to try to eat
        them both.   145
    In the very middle of the night the monsters exploded,
        the water exploded.
    Because of that the dew that covers our houses came into being.
They both were submerged.
    Taugi came up inside a small gourd,   150
        and Aulukuma inside the shell of a large tucum palm nut.
After that the water retreated.
    Nothing had happened.
    "He can't do anything with this."
"Well, Aulukuma," Taugi went,   155
    "I really desire our grandfather's wife.
        I want to lie down with her,
            to lie down with our grandfather's wife."

"Taugi, you're foolish.
     Don't you realize our grandfather is right here?"   160
          "Yes, you're right," he answered.
Before dawn he arrived.
     Sagangguegï arrived.
     Buh ah! He had killed so many.
     He had shot *tifi* and *tate* fish!*   165
She cooked some of the fish,
     his wife did.
Then she brought them their food,
     tate and *kagikagi* fish.
"Quickly, Aulukuma,   170
     go get our grandfather the Trumai people's pet, the
     Cormorant,
          so he can eat this dangerous food.
               This stuff here makes us choke."

The next day they left after they had slept two days,
     Taugi and his companion had slept two days when they went
     away.   175
Then they slept five more days,
     and they returned once again.
"Well, Aulukuma," he went,
     "Let's break the water our grandfather has stored here, his
     water."
          "All right."   180
"Be sure to watch carefully!"
     "All right," Aulukuma answered.
          "He will remain as he is, he will remain as he is."
     "Let's go once again."
They came once more and they arrived.   185
     "*Koh!*" as they arrived.
     "Taugi, Taugi, Taugi, Taugi!"
"Well, Grandfather," he went,
     "Because we two want to teach you something of ours,
          I've come to you with your grandchild.   190
               So you will learn about it."
"I see. That's certainly all right with me," he answered.
"Because we want to teach you I've come to you with your
grandchild."
     "All right," he answered.
"This thing almost destroyed me,   195
     destroyed me."
"Did it indeed?" Sagangguegï answered.
"It will happen tomorrow at dawn."

The next day at dawn,
   "Come on, everyone."   200
Taugi wanted Sagangguegï to pierce his ears in the plaza,
   Taugi wanted him to pierce his ears.
"You should do it," he said to Saganggguegï,
   "Go ahead."
His spear thrower was set,   205
   set in his bow.
"I want to do him in right now," Saganggguegï said to himself.
"You must really watch carefully! Watch him carefully,"
   Taugi told Aulukuma.
      "Watch carefully since you are the weaker.   210
        Go ahead!" he told Saganggguegï.
Saganggguegï began to aim,
   and he aimed.
"Go ahead!" Taugi went,
   and Saganggguegï shot Aulukuma.   215
      His neck was slit by Saganggguegï and he died.
"Now me!" he told him,
   Taugi said.
      Saganggguegï pierced his ears.
      Since then all my people have it.   220
"The other side now, the other side!"
   He finished, but he didn't kill him,
      not at all.
      Only Aulukuma had died.
"All right," Taugi said,   225
   "Grandfather," he told him,
   Taugi said,
      "Now I want to do the same to you."
"Akah, it's already been done, I've been made."
"Never mind, let's do it in any case," Taugi went.   230
   "No."
"I do want to do the same to you. Come on!"
"All right," he answered,
   "Go ahead if you wish."
Then Taugi shot him.   235
   When he shot Saganggguegï he died.
      He didn't move.
      "So he will remain."
Then Taugi put Aulukuma's bones together.
   When that was done he went for Nguke the Termites.   240
      "Grandfathers, look at your grandson."
      Tsïka tsïka tsïka tsïka, they put all the bones together.

Next Atsigi Termites placed them exactly together and Taugi
covered Aulukuma with *kedyite* leaves.
　　"Achoo achoo," he sneezed,
　　　　and he became well again.　　　　　　　　　　　　245
Aulukuma stood up.
　　"Say, I must have been sound asleep."
　　"No, you weren't. Your grandfather killed you."
　　　　It was over after that.
"So he will remain."　　　　　　　　　　　　　　　　250
"Aulukuma, go get our grandfather Kwatïngï."
　　"All right," he went.
"And you must be sure to bring our relatives to me."
　　Mbambangisï,
　　Kwatïngï,　　　　　　　　　　　　　　　　　255
　　Kangangatï,
　　Kangangafanga,
　　　　and then Nafïgï.
　　　　　　Such are they.
Also Atugua the Whirlwinds,　　　　　　　　　　　260
　　Upidyu,
　　Zhakwikatï,
　　　　and Kwambï.
　　　　All of the powerful beings traveled together to release the
　　　　waters.
"All right," he said.　　　　　　　　　　　　　　265
　　Taugi made Upidyu's burity headdress,
　　　　that of Zhakwikatï,
　　　　and then Kwambï.
　　　　　　He made them so that when the water was released,
　　　　　　the monsters wouldn't eat them.

Tute wanted to kill Taugi,　　　　　　　　　　　　270
　　Tute did.
　　　　He wanted to exterminate him.
"Something should be done about him, everyone. Come here.
　　Let's kill him."
　　　　Because of what Taugi had just done to their leader,　　275
　　　　to Sagangguegï.
　　　　　　"Be just as he is.
　　　　　　Be as you wanted him to be.
　　　　　　　　Die as he did!"
　　　　　　　　Tute felt murderous.　　　　　　　　280

Following that they all arrived where he was.
　"Come now, I'll give you what your leader kept for himself.
　"Don't act yet, Grandfathers," Taugi told them.
　"All right."
Then they all came into the house.　　　　　　　　　　285
　"This is it," he told them.
　There was the water, all lined up.
"Taugi, give me some to bathe in," Kofongo the Duck said.
　"All right, go ahead," into her water bottle.
　　Into her water bottle.　　　　　　　　　　290
　　　Pupupu it was a small one.
"Now me," Ndïtï the Motmot said.
　Into her water bottle.
"Now me," Embisa.
　"All right," Taugi said.　　　　　　　　　　295
　　Embisa had a large water bottle.
　　　Pupupu.
"Now me."
　It was Fïnggegi.
"Not you.　　　　　　　　　　300
　You'll be the only one to stay as you are now.
　　The only one."
"All right, that's how I'll be."
"Now me!"
　Tute the avenger spoke.　　　　　　　　　　305
Pupupu into his water bottle.
　Tute had brought a very large one.
"Me, too," Ogo the Storage Platform said.
　"All right."
　　Into a small one.　　　　　　　　　　310
"Me, too," Taugi gave water to Ema.
　"Well, that's too much.
　　The Mortals won't be able to find you if you're that way.
　　Mortals won't be able to see you."
"All right. That's how I'll be."　　　　　　　　　　315
"Just enough to wash your face.
　That's all," he said.

Then Taugi tapped them.
　He did that to the largest caldron.
　　This was Tuwakuegï the Water Monster.　　　　　　　　　　320
　　That's its name, Water Monster.
　　　It is water.

"Move farther away," the others said to Atafa the Dove,
  Dove was perched on it.
    He took a sip of it.   325
"Well, beware Water Monster doesn't eat you," they said to him.
"All right.
  Look, it's certainly Water Monster who would do that.
  It would flood almost to the sky.
    Not like some closer flood."   330
Then Taugi tapped the one beside it *tuk tuk tuk.*
  There was water inside.
  Dove took a sip.
  "Move farther away lest the Culuene should eat you."
    "I think that's a river."   335
Next another one,
  a smaller one *tuk tuk tuk.*
  Another sip.
  "Move farther away. The Culiseu River will eat you."
    "This is actually the Culiseu River," Taugi said.   340
Next Tïgïïñï, the narrow one, the 7th of September River.
  Tïgïïñï will eat you."
    "This is actually the Tïgïïñï River, Aulukuma."
Next Tanggugu, the Tanguro River.
    "This is actually the Tanguro River."   345
Next Tingufugutiñe the dark one, the Ronuro River.
    "This is actually the Ronuro River."
Next the Agapaga, the Araguaia River.
    "This is actually the Araguaia, the Araguaia River."
Next the Parana.   350
    "This is actually the Parana River."
Next Angafuku, the upper Tamitatsalo.
  "Beware of the Angafuku eating you."
Next a creek.
  "Beware of the creek eating you."   355
All things of that sort were contained in small vessels.
  The Water Monsters were contained in large caldrons.
    That was how it was.
      They say that for a long time no one knew about it.
Then the Dove.   360
"All right, Grandfather,
  go take your mouthful to my place,
    to Mogena."
      The Dove's Mouth was filled,
        filled with the water it had been sipping from the pots.   365

So it went,
　　it went,
　　　　but it couldn't do it.
It spit all the water out.
　　Because of that the Kamaiura Lake exists now. 370
　　The Kamaiura Lake.
"I'll take this one away,"
　　Taugi said.
"I must leave with this one,
　　with the Culuene River." 375
　　　　Taugi took it far, far away.
Aulukuma went with the Culiseu.
Next Kwatïngï,
　　far away with Tisanguiña,
　　　　far away, yes. 380
Next Yanama with the Ronuro.
Next Ñafïgï to an unknown place,
　　far from here.
Next Mbambangisï on the Tïgïïñï.
When that was done, 385
　　"Come on,"
　　　　the Tapir took Angafuku and the creeks,
　　　　　　everything else.
"All right, all these will go to the place where I live.
There they'll all run together," 390
　　Taugi said.
　　　　"At my place,
　　　　Mogena."
　　　　　　Taugi's settlement is Mogena.
　　　　　　　　It's right here. 395
"Go far from here," Taugi said,
　　"All of these will go to my place,
　　　　there they'll all run together."
　　　　"All right," the others said.
"Leave this one here, don't break it, 400
it's Water Monster.
　　　　Don't,"
　　　　　　the Dove warned him.
Then while the others got ready to spread the water,
　　"All right," 405
　　Taugi hit the caldron *tuk! tuk! tuk!*
Puh! the water growled and came out,
　　going all over, far away from there.
The others all flew away,
　　they went away. 410

A huge lake appeared.
   This became what is found at your city,
      at the Christians' city.
         That is what that was.
The water almost drowned Taugi. 415
   The others came to the shore.
   "Come on over here," Aulukuma said,
      "Where could our older brother be?" he asked about Taugi.
        "Where is our brother?"
They saw him swimming hard on top of the plaza. 420
   Taugi was going back and forth on top of the plaza with the
   water's container covering his face.
   "Come over here, everyone, come on."
First Zhakwikatu *pïpïpï*.
   He couldn't reach him.
Then Pidyu. 425
   Nothing.
Then Kwambë.
   He couldn't help either.
"I'll do it,"
   Tomoño said. 430
     "With our older brother.
       "We'll move opposite each other," he said.
He began to sing:
   "*Kaminau*, 'Leader.'"
Taugi heard his name being sung. 435
"Well, Taugi must have died," they said,
   but he had just heard them,
     and he went in the direction of Tomoño's singing.
"Come on over here,"
   and he arrived, 440
     Taugi arrived.
"Well, Taugi," he said,
   Aulukuma said,
     "You've come back again, haven't you?"
"Yes," he told him, 445
   "I have come back again, haven't I?
   I'm sure I almost died there.
     The water certainly wanted to exterminate me."
Then he said to his brothers,
   "Go away. 450
   These must all run toward my place."

For the very first time he brought it,
    for the first time,
        Taugi did.
            Taugi was the one who brought trash into the plaza for
            the first time.* 455
He had a great many fish.
Then Aulukuma came on the Culiseu River.
    Aulukuma came to grill his fish catch there.
        Aulukuma came.
            He too had many grilled fish. 460
His grandfathers and his younger relatives were still going,
    they were far from there.
They were still far away,
    going as tributaries flowing into each other.
        They were still coming right toward them. 465
The very first one to come was Mbambangisï,
    on the Tïgïïñï.
After he came,
    then Yanama.
Then Ñafïgï and the Tapir after that. 470
    Then all merged at Morena.
Ñafïgï had made a magnificent one,
    Ñafïgï is its inventor.
That river is far away in another country.
    It flows in one direction 475
        and then it flows in the other direction.
            She made it that way.
                Ñafïgï is its inventor.
Finally the water became as it is now.
    It was done. 480
Because those others had begun to talk about our being without
water,
    Taugi broke it.
    He had no water.
        There was no water at all.
    Sagangguegï was the only one who owned water. 485
    The Ani Women were the ones who told Taugi about water.

That's all.

Notes to "Sagangguegï"

This is as much a story of the origin of the rainy season, as it is of the association of rains of varying duration and intensity with different constellations.

The names of the beings who received or were denied water are the names now given to various constellations whose appearance on the southeastern horizon marks each segment of the rainy season. The Ema (the Pleiades) was given only a small amount of water with which to wash her face; hence, a short rainy season occurs in the dry-season months of June and July. (See Appendix.)

lines

88   "Yes, you did": They agreed Aulukuma had warned them against telling Taugi, but didn't agree they should not tell him.

165   *tifi* and *tate:* extremely bony fish.

455   "trash into the plaza": that is, fish bones left over from meals distributed in that central location.

Women Bathing and Drawing Water at Aifa Lake, 1980

The Lake Community

Told by Kakaku at Aifa. February 25, 1979.

Notes appear on page 157.

Listen.
   Taugi placed water inside a tree trunk,
      Taugi did.
      Then a Dawn Person found it,
         he found it among his manioc plants,   5
         he found it.
            He found the water.
   Then the Dawn Person went there,
      to shoot the fish that were there inside the log.
      The next day, the next day,   10
         that was how he went,
            how the Dawn Person went to shoot them in the water.
   His brother-in-law asked about it,
      his brother-in-law.
      "Where does the father of our son go?" he said to his sister.   15
      "Where does the father of our son go?"
      "He just found some water,
         he found some water among the manioc."
            The Dawn Person was speaking to him about it being in
            that place.
      "All right, I'll go see," he went,   20
      "I'll go see."
      "Go if you wish," she said.
      "It's there among the manioc."
      "Very well,"
      and he left.   25
   Then he shot some fish,
      ketïti, wagiti, all kinds.*
   He shot at a giant *dyofi,*
      the Dawn Person did.
   With his arrow he pierced it,   30
      with a sharp one.
   When that happened,
      tuk! he shot it again, *tik!*
         It fled farther inside the log,
         into a side branch.   35
   Swimming from side to side,
      it kept trying to escape once and for all.
   Doing that it went up farther and farther,
      until the tree burst open and it flooded, *tuk!*

Monsters ate him,   40
    they ate the Dawn Person,
    and he died.
His brother-in-law had been in the manioc fields.
    "Where is my arrow?" he asked his wife.
    "I'm sure your brother-in-law took it a while ago," she said.   45
    "Where is he still?"
    "At the water you discovered, he went to the shooting place
    among the manioc."
    "What made him do that?" he asked her.
    "He's done for, I'm sure.
        Monsters will eat him."   50
            The other one had just died.

Then all of the settlement's community died,
        every one of them.
    It became Lake Tafununu.
    They all died,   55
        every one of the people died.
    Next it spread to Angafunga,
        the giant *dyofi* spread it.
    There were people at that place,
        so they all died.
    Next it spread here,   60
        toward Aifa.
    Here there were people,
        so they all died.
    Next it spread to Mïgiyape,   65
        and as a consequence the people there all died.
    There it hid itself,
        the same one I spoke of earlier hid itself.
            The giant *dyofi* hid itself.*
            It became the Lord of Lake Mïgiyape.   70

All the people died.
    When that happened, someone fled with his sister in a canoe.
        The two were still children then,
            a female and one male,
                when they fled in a canoe.   75
                    The waves kept washing them away.
    When it became like this again,
        they came toward land.
            They remained there.

Then they were thinking. 80
  "What are we to do?"
    They didn't have any food.
      "What are we to do?"
Taugi came to them.
  "Now, look at us here." 85
  "My grandchildren, you must make love."
  "Oh no! How could we do such a thing?"
    They were embarrassed.
  "When you make love, I'll bring you fire and manioc bread, so
make love right away."
    "Oh, no!" 90
      He then went away,
        Taugi went away.
Then he came back to them.
  "Have you made love?"
  "No." 95
  "You must make love, make love.
    Afterward I will bring you fire and manioc bread."
  "Oh no! How can we do that?"
    Then the other went away having told them what he wanted
    them to do.
Then they remained there, 100
  hungry and cold.
  They began to think about what he had told them,
    so they made love.
      Just once.
Then Taugi returned once more to them. 105
  "My grandchildren," he said,
    "Over there are fire and manioc bread."
      They ate it right up.
  "You must keep making love.
    When you make love I will bring you a house, 110
    hammocks,
      and a clay griddle."
        "Very well."
Then they made love again.
  And once again, they did as before, 115
    they made love.
Afterward they became relatives.
  She became his wife.
    His sister became his wife.

Then they made love,   120
   over and over they made love.
      A female resulted,
         then a male.
Then more children resulted,
   a great many people resulted.   125
They were Lake Community,
Tafununu Community.
   Those people were Tafununu Community.

Listen.
   It was during the Beginning when a Dawn Person found water.   130
   Since then there are lakes here.

Notes to "Lake Community"

In the Upper Xingu Basin are several large pluvial lakes, whose origin is described in this story. From south to north, as they were created in this myth,
these lakes are: Tafununu; Angafunga, now the site of a settlement of survi-
vors of Dyagamï and Wagifïtï settlements; Aifa ipagi ("Aifa's lake"), the site of
the present Kalapalo settlement; and Mïgiyape, formerly occupied by the Trumai, now the home of another Dyagamï-Wagifïtï group. (See map, page 140.)

lines
27   *ketïti: Curimatidae sp.* (the Portuguese *curimata*)
          wagiti: Brycon sp. (the Portuguese *matrinxõ*)
69   *dyofi: Boulengerella cuvieri* (the Portuguese *bicudo* or *pirapucu*)

The next story is about Kutsafugu, Taugi's companion during the ear-piercing ritual. This means he was an older man who had been initiated earlier, and who had been selected to hold Taugi during the latter's own piercing. A youth's ear-piercing companion carries the initiate on his back into seclusion after the ordeal, and lies with him in the hammock during the first few days of isolation and fasting. The relationship between the two men is thus a very intimate one, the success of the ear-piercing and the quality of the initiate's dreams having much to do with the character of the ear-piercing companion, especially his own power. The power of the older man is "built upon" by the dreaming of the younger.

Given this bond, Kutsafugu is a person who, "because of his own power," can handle Taugi's childish pranks and turn them to his own advantage. What we are told about Kutsafugu in this story is that he has power similar to Taugi's, a capacity to penetrate, resist, and even mock illusion. As Taugi's deceptions continue, Kutsafugu must more and more become an active agent. After leaving Taugi, with whom he is rather passive, being acted on rather than taking the lead, he has to wrestle the demonness Ñafïgï. In the end, he is an aggressive planner, setting out to destroy his Jaguar enemies. Kutsafugu overcomes them with a deadly use of power, which contrasts with Taugi's flippant and compulsive tricks.

Kutsafugu

Told by Ulutsi to his daughter Moge at Aifa. July 7, 1982.
Notes appear on page 174.

Now I really should have told her about someone else. It really
should have been this other person.
    In fact, had I made the choice myself, I would have begun with it.
So this time it's this one.

"You must urge my ear-piercing companion to bring me my arrows.
    Quickly."   5
"Very well," the other answered.
"Urge him and he will bring them."
What I'm talking about are arrows made from the ribs of palm leaves
from a very long time ago when Taugi was still a child, Taugi was,
    and even though they were made from wild plants they were still
    his weapons.
        Still his arrows.   10
        These are called *kangangatï* arrows.
        Yes.
"All right," someone said.
    "I will bring them to you without fail just as you say."
"When you arrive there,   15
    'It's Wahatsi who called for you,
        your ear-piercing companion.'
    Urge him to come and bring my arrows,"
        he continued,
    "And bring my arrows."   20
"All right.
All right.
    I'll certainly go right away just as you wish."
Then at dusk, so, the other went on, so
    the other went on.   25
    It went on alone by itself.
Through a lake, through one like this one here,
    like the place where water is drawn.
    The bathing place,
        Taugi's bathing place.   30
        Taugi's bathing place.
    Tiki from the place where water is drawn, from the place where
    water is drawn, across toward the other side.
That's where Kutsafugu was.
    He was there at his own bathing place.

Then, from where it was in the middle of the lake, after that Canoe
Monster came toward him. 35
    Canoe Monster.
    Pupupupu that was called *agakuni.*
Pupupupupupupupu tha-at way, *tiki* it landed right there.
"Kutsafugu," it said.
    "Come along," it said. 40
    "I've come because I must escort you.
    I've come because Taugi sent me."
"Not me.
    Not me."
"You're wrong to say that," it answered. 45
    "I've come because I must escort you."
"Not me," he answered.
    "Not me."
"Very well," it said.
    And it went out to the middle of the lake. 50
"Kutsafugu," it said.
    "If I had brought you out here, I would have sunk down to the
    bottom after that,
        I would have sunk."
He knew about it,
    he also was a powerful being. 55
    Yes, Kutsafugu.
He was Taugi's companion.
He was Taugi's ear-piercing companion.
    Because of his own power, they say.
Then, this time it was someone different. Alligator. 60
    This time it was Taugi's own canoe.
    Alligator.
Moh hoh, it was huge, what I'm talking about was as wide as this.
[Ulutsi gestures to indicate a great width.]
Tititititi it moved away from the place where water is drawn
tititititi it moved toward him. 65
Tiki. It was beside him.
"Kutsafugu," it said.
"Come along," it said.
[Breathily, as if casting a spell:]
"Get in this time, get in. 70
    This time get in, he's the one.*
    He's your escort, he's your escort."
"All right," Kutsafugu said.

Then *pok*, he sat on its back.
    Pok, he was ready.
    So, *tititititi* it moved on. Out to the water.
    "Kutsafugu," it said.
      "What?"
    " 'What an ugly lumpy head he has,' say it to me.
      'What an ugly lumpy head he has,' say it to me."
    "Oh no, your head's nicer than that.
      Oh no, it's nicer than that.
    I thought you had a smooth head.
      A smooth head."
        Alligator was lying heartlessly to him.
    "All right," it answered.
Next it went *titititititi* farther on out.
    "Kutsafugu," it said.
    "What?" he answered.
    " 'Those things poking out of him are really ugly,' say it
to me.
      'Those things poking out of him are really ugly,' say it."
    "Oh no, you're nicer than that.
    Actually, your teeth seem nice and straight to me."
    "Very well."
    It had no mercy, and wanted to exterminate him the way alligators
do.
Next *titititititi* it moved even *farther* on.
    "Kutsafugu," it said.
    "What?" he said.
    " 'That crooked thing of his is really ugly,' say it to me.
      'That crooked thing of his is really ugly,' say it."
    "Oh no, your tail is nicer than that.
      On the contrary, it's nicer than that.
    Actually, your bones lie beautifully in place.
    Your tail is a beautiful thing. Actually, your tail lies straight in
place.
      It's a straight one."
    "Very well."
Tititititi. It moved even farther away.
    "Kutsafugu," it said.
    "What?"
    " 'What an ugly strong smell he has,' say it to me.
      'What an ugly strong smell he has.'"
    "Oh no, your fragrance is nicer than that.
      What a nice smell."
    "Very well," it answered.

When it wasn't very far from shore,   115
   "Kutsafugu," it said.
   "What?"
   "'What an ugly lumpy head he has,' say it to me."
And so, almost there, "What an ugly lumpy head he has!"
    Puu tiki, he flew off toward that place over there,   120
    he flew off and landed on the shore.
There at that place,
   "Kutsafugu," it said.
    "This-is-what-I-would-usually-do-to-youuuu . . ." *PUH*
   but this time THAT HEARTLESS ONE WENT ON.   125
    And so it went on.
That was Alligator.
That was Taugi's canoe.
   Taugi's canoe.

And so Kutsafugu went on the path.   130
   Titititi tikii he walked up to the house.
   I don't know where Taugi was.
   His wife hadn't left their house.
"Well, Wahatsi," he said,
   "As you see, I'm still waiting."   135
   "Yes. I have no idea where he is.
    I have no idea what he's been doing."
   "All right," he answered.
And so Taugi's wife led Kutsafugu over to his sleeping place.
   And so he waited near the doorway, near the doorway.   140
   He was lying down in his hammock, he had lain down in his
   hammock.
He was still waiting when a snake came toward him along the rafters
of the house. Think of it, a SNAKE.
   A snake came crawling *titititititititititi* close beside him, along
   his hammock cord.
   "Well, Wahatsi," it said.
    "I'm certainly here, and so are you.   145
    I'm certainly here, and so are you."
    That's *just* what it said to him!
   "I'm certainly here, and so are you."
   "All right," Kutsafugu answered,
    and it went back the other way.   150
    And it went back the other way.
But the next time he came back toward Kutsafugu
   looking like a person now.
   "*Here's* my ear-piercing companion!"
   "Of course I'm here," Taugi answered.   155

"Wahatsi," he said.
  "What?" Kutsafugu said.
"You're certainly here."
"I'm certainly here."
"I really did send for you.   160
So you could bring me some arrows."
"All right, here they are," Kutsafugu answered.
  "Here they are."
"Very well."
That was all. Then,   165
  their dusk fell.
They sat telling each other stories.
Taugi's wife was making manioc bread.
  A very, very small piece.
  A very, very small piece.   170
"Wahatsi, eat this."
"All right."
He was about to eat it all up *kukukuku,* when out it grew, very big.
  It was very big.
  While he was still eating it, it grew bigger.   175
A baby's spoonful of manioc soup.
  "I'll drink it all up."
It grew larger when he drank from it.
  Now it was something large.
  A bowlful.   180
Then they stayed there, telling stories.
That was all.
And so they slept,
  they slept.
After they told each other stories.   185

The next day,
  "Wahatsi," Taugi went.
  "What?"
  "You must be hungry," he said.
    "Hungry."   190
  "Of course.
    Of course I'm hungry."
  "In that case let's go."
    The water's edge.
      They went to the water's edge.   195
  "Wahatsi," he said.
"In the beginning I didn't behave at all the way I do now,
Wahatsi."
  "I see."

Then "Kaaah," Taugi called out to the fish.   200
    "Kaaah," because he did that they came.
    They came *tititititi puk titititi puk.*
        Two of them.
    "Well, Wahatsi.
    Look," he said.   205
    "I certainly wasn't like this long ago.
        I certainly wasn't like this long ago.
    Take one of this pair.
        Be sure to take one of this pair."
        "All right," Kutsafugu answered.   210
    "Be sure not to eat its head," Taugi said.
        "Its head.
        You won't roast the tail, either.
        This part is what you'll roast, only its body.
            That's what you'll roast."   215
        "All right," he answered.
They came back,
    and cut open the fish.
        And he roasted the entire fish on the fire.
    Taugi himself didn't eat any of it.   220
    Kutsafugu ate only the body, this part of it.
    After he did that he gave the head unbroken to Taugi.
    He also gave the unbroken tail to him. That way.
But as for that other thing I just mentioned, his ear-piercing
companion *tak*
        broke the backbone of the fish into bits.   225
        He gave it to his ear-piercing companion.
    "Well, Wahatsi," Taugi said,
        "Why didn't you pay attention?
        'Don't eat its head,' I'm sure I've been saying that to you.
        'In the beginning I wasn't anything at all like I am now.' I know I
        said *that*, my friend."   230
        "I see."
    "Hi hi," Katsafugu laughed,
        "And *I* ate it even though you didn't want me to."
But even so Taugi picked up a cotton thread.
    Then he stuffed it inside the backbone.   235
    He worked on the spinal cord *tïgïtïgïtïgï* until he had made it
    whole again.
    And so he put on the head, and he put on the tail.
    It was ready.
    "Let's go down by the water."
        "Let's go."   240
            They came to that place.

Then *uuuupuk* Taugi threw him in.
After that the remains of what he had eaten swam off.
    So they swam off.
Then *pok,* he threw the remains of what his friend had eaten into
the water.   245
    Titsik they rose to the surface.
Those he had put back together, those he had put back together
swam off.
I don't know how he did it,
    he did it with his song.*
        And so they swam off.   250
"Look."
    "All right."
Then as they sat there,
    some piqui fruit that had already opened on the tree was there.
"Wahatsi, you'd like some piqui, wouldn't you?"   255
"Yes," Kutsafugu answered.
"There they are," Taugi went,
    "There they are."
"All right."
When Kutsafugu came toward the tree, *uuuu, kuuuu,* the fruit
dropped down.   260
    "You should roast it.
        You should roast it."
    "All right."
        Kutsafugu knew all about it, however.
He sucked on one *kukukukukukuku.* It was finished.   260
    The other one *kukukuku.* It was finished.
    "Here it is, here it is, Wahatsi."
    "All right."
Buh, and he threw it back inside the rind,
    Taugi did.   270

That was over. Then, at dusk when the sun was here,
    "Wahatsi," he said.
        "Go collect some wood.
            Some wood.
        Bring back our firewood."   275
    "All right." "I'm sure you'll find them.
    I'm sure you'll find them standing there.
            Them."
    "All right." He slung his ax over his shoulder.

And so he went on *tititititi*, over *that* way.   280
  Some other people were coming toward him.
      They were coming toward him.
  "Kutsafugu."
  "What?"
  "Where are you going?" "To collect firewood."   285
  "Very well, go on then."
As they went on *titititi*, why they were coming toward him
once more.
  "Kutsafugu." "What?"
  "Where are you going?" "To collect wood."
  "Very well."   290
Another time as he approached a place again people were coming
toward him.
  He had nothing. Now he was tired.
  He came back without any firewood.
      Without any firewood.
Tikii. "Wahatsi. Anything?" "No, nothing.   295
  But there certainly were a lot of people there."
  "So you came across some people, did you?"
      "Yes, that's what I said," Kutsafugu answered.
  "They're the ones," Taugi said.
      "They're the ones.   300
  Next time chop at their ankles.
      Chop at them!"
  "All right."
The people were there again.
  Tititi, "Kutsafugu," they said.   305
  "What?" "Where are you going?" "To get wood."
  As he passed by, Kutsafugu chopped at their ankles,
      tsok! budududu bum. One fell down flat.
  Then he cut it up into lengths.
That was done. So he tied up the wood.   310
  When he had walked slightly away from it,
  uumm, it stood up.
  And it ran away to the house.
Really.   315
  This is a tree.
  This is a tree.
      Yes.
  It was Taugi who did this to our firewood long ago.
  It changed into a person.
      Yes.   320

He had accomplished what he set out to do.
"Anything?" "Yes, look, this is it.
        Look, this is it."
That was what Taugi had spoken about.
"'I know that in the beginning I wasn't anything like this at all,' I
    remember saying that to you.   325
        Now I'm like this.
            Now I'm like this."
        "All right," Kutsafugu answered.
He slept twice.
    "Tomorrow I must leave, Wahatsi.   330
        Tomorrow."
    "All right, go then.
        Go then.
        But I remember I really sent for you so you would bring me my
        arrows."
    "Very well," he said.   335
        "That was why when you did that I brought them to you, just
        as you say."
            "Very well," Taugi answered.
    He went away after that.
The next day when the sun was over here Taugi gave Kutsafugu
some gourd bowls.
        "Take these, Wahatsi."   340
        "Very well."
Next after that, once again, a toucan feather ornament.
    "Take this, Wahatsi."
    "Very well."
Next, once again, he gave him what we tie onto our hats.   345
        Those tail feathers of our piercers that we wear.*
    "Take this, Wahatsi," he said.
All his swords.
    They were rather tall, like this.
    "You will use them to kill your enemies.   350
    Take these, Wahatsi."
        "All right."
    He was giving him everything he owned.*
The next day they stood together.
    "I'm going right now, Wahatsi."   355
    "Go then,
        go then."

He was going to meet Ñafïgï, who by that time must have already
been there.
    Ñafïgï must have already been there when he left.
      Taugi also went. 360
He knew about Ñafïgï, he knew she had already come to
Kutsafugu's settlement.
    I don't have any idea how Taugi went there.
She devoured all of his followers, Ñafïgï devoured all of Kutsafugu's
followers.
    Ñafïgï devoured all of Kutsafugu's followers.
      Every single one of his followers. 365
      Mbisuk!
        That was what happened when she ate them.
        Yes.
Then Kutsafugu traveled toward that place.
    Popopopopopo, 370
      Taugi's ear-piercing companion was paddling *pupupupupupu* by
canoe.
        Still by canoe, still by canoe, still by canoe, still by canoe . . .
The sun was still just barely showing above the horizon
    when he landed.
He still was on the other side. 375
He still slept,
    still on the other side.
Taugi wanted to go get all of his possessions back.
    Yes.
The next day while it was still dark Taugi went to get his own
possessions. 380
    Mbisuk Kutsafugu had taken away all of his possessions,
      but he planned to use them to kill his enemies.
    Swords, tall ones like this.
And so after that *tititititi* when the sun was here,
    Kutsafugu walked to his own settlement. 385
Tikii he came onto the entrance path.
Next he went on to his own settlement.
There she was standing in the middle of the entrance path.
    She came toward him then.
      Ñafïgï. 390
"Ah ha ha ha," she tried to grab him as she came toward him,
    and he slashed at her with his sword.
Pum she died when he did that.
Then, appearing in another place, she came.
    Once again she came toward him. 395
      Ñafïgï once again.

As she tried to grab him,
　　tsiuk bom, again she died when he slashed at her.
　Then when he had almost reached the house circle,
　　she came toward him again.　　　　　　　　　　　　　400
　She came toward him again, and when she tried to grab him,
　　tsiuk, bom.
　He slashed at her.
　　　He slashed at her with the sword.
That was over, think of it.　　　　　　　　　　　　　　405
Next *tiki,* into his own house.
　Tiki, no one was there.
　　Mbuuk! there weren't any people there.
　　　None.
　　　Nafïgï had eaten them all.　　　　　　　　　　　410
　So he sat there sadly . . . .
Then at dusk,
　"Something's got to be done . . . something's got to be done . . . ."
　　Nothing happened.
　"Why did she have to do this to them?"　　　　　　415
The next day again, "Something's got to be done . . . ."
　　The next day again, "Something's got to be done . . . ."
Then Taugi felt pity for his ear-piercing companion.
　"Well, what happened to my ear-piercing companion?
　I'll go to him," he said,　　　　　　　　　　　　　420
　　but only in the middle of the night.
　He chopped at the house posts, *pisuk, pisuk, pisuk.*
　　In all the other people's houses.
　　　He chopped at their house posts,
　　　Taugi did.　　　　　　　　　　　　　　　　425
The following day before dawn, at the beginning of the day.
　"Something's got to be done . . . ," Kutsafugu said.
　　"Something's got to be done, got to be done, got to be done,
　　got to be done.
　Well, so! They must be here," he said.
　"They must be here," he said.　　　　　　　　　　430
　　"They must be here."
Then he went outside.
　"Come here to me, come here to me."
　"All right," *uuuh,*
　　whereas before there were only a few, now there were a good
　　many of them,
　　　many people.　　　　　　　　　　　　　　435

Next he stayed there, he slept, he slept, he slept, he slept.
　　Now everyone was murmuring.
　　　　They were murmuring.
　　Those were the house posts.　　　　　　　　　　　　　　　440
　　　　Their own house posts.

He slept, he slept, he slept, he slept, he slept,
　　and on the sixth day, "Well! My brothers," he said.
　　　　"My brothers."
　　　　"What?"　　　　　　　　　　　　　　　　　　　　445
　　　　"Let's go traveling about to some place far from here.
　　　　Let's go traveling about right now."
　　　　"Let's go as you say," they answered.
　　　　"Let's go as you say."
　　So they all came together.　　　　　　　　　　　　　　450
　　When they were all together,
　　　　every one of them went,
　　　　　　all of them.

Well, when the sun was here they were arriving at an empty place.
　　　　They were arriving at the settlement of the Jaguars,　　455
　　　　　　the settlement of the Jaguars.
　　"Hoh!" *Tik tik tik tik tik tik.*
　　　　When they arrived each one of them went into the ceremonial
　　　　house, *dududududududu* so many of them!
　　　　No one was there.
　　　　　　No one was there.　　　　　　　　　　　　　　460
　　　　The others had all gone off somewhere to hunt.
　　　　　　To hunt.
　　　　Only one of them was there all alone.
　　　　　　All alone.
　　　　　　One of their women was still there by herself.　　465
　　　　"You must go.
　　　　You will tell the others."
　　Tututututu. She ran, "Kah kah kah."
　　　　"Here comes someone to warn us, here comes someone to warn
　　　　us."
　　　　He himself, he himself, Kutsafugu,　　　　　　　　470
　　　　　　he went on top of the house, up here.
　　　　　　Up to here.
　　　　　　Why, he went on top of the house.
　　　　His necklace.
　　　　　　His necklace.　　　　　　　　　　　　　　　　475
　　　　Teh, how bright it was!
　　　　　　Bright.

He was a powerful being.
   A powerful being.
Then at the other place,   480
   "Kaah." "Here comes someone to warn us."
   "What are you doing coming here like that?"
   "You've got to come right now.
      Right now."
   "Why do we have to do that?   485
   Have some of those who devour us come to our settlement?"
      "They have.
   They've gone right inside the ceremonial house!"
"All right!" They all went back after she told them that.
   They all went back after she told them that.   490
   Why, to their settlement.
   They made no noise as they arrived.
      Silently.
They were ready. "All right!" The Jaguars all stood outside now.
   They all stood outside after they arrived,   495
      and finally they closed up their houses after they arrived.
   They killed the others after they closed up their houses.
      Kutsafugu was still up in the rafters of one of these houses.
      Kutsafugu was, still.
   While every one of his followers was being killed by them,   500
      they killed them.
         The Jaguars did.
"All right!" The people had all come together in a single place.
   Since they were all in one place, the Jaguars killed them,
      pok pok pok they jumped on every one of them.   505
      Since they were all together inside.
   Well, the Jaguars boiled them.
When the sun was over here, an old decrepit Jaguar approached.
      An old decrepit one.
      An old decrepit one.   510
   Uuuh he slinked inside the ceremonial house, along the walls.
      The old man slinked in uuuh along the walls.
   From where he was Kutsafugu watched him.
   He was nothing special to look at, just a sooty one.
   He was looking at himself all over.   515
   "Teh I'm really still nice and bright, despite what they say."
   The gleam from Kutsafugu's necklace had just brightened him up.
      It had just brightened him up.
      (He was a powerful being, I remember telling you that a while
      ago.)

While the old Jaguar painted his legs, 520
   "You've certainly been saying 'Sooty' to me enough, Children,"
he said to himself,
   "But I'm still nice and bright, am I not?"
While he was doing that *padah!* Kutsafugu dribbled some dust
down on top of him.
   On the other, the one who had come inside.
     The Jaguar who had come inside, 525
      while he was still inside.
   Padadah he dribbled some dust down.
So when the Jaguar looked up, there was Kutsafugu!
   Yes.
"Oh! Children!" he said. 530
   "Children, there's someone here!"
"Where?" the other Jaguar asked.
"Here!
   Here he is, on top of the house!"
So all the others came toward him. 535
   All the others came toward him.
Then *titititi* they ran on.
   Along the rafters.
Kutsafugu grabbed one, *tsiuk, puk,*
   he slashed it and threw it down. 540
   Pupupupu tsiuk.
"All right now!" *Pupupupu tsiuk,*
   some others went *tsiuk.*
   They went along the top of the house, *tsiuk.*
   They went up this way, *tsiuk.* 545
Tsiuk pom, tsiuk pom, tsiuk pom, tsiuk, he slashed at the pile of
Jaguars
   with Taugi's sword.
   He was Taugi's ear-piercing companion.
   He was a powerful being.
   He was Kutsafugu. 550
   Kutsafugu.
Tsiuk, tsiuk, tsiuk, tsiuk,
   mbiih, until they were all dead.
   He had slashed them all.
     That was the reason all his people had gone there. 555
"I'm coming to get you all!" he said. *Tidik* he jumped down.
   Tidik, he jumped down after that.
He ran over to the caldrons and spilled the others out,
   he spilled out all his followers.

Puh puh they had begun to weaken while they were being cooked.   560
Puh puh he went spilling them out of every one of the caldrons.
  He spilled out his followers.
  From where they were inside the caldrons.
 Those the Jaguars had just begun to boil up, I mean.
   Kulukulu, that way.   565
   They had just tried to boil them up.
But they had almost cooked them, but they had almost cooked
them.
Since their flesh had already begun to be boiled off their bodies.
Next, into the house.
Tsiuk, he went slashing at their women *tsiuk, tsiuk, tsiuk, tsiuk.*   570
Only one pregnant one was able to escape.
   Only one.
      A pregnant one.
  Once again he came back to the others.
Next he arranged his followers,   575
  he took them out of the caldrons.
And he lined them up, he lined up those he had taken out,
  he lined them up, and they were ready.
Then he covered them all with *kedyite* leaves, and they were ready!
  Then he uncovered them and they had all begun to breathe.   580
   They had all begun to breathe, they had all begun to breathe.
   Mbiih, all of them had begun to breathe.
   Every one of them.
      Yes.
(He was a powerful being, I remember I told you that a while
ago.)   585
   Kutsafugu.
  He was Taugi's companion.
  Because of his own power.
Mbiih, they all stood up.
  Then this time they were victorious.   590
   They were eating the Jaguars, they grilled them well.
   How well they grilled them all.
   Now, this time they were victorious.
That's all.
  After all that happened to them, they came back the next day.   595
   To their own settlement.
      Yes.
It's over. That's certainly all there is to that.

Notes to "Kutsafugu."

An earlier and incomplete translation of this story was published in Basso, 1985.

lines

69-71   Taugi is blowing a song spell to make Kutsafugu climb onto the Alligator canoe. Since Taugi can be in more than one place at a time, it may be that Alligator and Taugi are the same. However, this is not suggested by the narrator, as is usually the case. What is most interesting, though, is the conversation between the two. Kutsafugu is being tested by Alligator. As Taugi's ear-piercing companion, his power is capable of withstanding the trickster's capriciousness.

249   "his song": a musical spell

345-346   "what we tie onto our hats"; "our piercers": that is, feather ornaments made from the yellow feathers of the olive oropendola (*Gymnostinops yracares;* the Kalapalo *kïngua*). Ulutsi could not use the Kalapalo word because he had to avoid an in-law's name.

353   An uncharacteristic gesture, obviously deceptive, since Taugi tries to regain his possessions.

Deception serves Taugi well when he desires to make the human condition more satisfactory. However, at least from a human perspective, he shows the world to be not only unpredictable and capricious, but absurd and even extremely dangerous because of that deceptiveness. The disorderly, unrepeated, unpredictable, and dangerous aspects of Taugi are the sources of all that is difficult and troubling about human life: the hatred in people's stomachs and the bitter finality of death. Taugi's most notorious inventions are evil, occult tools people use to kill one another: the "dart" (a magical missile used by witches) and mechanical disguises inside which witches travel as if they were jaguars, snakes, macaws, and giant fish.

This strong aversion to Taugi appears in a horror story about men who use jaguar disguises to kill people. These are Taugi's invention, and like all of his creations, have the quality of backfiring on their users. As he spoke, Kudyu noticed that his story was frightening his wife and sister-in-law. But he had become so caught up in the horrible mood engendered by images of jaguar sorcerers that—once he realized the children were swimming at the lakeshore—he continued with a second, even more vivid horror: a man grotesquely devoured by jaguar sorcerers piece by piece.

Kudyu

Women Kill Jaguar Sorcerers
Told by Kudyu at Aifa. July 5, 1979.
Notes appear on page 182.

Listen now, listen now.
Well, someone was speaking.
  "Now, Daughter," she said,
    "Daughter."
  "What?"   5
  "We should go,
    let's take care of our salt plants,*
      let's take care of our salt plants."
  "All right, as you say, let's go."

Then she made their food,   10
    she made some food.
  "We'll just filter the salt solution,
    we'll filter it."
  "All right," her daughter answered.

Then the people told someone else about the two women.   15
    The people told someone else about them.
  "That woman just left with her daughter to work the salt plants,
    to work the salt plants."
  "I see," he said,
    "I see."   20
Then he told yet another person.
  "Friend."
  "What?"
  "Let's go eat that woman and her daughter, let's go eat that woman
  and her daughter at that place way over there."
  "All right, let's go as you suggest."   25
  "So they will remain,
    so they will remain," they told each other,
      the Dawn People said,
        the Dawn People said.
          "All right."   30

Then they also left
    and they went on to the same place as had the two women.
  This was how they did it.
    They went underground,
      they went underground beneath a small mound.   35
    There they took on the appearance of jaguars,

the appearance of jaguars.
Dogfish teeth were their teeth.
  These were tied on firmly with agave fiber.
Inside here was some cotton, *ta!*
  packed firmly inside so they could walk on their elbows.
"We must dress ourselves now," was what they told each other,
  was what they told each other.
    "We must dress ourselves," they told each other that.
      That was so their footprints would be those of the
        jaguar.
That way their footprints could be just like the real ones,
  just like the real ones.
Their bodies were those of the jaguar,
  the jaguar.
They were the makers,
  they were the makers.
Not every one of us has this,
  only witches have it.
    Witches use it to travel about,
      they are the makers.
Taugi invented it,
  Taugi invented it.
    Because he planned for us to be killed by it,
      to die.

Listen, listen.
Then he went on,
  he went away inside his disguise.
    The other man also went away like that.
When it was dusk, the sun was over there,
  they came to where the salt plants had been left in a large pile,
    ready to be processed.
      The women will hide beneath it,
        they will hide beneath it.
"Go ahead," one man said.
  "You go on one side and I'll go on the other side,
    the other side.
We must enter the house from each side.
  I'll be here on this side.
    Be sure to do it that way."
"All right, that's what we'll do," the other said to him.
His friend said to him, "Let's go," he said,
  "They've only gone a short way over there," he told the other
man,
    well, that's what he told the other man.

40

45

50

55

60

65

70

75

Suddenly the women heard them,
    they heard them.   80
        "Um! um," a man was howling.
            One of the friends was howling.
            One of the friends was howling.
Once again they heard him do that as the two kept coming farther
on to eat them,
    they went on.   85
        To eat the women.
            To eat the Dawn People who were at the salt plant
            pounding place.
They went to eat them,
    they went to eat them,
        the Dawn People came farther on.   90
Then while the women stayed there,
    while the women stayed at the place they had come to,
one of them heard the jaguars in the distance,
    she heard the jaguars in the distance,
    far away.   95
"Listen to that!" she said to the other woman.
    "Listen, Mother!"
"It's nothing, they're traveling far away from here, they don't know
we're here.
    Far from here,
        they're far from here."   100
    "All right," her daughter answered.
Then very soon after they were very close!
    They were very close indeed!
        They were close,
            one coming from each side.   105
"No, Mother," she said,
    "No, Mother.
Don't they seem to be people,
    like people?"
"I don't know, maybe so,   110
    We'll soon see."
Then after a short while,
    "Um um um," from close by.
    "No, dear child," her mother said,
        "Your younger brothers must be coming to devour us,   115
        your younger brothers.
            To devour us."

"Come on, let's go,
   let's hide over here,
      let's go underneath it." 120
         She spoke about that thing,
            the pile of salt plants.
Tsuduk tsuduk!
   Quickly they both went underneath the pile,
      deep inside it. 125
         They burrowed farther into the salt plants.
Then the others came.
   All the while they were snorting heavily.
They entered the house.
   "Eh he he," they really snorted as they came, 130
      because they had run all the way.
One entered from this side,
   his friend from the other.
      Tududu tududu they entered the house.
A fire was there, 135
   so they came right to it.
The women's hammocks were empty although it was dead of
night,
   it was dark when they came.
      It was dead of night.
They looked all around them. 140
   The friends looked all around them.
   On each side of the house,
      then in the house rafters,
         in the rafters.
They searched carefully for the women, 145
   but the mother and her daughter had already hidden in the pile
   of salt plants.
      They stayed there.
         They sat this way, face to face.
            They sat this way, huddled together,
               hidden in the salt plants. 150
"They're here!" the women whispered to each other.
   "They're here!"
      They had heard the others.
"Now, look. I kept telling you they were people.
   I kept telling you that!" one said to the other. 155
      The woman spoke,
         the Dawn Person spoke.
            "I kept telling you they were people,
               I kept telling you they were people!"

"There's no one here at all,   160
    there's no one here at all," one of the men said.
    "They must have run away, because of what they heard,
        they must have run away.
            They ran away because of what they heard.
    'We must be silent!' I'm sure I told you that,   165
        'Don't growl.'"
"Where could they have gone, where?"
"Oh, let's go to sleep now, we'll sleep," he said to the other man.
    The friend spoke.
Then they removed their jaguar disguises.   170
    Kï kï kï kï, both of them *kï kï . . . aapok!*
    The other also put his disguise down *buk!*
Now, they began to tease each other,
    they joked about women.
"Why weren't we able to eat them?" one asked the other.   175
"Let's go to sleep now,
    let's go to sleep."
"Let's lie down in their hammocks."
    "All right."
One of them lay down in one hammock,   180
    and the other lay down in the one belonging to the daughter.
    There they remained talking, talking, talking,
        joking about women.
Sleep touched them and they slept,
    and they slept.   185
Because the others had blown spells on them.
    "Sleep, sleep," the women said,
        the Dawn People said,
            so the others fell sound asleep.
    "Dooo," they kept snoring.   190
        They kept on sleeping.
"Dear child," her mother told her.
    "Let's go, let's go.
        They're sound asleep."
            "All right."   195
They crawled out and stood up.
    They came out from where they had hidden themselves in the
    pile of salt plants.
    kï kï kï kï kï, the men were still asleep.
        They had put the things by which they had almost eaten
        the women—those jaguar disguises—nearby.   200

"Dear child," her mother said.
"What?"
"Your younger brothers will remain as they are,
    your younger brothers will remain as they are."
"All right, let's go," her daughter answered.   205
    That woman went inside the skin.
Really!
    Then her mother also *gïdïdï.*
    The owners,
        the owners were sound asleep still,   210
            the men didn't move.
    "Let's go!"
    "That one over there is yours and this one is for me."
        The men were still sound asleep,
            the men were still sound asleep.   215
The women jumped on them,
    they jumped on them and began to gnaw on them,
        they began to gnaw on them,
            they began to gnaw on them.
    "Ah . . . haa!"
        Bom! the men fell down,   220
        they fell down,
            and the women ate them after that happened,
            they ate them after that happened.
    This is a story about it.   225
    "Too bad, too bad,
        stay as you are, stay as you are," the women said to them.

Then later they told the other people,
        they told the other people.
    They returned home afterward,   230
        they were sobbing when they did that.
        They had eaten the others up,
            they had eaten them.

Do, listen well!
    This is a story about it.   235
  Some of our ancestors made jaguar disguises.
    Taugi was the inventor,
        Taugi made it.
        It's called "their disguise."
    That's a monstrous apparition,   240
        because if we see it we die,
            we die.
            That's how it has been since it was first made.

This story makes us very tired,
  it's forbidden to us.   245
A small child never wakes up,
  our offspring sleep constantly,
    they're always tired.
      Taugi arranged it that way.
When the sun is here,   250
  when the sun is setting,
    only then do they wake up,
      that's how our offspring are,
        they don't get up.
I don't tell my children this story.   255
  That's how it is.
This is a story about it.
  The others had died, see. They died.

That's the end of that.

Notes to "Women Kill Jaguar Sorcerers"
line
7   "salt plants": water-hyacinth leaves and stems are dried, burned,
          and filtered to make a coarse salt used to flavor fish.

"Lies About Himself":
The Varied Character of the Trickster Taugi

Taugi is a dangerous and angry *itseke*, or "powerful being," though he is human in many respects. He is by no means the most awesome of the powerful beings, nor one who can fully transform and destroy. Kalapalo sound symbolism links *itseke* with music. In its multiplicity of interpretation, music is associated with the hyperanimacy and transformative abilities that are the *itseketu* or "power" of these beings. Thus, Taugi is unable to make musical instruments; he has to obtain them through trickery. People don't want to give him their ceremonial flutes, neither the *kagutu* nor the *atanga*, each of which is closely identified with masculine erotic aggression. (This might mean if he got them he would become uncontrollably powerful.)

Taugi uses his intelligence, either maliciously inventive or imaginative, against powerful beings, and against his skill they seem almost helpless. Taugi succeeds when he deceives powerful beings for the good of humanity, that is, when he acts in the interests of others, his "children." Thus when he seeks the elements essential to human life, light, fire, and water, he overcomes their diffident owners or guardians or sources. He fails in his quests, or is even duped in turn, when he is stupidly consumed by obsessive greed, envy, or sexual jealousy. These ludicrously inappropriate or excessive feelings hinder the effective functioning of his powers of creative insight and cunning. For Taugi never overcomes his adversaries by overt force or moral persuasion. He is sometimes called *tikambïngïmbïgï*, "someone who doesn't tell about himself," and the one who "baffles" people (*enggugikïgïïñe*). As his name Taugi (from *taugiñe*, "lies about himself") implies, Taugi acts mainly through concealment and deception, through verbal and visual subterfuges.

Taugi (and, less frequently and successfully, Aulukuma) is not only verbally disposed to deceive, he is corporeally deceptive and visually illusive. Both twins have the ability to conceal their gender and their age. Taugi is unique in being able to take on more than one form at once. He can create a second self in the form of an alligator, a tapir, a cricket, or a catfish, while pretending at the same time to watch innocently while the creature violates or destroys something. In these instances, Taugi exists side by side with an objectified agent who puts an important aspect of Taugi in the foreground: the action, disclaimed and of which Taugi appears guiltless, may be violent aggression, gluttony, lechery, or sheer vengeful destruction. In these stories, there is a clear sense of a trickster intelligence that is speculative, eccentrically playful, idiosyncratic, and guiltless, an illusory consciousness in which the things of the world, including Taugi's own self, can never be taken for granted or trusted, nor assumed to be fixed and assured. Compared with Kwatïngï and all the other characters whose action is described as persistent and repetitive, Taugi almost never tries to repeat an action. When he does (as in "Mbambangisï") he fails. It is almost as if repetition in Taugi's action has a hindering, limiting effect, just the opposite of what it accomplishes for human beings. In Taugi's case, creative imagination that is successful is connected to his erratic, unpredictable ways.

Looking at the specific relations Taugi has with others, we see he can represent any and all of the Kalapalo male categories: husband, brother, lover, grandfather, father, son, leader, shaman, and witch, especially as these labels indicate ideas about different configurations of character or personality. It is as a small child (a "son" or "grandson" in the stories about Kwatïngï) that Taugi adopts the most complex and implacably self-contained personality. Here he shows an acute self-consciousness: he acquires names, puts himself forward by demanding to be seen and heard, engages in outrageous acts of revenge and invents occult ways to make people die, and, more positively, penetrates the deceits of others. Sometimes, too, he forgets his goals, thinks in a disorderly way, tries out alternative roles, and otherwise seems flighty and unpredictable. It is thus in his role of child that he appears the most uncompromisingly unique, destructive, and disorderly. The older he is, the less directly violent and antagonistic he is, but he is apparently also less capable of revealing other people's deceits to themselves—less aggressively insightful, perhaps. As a "grandfather" to the Dawn People, he seems to be a commanding figure of potentially immense destructiveness. Dressed in a gleaming headdress of oriole and macaw feathers, his fearful appearance signals his confrontational motive when he visits others. Usually on these visits he only intimidates people into doing him some favor or other, and doesn't actually use his power. So frightening is his power's potential, people say they are "done for" as soon as he appears in the settlement. But he is also called a "father" to humanity. In these cases, he is kind and helpful, and wins respect for the advice he gives. This occurs, for example, in the stories of the "Original Piqui," and "Tukusi, the Pubic Hair Thief," which is about the origin of corn. In the sole story where he appears as the father of a son, his carelessness results in his son's murder, after which he tries unsuccessfully to take revenge on the being who caused the boy's death. And, finally, Taugi is said to be present at people's funerals as a father, mourning the death of his children. First as a son, then as a father, he enacts the complex feelings Kalapalo associate with grief: sadness, anger, lust for revenge, resignation.

The Original Piqui

Told by Muluku at Aifa. February 8, 1979.

Notes appear on pages 191–192.

Listen.
   They were the wives of Ugwanagï,*
      Ugwanagï was the name of their husband.
         Ugwanagï.
      His wives' names were Nzuengi, "Cicadas."   5
   They went to get manioc,
      his wives went to get manioc.
     "Let's go get manioc, my sisters."
      "Let's go, as you say." There were five of them.
So they went on.   10
     Then after they were finished there they came home.
Again the next day they went.
   They were discovered by Tafingakuegï the Alligator.
     He came to them.
 "Why are you all here?" he asked them,   15
     "Why are you all here?"
"We have just come to get manioc," they replied,
        the Cicadas said.
           "I see," he answered.
"All right now."   20
     He had the right to make love to them because he was their
cousin.
     Alligator had the right to make love to them.
Then because of that he committed adultery with the other man's
wives,
     Alligator made love to them.
     "You can be sure I'll always come to you," he said.   25
       "Repeatedly."
         "All right," they answered.
     "Kaah! you must be sure to call me," he said.
      "All right," they said.

The next day they went again,   30
      and they came again.
        "Kaah! Alligator, come make love to us again!"
       and he came to them.
The next day,
     the next day,   35
     the next day,
      he was always there to do that to them.

It was Akugi the Agouti who told their husband.*
   "Friend," he said,
     "Do you know what's happening?" 40
     He knew nothing.
       Agouti spoke to Ugwanagï.
     He knew nothing.
"Well, I'm sure someone has touched the mothers of our
children," he said.
     "I see," their husband answered. 45
      "Tomorrow you must go see."
      "All right," the other said.

The next day they both went to see.
     "That's who it is," Agouti said to him.
   Then "Kaah!" they went, 50
     "Sakangangatë, kaah! Sakangangatë, kaah!"
     That is his name,
     Sakangangatë.
   "Kaah! make love to us once more," they said as he came to
them.
   He made love, 55
     he made love to their oldest sister,
     he made love to their next born,
     he made love to their next born,
     he made love to their next born,
     their last born . . . and then he fainted. 60

Again the next day,
   "Look," Agouti told him.
   "That's what he is always planning to do here to the mothers of
our children."
   "Tomorrow I'll come here to kill him, tomorrow."

Then the following day the women painted their bodies and their
foreheads with red paint, 65
     his wives painted themselves.
When the sun was here they all went away once again.
   "We've got to go now," they said to their husband.
   "Go then, I'll stay here."
Then they went away and they arrived. 70
     "Kaah! Sakangangatë, kaah!
     Come make love to us now! Come make love to us!"
     Nothing happened. He was sleeping.
   "Sakangangatë, kaah!"
   He didn't come to them there. 75

"Come to us right now!" they said.
"I must have been fast asleep there,
  I was asleep."
    "All right," they said.
Then he made love to one of them,   80
  he made love to the oldest sister,
    he made love to the next one,
      the next one,
        and when the last one was finished . . .
        he fainted.   85

While he was still unconscious,
  their husband shot him from above,
    Ugwanagï shot him with a small palm arrow *tsik!* into his
    ear,
      and he died.
        Afterward their husband went away.   90
"Get up, get up!"
  But he didn't move,
    he was already dead.
"Come on! It's been too long. Come on!" they said to him.
  Nothing happened,   95
    and so they began to grieve for him,
      they grieved for him.
  "What could have happened to him?" they said.
    He didn't get up,
      so they all wept.   100
"We've got to do something about him," so they buried him.
  "Oh, what shall we do with our younger brother?" I'm told she
  said,
    the oldest sister said.
  " 'You always do this to our younger brother,' I do know I've
  said that to you before!"
    That was not what happened this time,   105
      he had died.
  Unfortunately you must have done that very thing this time.
  Probably when he was making love to you."
    That was not what happened, however.
      He had died.   110
At dusk they arrived at the house,
  They were all weeping.

The day after
and the day after they never went again to get manioc,
no longer,   115
because they grieved for him.
They were still grieving for him.

They slept,
they slept,
and after one month passed they went there.   120
Something had grown up from Alligator, it had grown up.
"This must be a sprout of something here," one of them said.
Each time they returned to it,
it had grown further.
Teh how beautifully red were the new leaf buds as it grew!   125
"This is really growing well now.
It couldn't become something for us to eat, could it?" Cicada
said.
Then it was fully grown.
Next it fruited heavily, *bah,* and the branches curved down with
the piqui fruit.
There was so much of it!   130
"Yes, now I really do think this will become something for us to
eat," she declared.

The fruit grew.
Bah! The branches were laden with it.
"Now I really do think this will become something for us to
eat," she declared.
Then they swept his grave,   135
beneath what had grown up over him.
Next it dropped,
the piqui dropped.
When it dropped they cut one after another open but there was
nothing much inside.
No, nothing.   140
"How did it get this way?" they asked each other.
They cut some more of it open but there was nothing much
inside.
Then their youngest sister—her name was Afukagu—took a straw
and held it against her vulva.
Next she pierced the fruit with it and it became fragrant.*
She pierced it and it was ready.   145

"I can tell this last one's ready now. Here."
"What did you do to it?"
"I did it with this," she told them.
"Very well," they answered.
    Now it had become ripe.   150
"How did it get this way?" Cicada asked.
A parrot who was Taugi's pet had sat there on the tree.
    On the piqui tree.
        It had come to eat the fruit.
Later when it relieved itself,   155
    he saw it, Taugi saw it.
    "Where did this come from?" Taugi said.
        "Where did my pet go before?"
Then Taugi tied it to a string.   160
    Holding on, Taugi went with it to that place.
    It perched there,
        buh on the piqui tree.
"So this is where it came to,
    to this place."   165
"Now, Taugi," Cicada said.
    "Look at us for a while and figure this out."
    "What have you all done, what?"
"Look at this pulp for a while."
    Why, there was pulp piled up all over.   170
"What do you think we did wrong with this? What?
    We took it outside to dry in the sun.
    That didn't work.
    It got mold.
    We smoked it on a grill.   175
    That didn't work.
    We even tried roasting it over the fire after that.
    That didn't work.
    We even tried roasting it over the fire after that.
    That didn't work.   180
What should we have done?
    Keep looking, Taugi,
        look.
        Figure it out for us," Cicada said.
        "All right," he answered.   185
"What should they have done?" Taugi was saying.
    "Do you remember where he came from?
        How did he come to you?"
    "He came out of the water."
    "I see," he replied.   190

"From what you've told me, I'd say you must put it back in
the water this time," he told them,
Taugi said.
"Into the water."
"All right," they answered.
"All right, weave us some holders,   195
weave some holders now."
So then Taugi made them.
When that was done he collected *uwanapagë* leaves.
They held the pulp inside.
Then it was held inside.*   200
When it was ready,
"Take this back into the water," Taugi said,
so they carried away the basket of piqui.

After they had slept three nights,
they went to look at it.   205
Teh, it had become delicious preserved piqui pulp.
"All right, let's look at it right away!" he said.
He unwrapped it.
Taugi desired it.
He desired it.   210
"Oh, Aulukuma," he said.
"Oh, I've never drooled as much as I am now," Taugi said.
"It will always be this way.
Those mortals who don't think they'd like it will crave it."
"All right," his younger brother answered.   215
"It's ready.
This is the way we must do it,
this is how we will do it," Taugi said.
Then, *mah!* greedily they all ate it up.
"All right now," they said.   220
"Here." They packed more of it into holders.
"Here."
There was so much of it!
Taugi was going around with Tïkitse the Cricket.
As he did so, a storm appeared.   225
He waited for Cricket to go on.
Cricket went on. *Ku ku ku ku.*
"River Bank Community is constipated," he called out.*
Cricket was speaking.
Taugi was listening to him.   230

Taugi disliked him.
"I'll go watch him," he said,
"I'll go watch.
Let's go look, Aulukuma," he said.
"All right," his younger brother answered.   235
They approached, "*Koh koh koh.*"
Storm clouds gathered.
"*Koh koh koh,*" they approached once again.
"Oh, River Bank Community is constipated," Cricket
said.
He rested beneath the tree.   240
Then the wind came *koh koh koh* and the piqui dropped.
Cricket desired it.
As he began to pick up the falling fruit, Taugi used one of them
to crush him.
When Cricket was crushed,
Cricket's body,   245
he died.
"Why, Cricket has just been crushed by a great piqui fruit,
he is dead.
The piqui crushed him.
Why, he will stay the way he is. This time Taugi crushed him. 250
Why, because you spoke to him that way he did that to you."
This was how piqui came into existence.
All the piqui came from that other person's body,
from Alligator's body.
That was the original piqui.
The original piqui.

Notes to "The Original Piqui"

In another version of this story that I heard, the Cicadas first make love to
Tapir, who is also killed by their husband. From his body grew various wild
fruits the Kalapalo eat.
lines
2   Ugwanagï is Agagati the Tinamous (possibly *Crypturellus parvirostris*).
         Muluku did not use this latter name because it is owned by a person
         to whom he owed respect, someone whose names he could not use
         in speech.
38   Here, as in the story of Kafanifani, Agouti is a sneak and a spy. This
         rodent has the habit of foraging stealthily around Kalapalo houses,
         scrounging in the garbage mounds that ring the settlement.
143   Having pierced the fruit with a straw that she had introduced into
         her vagina, Afukagu created the odor of ripe piqui.

193–198 When they process the piqui fruit for storage during the height of the harvest (October–November), the Kalapalo first boil the fruit, scrape off the pulp, and then pack it into cylindrical baskets made of woven bark and lined with these large, resilient leaves. The baskets are placed in a shallow stream where they may be kept for as long as a year. The fruit ferments in these containers, but remains non-intoxicating since the alcohol is dissolved in the water that continuously flows over the containers. When the food is needed, the baskets are removed and split open, and the pulp is mixed with water and manioc gruel to produce an excellent, sour soup (called *intsene*) that is served cold. During the period of intensive harvesting and processing, unfermented piqui pulp is made into a soup with the taste and texture of Wheatena.

228 Because they didn't eat enough piqui, the community members' stools were hard and black. Cricket mocks Taugi, whose settlement is located beside the Culuene River at Morena. In fact, Cricket is Taugi, who can be in more than one place and one form at a time. So Taugi is actually mocking himself, and in the end foolishly trying to exterminate his self-mockery.

Fufitsigi
Told by Ulutsi at Aifa. July 6, 1982.

A Dawn Person went, he went to throw *taka* traps.
  He kept doing that with them.
When he was finished, someone came toward them,
  Fufitsigi.
He came at night to draw the traps out of the water.   5
  To draw them out, he would carry off all that was inside them.
    He would carry off all that was inside them.
When he was done,
  the other person came there to draw them out.
  The owner would go there when it was daylight.   10
  And he came back, without anything at all.
That kept on happening to someone, to Taugi, he himself was the
one that was happening to.
  Yes, that's right, just as you say, it was Taugi, Taugi.
    There was nothing.
He would go,   15
  just a short time after that,
    and again just shortly after that.
There was nothing,
  nothing.
"What happened here?   20
  Who took out my fish?
    What happened here?"
"Well. You," he said
  to Kwakwagï,
    Kwakwagï the Potoo Bird.   25
"Keep a watch out," he said,
  "Watch this.
Watch to see who takes my fish out.
I don't know who keeps coming to take my fish out,
  so look."   30
  "All right.
I'll go there just as you say," so when it was dark he flew away as
potoos do.
  Uuupok, he landed on a nearby tree.
He sat above the *taka* dam, on a tree.
  On a tree.   35
Here on the dam, *piïï* he settled on top of the log supporting the
dam, *poki.*
  There he was, on top of the log that stuck out from the dam.
He waited, waited, and waited,
  until, when it was pitch dark, "Tsiii," someone went.

"Here comes someone!" Potoo said, 40
    Kwakwagï said.
Fufitsigi alighted while the other still sat there.
    He put his necklaces there,
        Fufitsigi did.
            That was what he always did. 45
The necklaces that he owned were long pendants,
        which were still uncut.
        They hung this far down.
        They were still uncut.
        Those necklaces. 50
As he walked toward the fish traps *tititi* he took off his necklaces
and draped them carefully over the post,
        carefully.
    He took off his necklaces,
        pok he put down his necklaces, Fufitsigi's necklaces.
    He needed to use something like a tree. 55
Like that thing that stuck out just that way, they were on that log,
    as if they were draped around his own neck.
        Mbok, he put down his necklaces,
            his necklaces.
Gïdïk, they rested quietly there, they didn't clink together. 60
Tutututu, he went on through the water after that.
    Tutututu Fufitsigi went on to pull out the *taka* traps,
        to pull out the *taka* traps.
He started to pull out the *taka*, he started to go on through the
water *pupupu*.
    There they were. 65
        There were the necklaces that belonged to him. There were
        the necklaces that belonged to him.
With the necklaces, those necklaces, Kwakwagï went on in his
own way.
        To Taugi.
        To Taugi.
And then, "Why, Taugi," he went. 70
    "You're right after all.
You're right about some powerful being going around there.
        A powerful being.
        Fufitsigi.
    Look at this. They're his necklaces. 75
        His necklaces."

Then he gave them to Taugi.
  "Now these necklaces are mine," he said.
    "Now these necklaces are mine."
  "Don't be in a hurry to show them around.
    Don't be quick to show them around.   80
  And you're not to walk out without thinking.
    No."
  "All right."
Fufitsigi came back while they were talking to where he had put his
taka traps,   85
  Tsugutsugutsugutsugu tiki, he pushed his way through the water
  and stopped at that place where he had left his necklaces.
He was looking for his necklaces,
    but no,
  Kwakwagï had already taken them,
    they were already taken.   90
And so he went on after that.
  He looked for them, he missed them when that happened.
    He missed them when that happened,
      he missed them.
  There was a child of Taugi's who was this tall, like this.   95
    He was Taugi's son.
    Like this.
    Tallish.
Then, I'm told, that's all.
  A dry season passed.
  And then again a rainy season.   100
  And again a dry season.
  Again a rainy season.
  And he wore something like this, a tiny little one.
    That was his son's necklace.
Fufitsigi was still going around looking for it,   105
  he kept looking for it,
    he kept looking for it.
      He couldn't find it.
Taugi had forgotten all about him.
  He had put a tiny necklace on his son.   110
    Just one.
    One.
"Well! Here's my necklace, isn't it?
  Why, give it to me," Fufitsigi went.
    And he took it off the boy.   115

"All right now!"
And he blew a spell.
"Look," he said after that,
    and the boy died after what had been done to him.   120
He came, he came tottering from side to side,
    and he died after that.
"Look at this!" Fufitsigi had taken off his necklace after he did that,
    he had taken off his necklace.
Then, that was over.   125
He died after that had been done to him,
    so he died.
"How did my son get this way?" Taugi said to himself.
"How could the owner have done this to him?"
"He's the killer," he went.   130
    "He did that even though he took off his necklace."
        "I must do something."
He plucked out some hair from his son's head.
    He plucked out some of his hair.
"All right, I'll do it."   135
    He wound up what he had plucked out.
To whom did he carry it, what he wished to wind up?
    He himself, who had done all that.
    He himself, still.
    Taugi wound it up.   140
What had come from his son,
    the hair from his head.
He put it inside something like this, inside a large caldron.
    Why, he made his own *kune,* his revenge charm.
    He was taking revenge for his son's death.   145
The *kune* drew the other to him. "Tsiiii," he went as he always did,
    "Tsiiii," Fufitsigi went.
"Oh! Well! That's my son's killer all right," Taugi said.
    "That's my son's killer all right.
    My son's killer.   150
    That's him all right."
Tsaikï, he brushed against the thatch. *Tsaikï,* he went.
    Taugi spread open the thatch.
    The next day as well, again he came.
    The *kune* was hurting Fufitsigi,   155
        the *kune.*
And Taugi himself, he went to part the thatch.
    He would go to watch for Fufitsigi
        but it was no use.
            It was no use.   160

He would go to watch for Fufitsigi,
  but each time he came to part the thatch Fufitsigi would
  stupefy him.
    He would stupefy Taugi.
    Very badly.
Because of that he went 165
  to get Afasa.
    He wanted to capture Fufitsigi.
    He wanted to capture him.
  "Now, what brings you here, my grandchild?" Afasa asked.
  "Why, I've certainly come to you," he answered. 170
  "What for?"
  "You have to see your grandson's hair combings that I'm
  cooking.
    You have to see them right now!" Taugi said.
"I just don't know how to take care of him,
  I'm afraid."
    "Very well. 175
    Very well."
  So, they came back together.
Then, *tiki* inside the house.
  The sun was over here.
  They both continued to stay there in the house. 180
    That was all.
    It became dark for them after that.
Because that began to happen, Taugi built up the fire.
  "Now's the time to start watching for him!"
    "Tsiii," Fufitsigi went.
  "Here he is, go look, go look!" 185
    "All right."
Afasa went over to the wall of the house,
  to watch for Fufitsigi outside.
Fufitsigi came toward them while Afasa was waiting. 190
  Now, Afasa squeezed him hard after that but Fufitsigi weakened
  him, because he took hold of him so quickly.
Again Afasa squeezed him hard, despite what was happening to
him.
  He tightened his grip despite what was happening to him,
    but then Fufitsigi made him weak again.
    Bok, he threw him over. 195
    He threw off Afasa.
  "It's no use, I can't do anything to him. I'm so tired!
    He weakened me, didn't he, Taugi?
      I don't know who this killer monster is,"
        he declared. 200

"I failed when I tried to hold on to him.
    I failed.
        Yes."
Whom did he go to get next?
    Whom did he go to get the next time?
        He still wanted someone to catch Fufitsigi.
Ñafïgï? Was it Ñafïgï?
    I don't know.
    I guess that's who it will be.
        Yes.
        Ñafïgï.
"All right." He came to someone once again.
    "All right, tomorrow," and so once again.
Just like Afasa, she came there, and parted the thatch.
    She made an opening in the thatch, she made an opening in the
    thatch,
        so she could capture that awful thing.
    "All right," but nothing happened.
        When she took hold of him hard, I'm told,
            he weakened her.
                Nothing happened.
            He was the worst kind of monster.
                The worst kind of monster.
    "Well, leave him the way he is," Taugi said,
        "Leave him alone.
            Let it be.
You can see how he's overcome us.
    You can see how he's overcome us."
"All right," she answered.
"Let him be the way he is.
    Let him be the way he is.
Why, that thing that killed my son wasn't human at all.
    Not like a human being."
"Very well,
    very well."
That was all. He stopped it all.
    Taugi took apart his fire.
        Yes.
That's all.

205

210

215

220

225

230

235

Despite his acute self-consciousness, there are occasions when Taugi needs to be made aware of himself by an outsider. This occurs when his feelings are excessive and unsuited to the occasion. Then, Taugi is captured by his own self-delusion; he becomes obsessed with an idea, an illusion that makes his more material consciousness dissolve. These are instances of illusionary consciousness creating an all-too-encompassing prison of self-deceit, in which exaggerated selfishness inevitably diminishes insight and precipitates failure. In the narratives of "Mbambangisu" and "Kafanifani," sexual jealousy and envy come between Taugi and his fellows, and Taugi ultimately learns about the futility of these feelings: of the consequences of envy, jealousy, greed, and anger. Only at the climax of such stories does his acute embarrassment at his failure cause him to give up, or to begin to think more carefully about what is happening around him. There are, then, limits to Taugi's powers of insight and creativity. Taugi sometimes neglects to use his intelligence, as if, unlike other powerful beings, he must constantly develop his own power through active mental work.

In "Kafanifani," Taugi tries to bring back the Dead so they can visit the living. He fails because he forgets to use his magical power and tries to bluff his way to success as an ordinary person would. Kafanifani tricks Taugi by stealing his wives while they are performing an almost sacred service—the preparation of food for ceremonial visitors. This is as much a gesture of contempt as it is Kafanifani's way of showing disapproval of Taugi's plan to return the Dead to the living. Kafanifani upsets Taugi's attempt to maintain hegemony over life and death, though in the end he is permanently done away with by the more powerful being, who throws him into the sky.

In spite of this success, Taugi fails to return the Dead because his anxiety about his wives makes him forget to greet the visitors properly. Similarly, after the Dead leave in a huff, his continuing anxiety about finding his wives makes him forget to use his intelligent insight. Agouti, a much lesser being who is a sneak and a spy, has to remind him of this. When Taugi can reason unburdened by anxiety and jealousy, he uses his full powers of insight against his wives' deception (they prefer to stay with their abductor and try to hide themselves) and his equally powerful capacities of transformation to take revenge on Kafanifani. In a similar vein, his grandfather, Mbambangisu, must make him realize how limited he is and how futile is his envy of his brother Aulukuma.

Kafanifani

Told by Muluku at Aifa. February 8, 1979.

Notes appear on page 207.

Listen.
  Kafanifani cuckolded Taugi,
    it was Kafanifani.
  Why, because Taugi was trying to return those of us who had
  died,
    he was trying to return those of us who had died.   5
  "Now, something must be done, Aulukuma.
    I'm doing this so that our dead will return to us," he said.
  "I do want our dead to return, because the mortals are being
  used up,
    that's why I want the dead to return."
  "That's true, they are,   10
    that's true, they are."
  "Come here, everyone," and a messenger went on,
    the messenger went on.
      He went to Añafïtï, he went to the Place of Many Dead.
      Tititi.   15
      Tititi.
  That was all.
Then, I'm told he arrived.
  he arrived,
    their messenger did arrive.   20
  "Come here, everyone. Now, tomorrow your followers must do it,
    tomorrow they must do it."
  "All right, that will be fine." How they all cheered!
  "Tomorrow Taugi's guests will surely arrive,
    "Taugi's guests will arrive."   25
  "Why, the Dead are returning, the Dead are returning."
Then, shouting out the Dead were coming back in this direction,
    the Dead were coming back.
  "Come here, everyone," there were so many doing that!
  "The Dead are surely trying to return, the Dead are trying to
  return,   30
    the Dead are trying to return."
  "We must keep returning so we can remain here, we must keep
  returning."
  They were the Dead, those who had died. Yes.
Then I'm told, that was all.

So then cold manioc soup was being made, it was being made for
their entrance,* 35
    it was being made for their entrance.
        A huge quantity of it!
    His wives, Taugi had five wives,
        Taugi's wives.
    "Go ahead." So, Taugi's wives were making it for the plaza
seating of the Dead, 40
        Taugi's wives.
    It was being prepared for their plaza seating.*
        That was all.
    "They're almost here!"
        So now, the Dead were appearing. 45
Then *titi* . . . that was all.
Why, they were near the house circle,
        near the house circle.
    "Go on," well, they were getting ready. His wives went to get
water for mixing up the manioc drinks,
        Taugi's wives. 50
    "Quickly now, go get it!" *
        Kafanifani was there,
            Kafanifani was there. Kafanifani was there.
Since he just happened to be coming back from some place where
he had been fishing,
        from where he had been fishing. 55
    "Well, what are you all up to?
        What are you all up to?
            What are you all up to?"
    "Nothing," they answered.
        "This is for the distribution drinks we're mixing, 60
            we're mixing the distribution drinks.
        Why, Taugi's guests are surely arriving,
            Taugi's guests are arriving."
    "I see," he answered,
        "I see." 65
    "Where were you?" "Fishing."
        "I see," they answered.
    "Give me some fish."
        "Give me some fish."
    "Get it if you wish. 70
        Here, they're right here, get into my canoe."
        Into his canoe,
            the canoe.

Buk buk. So now, so he stole them from him, Kafanifani did. 75
   He stole Taugi's wives.
   Buk and away they went,
"Come here, all of you," nothing.
   "Come. Come here, all of you." By then the Dead were already
   close to the houses,
      close to the houses.
      Nothing happened. 80
   "Come here!"
   But now people were already talking about it.
   "Why, Taugi's wives have actually been stolen!
   Kafanifani has stolen Taugi's wives,
      Kafanifani did that. 85
   "Yes, he's really left!"
   That's all.
Then Taugi sped off to look for them,
   on the path to the water's edge.
   Then at the water's edge, 90
   mbiii, they had vanished,
      they had vanished.
   "Where in the world did they go?
   Why, they're really deceiving me the way they always do."
"All right," so he went on. 95
   While he was in the water, he submerged with them,
      Kafanifani did.
      Kafanifani did.
And he carried them away beneath the water, he carried away
Taugi's wives,
   he carried away Taugi's wives. 100
      So he stole them,
         so he stole them.
Pupupu . . . far away! And so he brought them up to the surface at
some unknown place,
   he brought them up to the surface.
   As he did that, their husband kept following behind . . .
   nothing. 105
   He was following them from far behind.
   Nothing.
Next they went on
   and he carried them off through a submerged log,
      Kafanifani made it happen. 110
   He wasn't a human being,
      Kafanifani.
         He was a powerful being.

Nothing.
Then Kafanifani carried them away. Taugi saw nothing. 115
     So he rested,
          he rested.
Then, "Why, we should go back, shouldn't we?" the Dead said.
     "We should go back, shouldn't we?
     All of you have made us wait and wait. 120
     Why, we must go back,
          we're going back."
               They turned right around.
     "We'll stay just the way we are, we'll never reappear,
          we'll never reappear, 125
               we'll never reappear.
     Let them be the way they are," they said to each other.
So they turned around,
     they turned around,
          they turned around. 130
     And the Dead turned around.
Then he arrived,
     Taugi arrived.
     "Have you found your wives?"
     "Not a trace." 135
          And so he arrived.
     "What a shame that happened.
     Your guests have all left."
     "Oh, so they will remain,
          so they will remain. 140
Now the mortals can't turn back,
     the mortals can't turn back.
     But I tried to do all that so the mortals would have to keep
     returning to us," he said.
     "To return to us always. I did it so that would happen to them,
     they would always return to us," he continued.
          "To return to us always." 145
               Yes.
     "Oh, so they will remain, so they will remain."
So now the others had left because of that,
     and they all went back the way they came,
          the Dead went back the way they came. 150
Then he went once again to look for his wives,
     Taugi went, *tititi.* To the settlement,
          to the settlement.
          to Kafanifani's settlement.

He was at his house, his house,   155
    Kafanifani's house.
Yes, so, he was fishing.
Next he came beside his wives, he came beside Kafanifani's wives.
    So, *tikii.* "Why, Taugi's here."
        "Taugi. What's the matter, Taugi?"   160
        "Nothing, nothing. Why, I came to see you,
            I came to see you."
        "All right," they answered,
            "All right."
        "Perhaps you've seen those who make my food around here?   165
            Those who make my food?"
        "We haven't, we haven't.
        They haven't come here."
        "All right," he said.
    So he went on.   170
Then the next day he searched around,
    the next day he went,
        to look for them,
            to look for them.
    Then nothing.   175
Again he kept going to look for them,
    to look for his wives,
        Taugi kept going,
        Taugi kept going.
Then as he arrived they were seated in the doorway laughing
at him,   180
        as Taugi arrived.
    "Ha ha," they were laughing at him,
        they were laughing at him.
"Here's Taugi!" they whispered excitedly to each other. "Here's
Taugi!"
They went over to their hammocks,   185
    so they went over to their hammocks.
Next they turned into large cooking pots,
    they became large cooking pots.
    They hid themselves from him.
Then, *tiki,* he came inside. No one was there,   190
    the place was empty.
    "Where can they be going all the time?
    Where are they?"
        There was no one there.
Since Kafanifani was fishing.   195
    He always went fishing,
        Kafanifani went to do that.

Then, that was all.
Then, he went away without his things,
        without his things.   200
    Taugi went on.
There was someone else who concerned himself with them, his
informer, his informer,
        Taugi's informer.
    That was Akugi the Agouti.
        That was Agouti.   205
"Well, Friend," he said, "Friend.
    Have you found your wives?
        Have you found your wives?"
    "No, I haven't.
        I haven't."   210
    "Now see here,
            see here.
        Look, you're not like me, you're powerful.
            You're powerful.
    What was it like when you would go there?   215
        What?"
    "When I went to them just like this,
        they would start to laugh.
    When I went to them just like this,
        they would start to laugh.   220
    Then as soon as they saw me,
        they would get up and go away.
            They would get up and go away."
"Now look, now look. What do you remember seeing there?"
"Cooking pots,
        cooking pots."   225
"I see," Agouti answered. "I should go back. I'll go get them.
        I'll be going, I'll be going," Taugi said.
So he went.
    "Why, I'll go tomorrow,
        tomorrow."   230
He had come to where they were.
    They kept laughing, they were still talking.
        He was ready.
    "Well, Taugi's here again,
        Taugi's here again."   235
He had come to where they were.
Nothing!

"Well, where are they? Oh, where do they keep going?
     Where?
        Oh, why is it so easy for you to do this?   240
           Oh, why is it so easy for you?" he said to them.
   Now, he snapped his finger on the pots. *Pisuk, pisuk, pisuk, pisuk,
pisuk.*
      "Ouch, don't, Taugiii," now they began to speak to him, I'm
         told, yes.
Now, that was all.
   "Well, come along, all of you,   245
        now come along."
   He had found his wives,
      Taugi had.
   "Now come along, all of you,
        now come along."   250
   And so he carried them off,
      his wives,
         Taugi did.
   His cuckolder, that was Kafanifani,
      Kafanifani did it.   255
   The other had kept trying to return to us . . .
      he had kept trying to return to us those of us who had died.
   Kafanifani didn't want that to happen.
         He didn't want that to happen.
      Otherwise, they would have always returned to us. That's what
      Taugi wanted to have happen to us.   260
      Afterward,
         afterward.
      But no. It didn't happen,
         it didn't happen.

Listen.   265
So they all returned home,
     so they all returned home.
   "Why, Taugi found his wives,
      he found his wives."
   "Now look, do think now.   270
      When you're powerless you're a failure."
That was all.

Following that, he threw him onto the sky.
      Taugi caused him to be on the sky,
         Taugi did.   275
   He threw Kafanifani
      onto the sky.

That's all.
Then, it was over. That's all, that's just all there is.

Notes to "Kafanifani"

Muluku's version of this story places great emphasis upon the message ex-
plaining why the dead no longer visit the living. The underlying idea—usually associated with Taugi's exploits but here also involving his cousin (*ifaŭ*),
Kafanifani—is that deception and trickery can serve as the cause of some condition of life now experienced by the Kalapalo. It is the Dead who actually
decide never to return, establishing their future conduct in utterances that are
also present in Taugi's quoted speech ("So they will remain," a declarative
effecting the future condition of whoever is the referent). So, although Kafanifani initiates the conditions that lead to the final effect (his deception is
to steal Taugi's wives so that the Dead will no longer return), it is Taugi himself who declares in the end that the Dead will "remain as they are" (lines
104–105). Hence, a hierarchy of power is suggested: at the summit are the
Dead, followed by Taugi, and finally by Kafanifani. Kafanifani's relative weakness is suggested by the fact that Taugi throws him onto the sky, where he
becomes the constellation Kafanifani (Beta Hydra and Gamma Hydra).

lines

34–35   "for their entrance": serving cold manioc soup to guests as they ar-
        rive at a settlement after a long, hot journey is an important event in
        the earlier stages of *egitsu* ceremonials.
42   "plaza seating": a second serving of food.
51   Taugi is speaking here.

Mbambangisï

Told by Muluku at Aifa. February 11, 1979.

Notes appear on page 213.

Listen.
    Taugi stole Aulukuma's wives.
        After that happened Aulukuma felt sad,
            so he went away to his grandfather,
                to Mbambangisï.   5
        He was grandfather to Taugi and Aulukuma,
            Mbambangisï was.
                So Aulukuma went away.
    Taugi tracked him but he saw nothing and he lost him,
            Taugi lost him as he tracked Aulukuma.   10
        The other had gone toward the river.
            Aulukuma went there.
                He rested there.
        "Where shall I go?" Aulukuma said,
            "Where shall I go?   15
                I'll go on to Grandfather," Aulukuma said.
    So he went into the water,
            Aulukuma went there.
        "Why, here comes our grandchild, Aulukuma is here!" they
said as he went on.
        When he came beside them,   20
            "You're here because your older brother has been tracking
you, your older brother."
                "Yes," Aulukuma replied.
        "I don't speak to your older brother.
            Now why is it that your older brother is always so nasty?"
            Mbambangisï said.
    He arrived.   25
        Then he stayed there for a very long time.
            He slept there many many days,
                Aulukuma slept.

Then Taugi went to look for him,
            Taugi went to look for him.   30
                There was nothing.
        "Why, my little brother has escaped me."
            Then he stayed where he was.

Aulukuma arrived,
    Aulukuma arrived.   35
  "Well! Aulukuma has arrived," Mbambangisï said.
  "You have come again, have you?" they said to him.
    "Yes," he said.
  "We don't speak to your older brother," they said to him,
    "Because of the way he is."   40
"Well, Grandson," Mbambangisï said.
  "I want to scrape you," he told him, Mbambangisï said.
    "All right," Aulukuma answered.
So, Mbambangisï scraped him,
  he scraped him all over.   45
When he was finished,
he collected some of the blood.
  It was beautiful.
When that was done he mixed in *tutu* fruit.*
Next he covered it all *bok* with *kedyite* leaves,*   50
  Mbambangisï did.
"This will become your own bird, your pet."
  "Very well," Aulukuma answered.
"You must take this, it's your own pet!" Mbambangisï said to
him.
  "Very well," Aulukuma answered.   55
"This is something to make your older brother envious later on,
so you will take it with you," Mbambangisï said.
  "Very well," Aulukuma answered.
Then *bok* with *kejite,*
  he placed that over it all,
  Mbambangisï did.   60
    Bok, bok.
Next he blew on it,
  he blew on it.
  Because of that it is one of our song spells.
Everyone—that is, all the people here have it, the curers have
it.   65
  Because of Mbambangisï, all the people here know it.
Then Mbambangisï uncovered it.
  Teh, it was a beautiful red!
  It had become *tafitsekuegï* the red macaw.
    That's what it became.   70
They live far away from here, all of them.
  Mbambangisï is their parent.
    He himself is their parent.
    Taugi didn't know about it,
      nor Kwatïngï.   75

Teh his blood had turned into something beautiful.
"Take this, it's your pet," Mbambangisï went,
"This is something to make your older brother envious, your
older brother."
"Very well," Aulukuma answered.
Teh! Truly it was done most beautifully.   80
It dazzles us.
There were two of them.
"Grandfather," Aulukuma told him.
"I really do want to leave now, I want to leave."
"Very well," he answered.   85
"Go then.
Take your pet with you, your pet," Mbambangisï said.
"Very well," he replied.
"'You must come here to me.' Say that to your older brother
with his envy-maker beside you."
"Very well," Aulukuma answered.   90
"You must give one of these to him.
You will give it to your older brother, the envious one."
"Very well," Aulukuma said.
"Now I want to paint you," Mbambangisï went.
"Very well," Aulukuma answered.   95
Mbambangisï painted his hair with red urucu paint.*
He also painted his body,
he painted his body with black genipapa paint.*
Then Aulukuma left.

Then at dusk he was arriving home,   100
Aulukuma arrived home.
Then the next day before dawn he brought out the red macaws.
Teh how beautiful were the red ones!
Next Taugi's wives spoke.
"Well! We didn't expect Aulukuma to arrive the way he did.   105
Aulukuma has just arrived."
"*Teh!* What do you think of those beautiful pets of his, Taugi?"
they asked him.
"Go ahead, look at them. Aulukuma has some pets.
Now, what do you think of them?"
Then he saw them . . .   110
the red macaws!
"Well, this must be an easy thing to do," Taugi said.
"Why, I think this is easy to do.
I'll do something about that, I'll do it."

Taugi molded some beeswax. 115
When it was finished,
  Taugi blew on it.
Then he placed *kedyite* leaves over it *bok, bok.*
Well, he uncovered it.
  Nothing. 120
That had become *tagipiso* the vermilion flycatcher.
"Oh, let it be. Now go far away!" he said.
"You will live behind the mortals' houses.
"How shall I do it?
  I think this is easy to do. 125
All right, this time I'll really do it!"
He took some dried manioc starch and he shaped it.
When that was done, he blew on it.
When that was done, he uncovered it but it was nothing. That
had become *kïngi* the spoonbill heron.
  Kïngi. 130
"Oh, let it be," he said.
"You will live where the mortals go fishing, so go far away
from here," he said.
He couldn't do it,
  Taugi failed.
    "So it will be!" he said. 135
      That was all.

Then at dusk, *teh!* Aulukuma appeared with beautifully painted hair
and genipapa paint on his body.
  Teh, how handsome he was!
"I think this is easy to do," Taugi said.
Next he put dirt on himself. 140
  Taugi painted his hair with it.
    Nothing happened.
  He failed to do it,
    Taugi failed.
      He knew nothing of red paint, 145
        nothing.
          "Oh, let it be this way," he said.
Next his younger brother arrived.
"Aulukuma, let's go outside at dusk, let's go outside," he said.
  "I want you to remove my tiredness." 150
Then Aulukuma came to him.
"All right now,"
  Taugi was already smoking tobacco.

Because of that, all our people have this now. They smoke
tobacco.
    Taugi is the only one who knew of it. 155
        No other powerful beings knew of it.
            Taugi is the knower.
"Taugi," Aulukuma told him.
    "Here is your pet, a red macaw."
        Teh, a beautiful red! 160
    "Very well," he answered.
    Aulukuma gave it to him because Taugi envied him.
Aulukuma also had arrows,
    arrows as well.
        His grandfather owned them. 165
Teh, with beautiful red feathering!
That was his kind of arrow,
    the arrow that's now associated with him.
"Take this with you, take your own arrows.
    This is an arrow," Mbambangisï had told him. 170
"Aulukuma, let's go shoot fish tomorrow.
    Let's go fishing tomorrow."
The next day Taugi and his companion left.
    "Very well," Aulukuma answered.
    Then they went on, 175
    they went on.
"Aulukuma," he said.
    "Stay here, we'll wait to shoot them here," he said.
        "Be sure to watch carefully."
Teh, the beautiful red feathered arrows! 180
    Teh, his arrow's feathers were beautiful!
Taugi didn't know anything about arrows,
    nothing.
        Only Mbambangisï knew about it.
They had traveled far to Lake Kalawti. 185
    There they were beside Lake Kalawti,
    Taugi and his companion stood beside it.
"Look, here comes a *tugufi* catfish toward us!" *
    Taugi came that way, inside it.
"Aulukuma," he told him, 190
    "Here comes a good one, here it is!
        Watch carefully!"
            "All right," his brother answered.
Tsïk! he shot it here on its side,
    Aulukuma shot it with his arrow. 195

Once again, *tsïk!* he shot it as before.
Once again, *tsïk tsïk tsïk,*
 Aulukuma shot many arrows at it.
"Keep shooting your arrows!"
Then, well, they were all gone *mboh!*   200
 Ku ku ku the catfish broke the arrows.
 Koh koh koh it broke them all.
"Why, this must be Taugi!" Aulukuma said to himself.
 "He's always envious of me."
"Aulukuma," Taugi told him,   205
 "That fish broke your arrows."
"Yes, that's so," his younger brother said,
 "Yes, that's so."
"Well, let me fix them right now."
Then Taugi put them together.   210
 Because he did that there are markings on arrow cane.
They were fixed now.
 Taugi remade them.
When that was done they both came back.
 Because all those things were to make Taugi envious,   215
 Taugi was indeed envious of them.

Notes to "Mbambangisï"
lines

49   *tutu:* a small orange fruit with pitted rind, said to resemble the naked
        white cheek skin of the macaws.

50   *kedyite:* a fragrant bush of the *Monimiaceae* family whose leaves are
        used in curing, and which are said to have animating properties.

96   "red urucu paint" (mïngi in Kalapalo): a fragrant body paint made
        from berries of the domesticated *Bixa orellana* widely grown in tropi-
        cal South America.

98   genipapa, *Genipa americana* (*anga* in Kalapalo): a dye is made from the
        unripe fruit of this semi-cultivated central Brazilian tree. When first
        applied to the body, it is a pale, translucent green, but after a while
        oxidation and skin enzymes turn it a brilliant black. This paint can
        only wear off; it cannot be washed off.

188   *tugufi: Pseudoplatystoma fasciatum L.,* known as *surubim* to Brazilians.

Twinship and Relative Age

As an older brother, Taugi is Aulukuma's teacher, adviser, tease, and fault finder. Aulukuma the younger brother is far less developed a character than Taugi, but the discordant relationship between them is quite apparent in the stories. Aulukuma is clearly more sympathetic to their parents, helping his father Nitsuegï to escape from the Fierce People, for example. Taugi, on the other hand, devises a way to kill his mother, and tries to do the same to his father. His relations with his younger brother are hardly any better. Aulukuma is often bullied and taken advantage of by his older brother, who steals his wives, destroys gifts to Aulukuma he cannot acquire for himself, and, when he warns Taugi about approaching dangerous monsters, criticizes him for his weakness and cowardice. "Fiery," "Sagangguegï," and "Mbam-bangisu" all begin by pointing out Taugi's smugness and the sneering pride with which he puts Aulukuma in his place. There is also a story about how Taugi cruelly uses Aulukuma in order to rid the world of Whirlwind. Although this powerful being has already had his ears pierced, Taugi insists on trying to do it again for him with a spear and spear thrower. He encourages Whirlwind to hurl the spear first at Aulukuma, setting up the younger brother to be killed so that he, Taugi, can revenge his death. Taugi decapitates Whirlwind, and then revives his younger brother. Aulukuma comes alive again, saying, "What happened? I must have been asleep." To which Taugi sneers: "You weren't asleep, you were killed, as usual."

Aulukuma, then, is in many ways more a human and less a powerful being than Taugi. His essentially naive and trusting nature, his inability to penetrate illusion easily, and his social conventionality make him reluctant to confront his enemies aggressively. Thus, he is weak and always the first to die when faced with monstrous enemies like Fiery. Taugi and Aulukuma seem to represent the inherent split the Kalapalo perceive in human nature: between selfishness and whimsicality on one hand, and sympathy, sincerity, and trust on the other.

Throughout South America, such developmental differences as exist between Taugi and Aulukuma (as well as others based on relative age and gender identity) are the source for symbolic uses of a brother or sister not only in mythic narratives, but in ritual drama and in politics. In these, and probably other domains, siblings become images that realize complex ideas about the relations between knowledge, power, sexuality, and moral judgment.

Siblingship is especially fascinating for the issues it raises about the dynamic role of personal growth and development. These issues include the significance of relative age; the relation between birth order and parental ties; the processes involved in sexual awareness; the selection, or avoidance and repression, of sexual objects; the problems of sibling incest; sibling taboos, such as avoidance of siblings after puberty or bans on speaking about the sexual life of one's sibling; and the persistence or sundering of ties with parents, to name but a few perennial anthropological fascinations.

There is something innately paradoxical about siblingship. Siblings voice solidarity and unity vis-à-vis society at large, but inherent in their identities are irreconcilable biological and ideological positions: these are the sources of their opposed and often highly antagonistic relationships.

The Kalapalo attribute to the first-born siblings capability, dignity, high rank (active hereditary leaders are supposed to be the eldest of a sibling set), and objectified knowledge, which comes from instruction through words and observations of the sensory world. We might say then that the older sibling is associated with a more focused material consciousness that is also potentially rule-bound, inflexible, and relatively context-free. On the other hand, to last-born siblings are ascribed self-centeredness and a highly developed sensitivity toward how others respond to them; magical, shamanistic insight and knowledge; and a physical strength that allows them to endure ritual pain and to confront powerful beings. This explains why Aulukuma can be revived each time he is killed by monsters, and why Taugi is the one to do the reviving. I suggest that these ways of symbolizing siblings may have to do with Kalapalo understandings of sibling development.

Like Aulukuma, the last-born feels a sense of being always left behind by an older sibling, and is somewhat unsure of his or her powers of intelligent insight. After other children are born, the oldest, like Taugi, has an easier time establishing an identity separate from the natal household and the parents. But the last-born is kept around much longer than the older children; the parents cling to the last child, seeing it as the most beautiful and morally good of all their offspring. Thus, a break with the parents is more difficult, both for the child and for the parents, who, for example, like to keep their youngest child in puberty seclusion as long as possible. Aulukuma conforms to this configuration, much as Taugi does to the model of the domineering, older sibling.

As they move through these psychosocial passages, young Kalapalo adults establish new contexts for the compassion, respect, and love formerly restricted to their own family members. The natal household may even be replaced as the locus of moral behavior and feeling; indeed, it is necessary for Kalapalo to be able to do this, for they usually marry into other households and sometimes outside of their natal communities. The last-born thus seems to be in a special kind of life situation. Relatives establish values about how people should treat each other, but with their family demands hinder the last-born from applying those values to strangers or outsiders. Since extending these values calls for a more encompassing moral sensitivity, the emphasis on heritage and pedigree comes to seem claustrophobic to the youngest. In Kalapalo myths, this claustrophobia is greatly exaggerated. Family life and common humanity are represented as opposed and irreconcilable. So we see in many of these Kalapalo stories the younger sibling doing what he or she can to resolve this: helping strangers as if they were family members (often against the wishes of relatives), or adhering to moral virtues despite an agreement among others in the family to effect evil.[3]

The paradoxes and ambiguities of Kalapalo siblingship are blown out of proportion in the case of twins, and are the source of the Kalapalo fear and disgust at the idea of having twins in one's family. Two people who appear to think so much alike, to anticipate one another's responses, to reason in such similar ways but (as in the case of Aulukuma and Taugi) with such different conclusions seem, like those powerful twins, to have an intelligence that penetrates dangerously beyond the insights of normal human beings. I say "dangerous" because twin intelligence anticipates and yet rejects the consequences of decisions, to the point of overturning rational judgment. Knowing in advance that evil will follow from their behavior, they act anyway, as if evil as such did not matter. This is, we might say, an overdetermined illusory consciousness. Notice as well how rarely the twins repeat themselves, how therefore inconsistent and unstructured is their personality. So strong is the feeling that twins cannot live normal social lives, that there is pressure against allowing even one of a pair to live. I happened to be told of a certain childless family who allowed this to happen and buried the weaker of their twins at birth. Tragically for them, people from other settlements complained until the survivor was also smothered.

Ñafïgï: The Horror (and Humor) of the Female Trickster

There is a cousin (*ifaü*) of Taugi, the demonness Ñafïgï, who is also a kind of trickster. In the story of Taugi and Ñafïgï, she is rendered relatively harmless (in a way amusing to listeners) by her male cousin, but we can tell from other stories about her that, if any mythological character is marginal, it is she. While described as essentially female, like Taugi and Aulukuma Ñafïgï can change her sex and age, and she has the uncanny power to appear to be any person she chooses. In many ways, she represents a warning about feelings that people need to guard against, not only sexual passion, but the intense, compassionate longing (*funita*) that is connected with close family relations. A man named Kofi once told me: "When Ñafïgï desires a woman, she becomes a man. When she desires a man, she becomes a woman. If a person who has a child thinks longingly about it, she appears as that child. She embraces the parent and then runs away. After she does that, the parent dies." Although Ñafïgï bears a child (in the story "Sakatsuegï"), her household is a bizarre—but again, funny—travesty of domesticity, and she is fundamentally a destructive being, not a creative one like Taugi. As Taugi's *ifaü* or "cousin," she is held up as a negative counterpart to him, a twisted likeness of the male trickster.

In the story of Sakatsuegï, Ñafïgï appears as an appallingly lewd, vampirish creature who captures solitary men and destroys them by poisoning them gradually with her genitals. (Storytellers are amused, however, by her compulsive sexuality.) Her repeated rape of men has ghastly consequences for her partners. By coupling with this monster, they gradually lose their vital seminal fluid and waste away. The original menstruator, she is repugnant to men for that reason, too, but her real danger comes from what is called the "poisonous pungency" (*pïngegï*) of her genitals. (This may be a consequence of her being the first menstruator; if so, this is another unfortunate side effect of Taugi's meddling.)

Notwithstanding these very female attributes, Ñafïgï is also male in character. A skilled hunter and a sexual aggressor as men are supposed to be, she is associated closely with biting and stinging pain, especially connected with male violence. The biting flies called *tugenggi* are said to be her nail parings scattered about, and, as Muluku describes in his story about her, her vagina originally held a stinging ant, a poisonous caterpillar, and a tiny piranha.

Ñafïgï thus embodies the qualities of sexual feelings that the Kalapalo most fear: the insatiable devouring female sexuality that seduces young men and jeopardizes their ability to survive by sapping their strength; and the aggression of male sexual passion that can so easily turn to rape. This doubly destructive sexuality is closely associated with destructive transformation, a trickster sensibility that makes no contributions to human welfare.

While all powerful beings are capable of transformation, Ñafïgï's powers of transformation are pervasive and multiple, a kind of aimless, destructive compulsion. She has the exceptional ability to travel through all features of the landscape. She can move through the air, underground, through trees, rocks, and water. No other river but hers can flow in both directions. Her embrace is deadly, she is terribly strong, and only the most powerful heros can throw her off them. While Taugi's tricks are all directed at specific aims, Ñafïgï seems always to enact senseless destruction, threatening her victims with horror and with death. Even Taugi cannot fully subdue her, and he uses her to terrify his own enemies on several occasions. The Fiery Brothers, for example, have only to see Ñafïgï and they are terrorized into submission. In a women's "birding" song, someone hears her husband's insistent lover (who calls herself his wife) say:

Look, look, my husband stands motionless
Ñafïgï's doing
Our husband is dead, once and for all
Ñafïgï's doing.

As if the listener herself had poisonous genitals.

Ñafïgï

Told by Muluku at Aifa. March 5, 1979.

Listen.
    There were five women named Ñafïgï who went to draw water,
        Ñafïgï went.
        They were teasing each other.
    Then as Kanuakuma drew near,   5
        "Who might my new lover be?" Ñafïgï said,
        "Who might my new lover be?"
            They were bathing in the water as Kanuakuma the
            Black Ibis drew near.
            He was a witch.
    "We know Kanuakuma has been your lover all along," the other
    Ñafïgï replied,   10
        "that man with the black penis," while Kanuakuma listened
        to them.
        They returned home.

Then they went to the forest,
    Ñafïgï went,
        all five of them went.   15
    Kanuakuma entered the house at dawn.
        "Where are your relatives?"
        To Akugefe.
        "In the forest, to kill birds for their food."
        "Very well, you must not tell them about me."   20
        "All right."
    Then Kanuakuma made witch's darts.
        He set their drinking vessels about him,
            four of them.
            Only one Ñafïgï was his lover.   25
            She was the only one he didn't poison.

Then at dusk they arrived home,
    Ñafïgï arrived home.
        Boh, they had shot monkeys and toucans,
            all kinds of birds.   30
            They arrived home.
    Next they drank,
    Ñafïgï all drank,
        with the witch's darts Kanuakuma had placed inside their
        drinking vessels.

At dusk they died,   35
   Ñafïgï died.
      All four of them died.
         Only one of them was still alive.
         Nothing happened to her.
"Get up," their younger sister said.   40
   "Get up, so you can roast what you've just killed."
   Nothing happened.
They were all dead,
   Ñafïgï had died.
It was Kanuakuma who had poisoned them with sorcerer's
darts,   45
   so they all died.
Then it was over,
   and they were buried, she buried them all.
Only one of them was left,
   one Ñafïgï was left.   50

Then Taugi heard what had happened.
   They were his *fisuagï,* women of his own age to whom he
   was related,
      Ñafïgï were his *fisuagï.*
Next Taugi came there.
   "I'm leaving right now.   55
   I will go mourn right away," Taugi said.
      "Very well."
Then when the sun was here,
   at dusk he arrived.
   "Our older sisters are really no longer alive, no.   60
      They are no longer alive."
   "No, they're not," he said.
   "Why, they will remain as they are."
He slept,
   Taugi slept,   65
      and she became his wife,
      Ñafïgï became his wife.
         Taugi remained living there.

Taugi then said,
   "I want to touch you right now, I want to touch you."   70
   "Despite what you say," Ñafïgï said,
   "If you touch me *sike* the stinging ant will bite you.
   Tefoko the stinging caterpillar and *fengi* the piranha will chew
   on you."

"Is that so?" Taugi said,
　　so they went to the water's edge.
Then he went to get some fish poison vine.
　　Next Taugi crushed the vine.
　　When that was done Ñafïgï sat down in the water with her
　　　legs apart.
　　The stinging ant emerged.
　　When that was done, then the stinging caterpillar,
　　　then the little piranha,
　　　　a very small fish.
　　　　　That was all.
"That's all," he told her,
　　Taugi said.
　　　Following that it was done.

They arrived home,
　　and after that Taugi made love to her since she had become safe.
　　　Because he wanted to do that.
　　"Ajah! Taugi, it's too much."
　　　She didn't want to make love so often.
　　Then he took the tiny piranha
　　　and put it *bok* inside her breast.
　　Because of that women menstruate,
　　　because of that,
　　　　Taugi did it.
He remained there afterward for a long, long time.
　　"Listen now to what I tell you," Taugi said,
　　　"I will make memorial posts for our older sisters."
　　"Will you?" she replied.
　　　"I was just going to say the same thing to you.
　　Very well, I agree you should make Ñafïgï's memorial
　　ceremony."
　　"Very well, you should do it, go now."
　　　The messengers left.

They were memorializing Ñafïgï.
　　But he really wanted to steal her *atanga* flutes,
　　　Taugi wanted Ñafïgï's flutes.
Then the guests arrived,
　　　the guests arrived.
　　Dawn People were who they were.
　　　They had arrived.
"All right, everyone come over here."
　　Taugi was looking for her flutes.
　　　There weren't any because Ñafïgï had hidden them.

75

80

85

90

95

100

105

110

"Come on," at dawn the guests then left to enter Ñafïgï's
settlement. 115
"Well, Taugi," she told him, Ñafïgï said.
"I have to do that so my flutes can be played by me alone,
so only I can play my flutes."
"Yes," he said.
"Where are they?" 120
She had hidden them under the house beams.
Then she took them down *tïki,*
Ñafïgï's flutes.
"Why, give them to me," Taugi said,
"Give them to me. 125
I've been wanting them badly, so you must give them
to me,"
he said to her,
and he stole them,
Taugi did,
he stole Ñafïgï's flutes. 130
He stole them.
He left, having done that.
"Let her remain the way she is."
It was over,
so the guests went away. 135
They no longer came there.
No longer was the memorial ceremony being held,
because they all left,
Taugi having stolen the flutes,
Ñafïgï's flutes. 140
"Let her remain the way she is," they said,
as they all left.

Then he arrived home,
Taugi arrived home.
"Here are my *atanga* flutes." 145
"Very well," his followers said.
He had arrived home.
Then he put them behind his back.
Taugi put his flutes behind his back and he lay down.
For a long time he remained lying down. 150
He pretended to be sick.
He was lying.
Someone told Ñafïgï.
"Taugi is dying, he hasn't gotten up at all."
"I'm going to see him right away," she replied, Ñafïgï said. 155

Then at dusk she arrived.
　"Taugi, it looks to me as if you're sick," she asked him,
　　"What is the matter?"
　"Look at me, you must look at me."
The shamans were there.　　　　　　　　　　　　　　　　　160
　They were powerful beings, those who were there.
　　Shamans,
　　　his own shamans.
　They were there curing him,
　　trying to do that.　　　　　　　　　　　　　　　　　165
　　　All the shamans.
　　　　They couldn't do anything because he was deceiving
　　　　them.
Mbah! The shamans were Whirlwinds and Giant Kiskadees, all of
them.
　Nothing happened,
　　he didn't recover,
　　　no.　　　　　　　　　　　　　　　　　　　　　170
Then *tikii,*
　Ñafïgï arrived.
　"Are you sick?" she said.
　"I'm not well at all."
　"What kind of pain are you having?　　　　　　　　　175
　　What?"
　"My legs are so very tired," Taugi said.
　"I see," she answered.
　　"Have you bathed yet?"　　　　　　　　　　　　　180
　"No, I haven't bathed at all," Taugi said.
　"I want to bathe you right now."
"Very well," Taugi answered.
Then she helped him to rise,
　Ñafïgï did.　　　　　　　　　　　　　　　　　　185
　"Ouch! I can't move my body at all."
　"All right, try harder," Ñafïgï said.
The flutes were right where he had put them,
　behind his back.
　"Here is what I'm looking for!" Ñafïgï said,　　　　190
　　"Here is what I'm looking for!
　　　This was what I was searching for."
　　　　She had left right after he had stolen them.
She who was the owner carried the flutes away.

After she left,
   Ñafïgï left,
      the other remained there,
         and he recovered because he was deceiving them about
         it,
            Taugi was deceiving them.

     He recovered,
       and the shamans went away.
         They all went away,
            the Powerful Beings went away after all that
            happened.

He was tricking them.

Female and Male Tricksters

Kalapalo tricksters mock and resist particular features of the Ka-lapalo world that pose more difficulties to men (especially, but not ex-clusively, young men) than they do to women. Foremost are the signs of relative social competence and power, which are disturbing ele-ments of a social world that portrays itself as collective in its goals and egalitarian in its functioning: signs that some men are wealthier, own magical objects, can easily dominate their fellows with aggressive sar-casm, and easily seduce beautiful women, including one's own wives. Considerably more focused is a man's concern with female sexuality. This concern centers on what he has learned is a conflict between his lust for women (which is continually overstimulated by what he sees and hears) and the condition of physical perfection that he must strive for if he is to avoid the scorn of his friends and family (but which he knows can only be achieved if he keeps from excessive con-tact with women).

The most powerful female trickster, Ñafïgï, became a sexually com-pulsive vampire in her relations with human beings, a kind of dread-ful counterpart to Taugi. The principal male and female tricksters have been clearly developed to complement each other, forming a pair of opposed yet necessarily related images. Taugi's character clearly is in keeping with the public buffoonery of many Kalapalo men, and the importance of deception and jokes in their relations with one another. Kalapalo women make far less use of such playful illusionary speech in public. Women's speech seems less artful and more "literal," al-though there are some very fine women storytellers. More important, women seem to be held more responsible for what they say. Their re-marks about other people provide the greater substance of the ironic Kwambï songs, in which both men and women throw back at the com-munity the gossipy lies they have heard about themselves. (I learned only one song—in over fifty—that characterizes this gossip as coming from a man.) Men, equally gossipy in fact, are not as frequently criti-cized for this as are women, an unfair advantage about which women have complained.

The only humanly female characters who engage in deception are Dawn People who turn a man's trick around to save themselves from horrible (but always eroticized) fates. In stories about female deceit (in this book, "Mïti" and "Women Kill Jaguar Sorcerers"), women use de-ception in order to save their very lives and to take revenge on the men who have mistreated them. Only rarely do women in stories use de-ception playfully to disconcert someone else; I am aware of this only because of the disgusting Dawn People stories women tell one an-other about strange compulsions in the distant past. They apparently do not use deception to accomplish the kinds of selfish goals associated with male deceivers like Taugi.

Women in these stories suffer from the same eroticized male aggression that makes contemporary Kalapalo women sometimes wary of men. Their caution is a counterpart to men's fear about what they believe are the dangers of insatiable female lust (a fear that seems to be fantasized in the stories about Ñafïgï). Just as there are few female mythological tricksters, Kalapalo women think of themselves as more reticent than men, and are far less involved with trickster-like behavior than men. The reason has as much to do with the differences in power relations between men and women, having to do with their roles and relations, as it does with the differences in power relations that are the result of social competence among men themselves.

Chapter 3

Dimensions of Deception

Weird, awesome, and outrageous though they may be, mythological figures like Taugi do seem very like real people, if we temporarily suspend our fascination with their extraordinary activities and special worlds, and focus more carefully on the narrative details, on how these activities and worlds are described. The *how* (rather than *what*) of the description makes it seem as if what is happening is almost like what goes on in the lives of ordinary Kalapalo listeners. The sense of familiarity has much to do with the way we learn about a character's feelings and intentions, which are clarified through what other people say, and the ways the character engages others in the story. Mythological characters like Kwatïngï and Taugi, Kangangatï and Kangangafanga, construct their special realities through activities, especially speech, that are organized and described in a "sensible" narrative form. This purposeful patterning constitutes a kind of interpretive matrix consisting of keys to the significance of the referential content, the "what" of the story. The discursive structure of a narrative (the "how") highlights what happens to particular characters, contrasts the settings in which events occur, marks events as distinctive, and links events together into hierarchically ordered segments.

Look again at the stories about Dyekuku's Daughter, and about Kangangatï and Kangangafanga. In each, repetition plays an important structural role. For example, incidents of travel back and forth between two places, between a central location and several surrounding places, or purposefully directed toward a single point (as we may describe the journey of the Made Ones in "Kwatïngï"), tend to link larger narrative segments. Traveling emphasizes not so much divergence or deviation from the action, but rather that the characters are experiencing something anew (in the stories with a long, single journey) or differently (when they move, as Kangangafanga does, back and forth between two different places—his own settlement and those of powerful beings—that are the loci of two different consciousnesses). Motion of the first or second kind reinforces expectations, as, for example, in the repeated search for Kwatïngï's father in "Dyekuku's Daughter," or the trip of the Made Ones in "Kwatïngï." The second kind leads to changes in the character's expectations, and the perception that he or she must formulate new plans. The units themselves are in groups of fours or eights (indicating the completion of a set, over either a short or long time), or in groups of five or nine (indicating accomplishment of a goal, also over either a short or long time). Finally, the frequent references in Kalapalo stories to events that indicate the experiencing of time (such as sleep, pregnancy, the movement of the sun across the sky, and seasonal changes) are themselves structuring devices. These serve as cross-references to consistencies, continuities, or changes in a character's feelings, motives, plans, or goal-oriented action.

Descriptions of such aspects of formal patterning in sensible or "significant" narrative form have to be complemented by methods that probe the organization of the discourse of entire texts. These reveal that the structures unfold in a dialogic context, in which the storyteller is aware of the audience as a listening, interpreting, questioning, responding group. Classical structuralist methods point to how the narrator develops a sense of place and event through purposefully patterned, and sometimes stereotyped, descriptions of actions. But discourse-focused analysis illuminates more sharply how the characters come to be palpable and understandable, even familiar, through the turns of phrase that are part of a people's conventions for narration, and through a clever storyteller's imaginative use of these conventions for special purposes. Such methods have led to the discovery of segment-hierarchies in Native American myths, of elements of narrative structure that emerge through performance and a narrator's distinctive art, and which, as Dennis Tedlock and Dell Hymes showed so nicely, are scarcely apparent in block prose presentations.[1] Revealed along with this structure are the poetic, historical, rhetorical, and explanatory sensibilities that together constitute the overall significance of a particular narrative form. The study of comprehensive themes and semiotic relations in myths, then, can really proceed only within a considerably more informed understanding of the narrative framework—the performed, emergent design of a text, which helps us, as well as the local listeners, to interpret what is being said. In the Kalapalo narrative tradition, quoted speech provides the focus for this kind of understanding.

Despite scholars' interest in the thoughts and feelings of Trickster (or tricksters), no anthropologist who has written about him seems to have considered how expressions of thought and emotion—the more predictable or continuous qualities of a trickster—might be actively accomplished through specific cultural resources, especially language.[2] Most important, considering how obvious it now seems from the many texts that have been published, the speech-centered nature of a trickster's activities has simply been ignored, even though it is through speech that such a character experiences his own identity and constructs personal, subjective meanings.

The careful reader will have noticed that a great amount and variety of quoted speech is used to construct Kalapalo stories.[3] Most events are in fact "speech-centered" in that conversational dialogues (like those between Kwatïngï and his nephews, or between Kangangafanga and Ukwaka) are the most important tool Kalapalo storytellers use to develop their characters and give meaning to their activities. Through conversation, narrators construct developmental differences in the characters' attitudes toward one another and toward activities that are taking place in the story. Important characters shift ground from one dynamic posture to another, as they change (or reinforce) their subjective interpretations of the appropriate personal role in collective activities. Their quoted speech (which constitutes these processes) thus forms a coherent narrative progression of the greatest importance, involving as it does the ordered integration of statements about feelings, goals, and enactments, and accomplishments or failures. Feelings— the emotional quality of experiences—are made to appear as motives, the efficient causes or reasons that precede the formulation of goals. To put it somewhat differently, goals are qualified and given shape through what are presented as motivating feelings. In another light, the way speech is quoted—what is said and how what is said points to something beyond the particular instance of speaking itself—reveals ideas Kalapalo have about language itself, its use as conversation, and its functions and consequences for thought and action. In short, a careful look at quoted speech in Kalapalo stories directs us to an understanding of how particular characters are conceived and related to each other, and how these conceptions suggest a broader framework of propositions about language, personhood, and society.

In Kalapalo stories about tricksters—those in which there are characters who are defined by and through their deceptions—the contrasts between different dynamic postures, represented by the developmental progression of conversations, are especially revealing. These narratives are in large measure about how deceptive speech is organized and enacted, how it "functions," what it can "do," and how it can be thwarted. The Kalapalo characters who cope with illusionary experience illustrate various strategies of perspective and action. Very different points of view about deception are juxtaposed both within a single trickster character and among various characters.

While, for example, there are rather detailed insights into the plans lying behind tricks, and how they can be accomplished, we learn also about the experiences of creating a deception, and, just as often, about how it feels to have a trick fail. On the other hand are the viewpoints of the dupes: what it feels like to be tricked, the consequences of such feelings as they lead to concrete plans for revenge or recovery, and how people come to accept being tricked. Sometimes, we see the consequences of a deception reaching over a longer period of time than that of the story itself, which may be one that includes the present or, like the Kwatïngï stories, "Sagangguegï," "The Original Piqui," and "To Get Erections," even all of human existence. These different points of view are made manifest by various kinds of tricksters and dupes, who display markedly different ways of acting out, contextualizing, and justifying deception.

Augïnda: Deceptive Acts of Speech

Before looking more closely at more stories in which these different viewpoints are represented, I turn to the Kalapalo concept *augïnda*, in order to consider more directly the role of language in modifying interpersonal relations during deceptive action. Much of the remainder of this chapter will describe Kalapalo deception in terms of its culturally constituted constituents: function, sound-meaning relations, and context. In this connection, I will discuss the importance of validation in Kalapalo discourse as a whole, the nature of "unvalidated" and "invalidated" speech, how "truth" and "falsehood" are expressed, and the problematic relationship of propositional untruth to Kalapalo ideas of deception. This discussion will serve as a basis for understanding the "how" of trickster stories, their play with Kalapalo ideas about validation and deception.

One important duty of hereditary leaders (*anetaü*) is to make traditional speeches at the beginning of rituals (*egitsu*) to which people from other settlements have been invited. Called *anetu tagiñunda,* the "talking of a leader," the speeches are performed by both host and visiting leaders at the time the invitation is presented to a community, and later, when the visitors arrive. The "talking of a leader" is distinguished by the fact that more than one person may speak at a time, by a distinctive rhythmic chanting and extension of vowels, and by considerable repetition of formulaic sentences.

The speeches are not oratorical, in that they contain no arguments or even much information, but rather seem to serve as indicators of hereditary-leadership status and allow the leaders to represent to one another each community's collective responsibility for the ritual. Most of the sentences include the validation-evidential form *wäke,* which

An Acceptance, 1982
The *anetaü* Muluku
and Kefesugu accept
an invitation to lead
Kalapalo to a ceremony
held by a neighboring
community.

A Speech, 1967
Kalapalo *anetaü* Kambe, Ulutsi and Muluku, speak before visitors to a trading
ceremony in Aifa. Reprinted with permission from Ellen Basso, *The Kalapalo
Indians of Central Brazil*, Holt, Rinehart & Winston (New York, 1973).

usually indicates to listeners that a speaker has verifying firsthand evidence from the distant past. In the leaders' speeches, *wāke* suggests that this evidence is traditional knowledge that has been passed down from leader to leader, and that, consequently, only one true interpretation can be made of what is being said about the ritual event. Everyone is enjoined to share that interpretation. There is, then, a strong sense of validity associated with these events. However, contained within the speeches are words and expressions that, whether archaic or esoteric, are not heard in other contexts. Leaders are expected to be "respectful" toward both their own community and the other participants, and modestly "controlled" in their speech and movement (all this is prescribed by the word *ifutisunda*). They should not brag about themselves or the people they represent, but remain modest and even self-effacing. To these ends, leaders use certain inversions and dissimilations. The use of both archaisms and inversions in leaders' speeches is labeled *augïnda kotofola*, "something of a deception,"[4] as in the following example taken from a leader's speech upon the arrival of ritual visitors (most of the speech consists of this line rapidly repeated many times):

a) *ngingoku timbegatigaaah igei wāke, ngingoku:* "This was how it was in truth, tradition says, when messengers were almost about to arrive."
(Substitutes *ngingoku* for usual *etiñï,* "messengers.")

b) from a leader's speech to the hosts upon his own group's arrival at a trading ceremony (*uluki*), which will be followed by a wrestling match:
Nago etiñafikitsi ingitafïngï ufeke: "Of those I've brought, none are capable of gripping you."
(Refers to his group's wrestling champions as if they were very weak.)

Another, similar use of speech labeled *augïnda,* in the formal conversations of people about to be related through marriage, has similes and flamboyant inversions substituting for expressions more commonly heard. These, too, are situations of great formality and respect (*ifutisunda ekugu*), of controlled emotion, and, especially, of self-effacing modesty:

c) *Wetaketsange igei talokimukefa eñïnei witsomi:* "I had to come here to you, because even though it might not work out, I want to try to be lazy."
(A son-in-law wants to do bride service, which entails very hard work.)

d) *Untsi, ah iñandsu etiñatitsïgï inambake:* "My young relative, drink this stuff your sister (i.e., wife) just washed her hands in."
(In reference to some freshly made, cold manioc soup, which a woman prepares by stirring with her hand.)

Augïnda can also refer to mistaken or incorrect speech, as when a person begins to correct a mispronunciation by first saying, "*afïtï, waugïnda"* ("No, I've spoken incorrectly"). And, the word also can be used to indicate that someone's feelings are being hidden through speaking, as in examples e and f below (both taken from a story about a man who pretended to be a loving husband, but actually wanted to turn himself into a monster), and g (the text of an ironic Kwambï song). The last example might conform to our own more restricted sense of "slander":

e) *Lepene etiñandelïko, kine kidyïlefa.* Then they prepared food to take along, and manioc bread was made.
   Kanga engetofotsïfa. That was for the fishing trip.
   Augïndafegei. He was lying.
   Tugufifegei eteluingolefa. Because he was going to leave in the form of a catfish.

f) *Ah, tïkombeki akagoi?* "Did your relative do something to you that you didn't think he should have done?"
   Afitï, wende tufatafisalongoko. "No, we mourned him there."
   Uwamilei? "What happened to him?"
   Afitïlaketsange ukuaugufïngïlefa efisüagïko anïgïlefa: "Your brother can't be lying to us any longer."
   Tëtikilefa kangai. "He changed himself into a fish."

g) *Tïkinawakiñalï efeke, itau-ni*
   Tïkinawakiñalï efeke, itau-ni
   Tïkinawakiñalï efeke, itau-ni
   Tïkinawakiñalï efeke, itau-ni
   Tila(ko)su uwipi tafandene ïngï
   Ñatuisu uwïpi augene ïngï
   How many stories do I tell about you? the women
   How many stories do I tell about you? the women
   How many stories do I tell about you? the women
   How many stories do I tell about you? the women
   I have three disreputable containers of gossip.
   I have five disreputable containers of lies.

All these examples suggest "substitution" for the purpose of concealment is a core meaning of *augïnda*. This is substitution for something that would be recognized in "ordinary" (*taloki*) talk: an expected and identifiable way of phrasing, changed by metaphor, pun, deprecation inversion, or use of alternative names; changed by irony (as in the speeches of hereditary leaders and between relatives by marriage); an interpretation of an incident (as in the self-slanderous Kwambï song); and, finally, where concealment of certain inappropriate feelings is called for (such as pride in being observed in a complimentary way, inappropriate shame, and undue resentment or outright anger), making these explicit. "Substitution" thus takes various forms, including discontinuity, inversion, metaphor, and dissimilation, but always seems to point to an enacted difference, to action that imposes an alternative but no less "true" sense of reality.

A second important aspect of *auginda* is that, by the means peculiar to Kalapalo discourse, it is unvalidated speech. To understand why this is so, we need to digress for a few pages to examine some general ideas the Kalapalo have about discourse and how they go about creating validation.

Validation in Kalapalo Narrative Dialogues

In narrative discourse (*akiñatunda*), in which someone tells of either mythological or more recent, even firsthand experiences, there is a process of text ratification or validation that seems to focus upon affirmation and approval of sensory content itself. By means of various standard responses to a narrator's utterances, a responder-ratifier ("whatsayer," *tiitsofo*) contributes substantially to the construction of the narrated text. The whatsayer shows the speaker that someone is paying attention and thus helps to ratify the importance of a particular descriptive strategy for telling about the action. The responses let the speaker know that the images he or she is constructing are understood, appreciated, and agreed with. Finally, the whatsayer diverts the speaker into new channels of explication that were not originally planned; these new strands of the tale enhance both the listener's understanding and the authority of the narrator.[5]

The narrator has to know that the images he or she is creating are not just understood but are also adding to the listener's appreciation of the story, even though it may be one the listener has heard many times before. A good performance of a narrative, according to the Kalapalo, not only communicates the story accurately, avoids extensive repetition, and provides sufficient detail to hold the listener's interest, it heightens experience through the construction of vivid word images (*futofo*, "used for knowing") that allow the listener to "see" (which is to say, think more vividly about) what is happening in the narrative.

Consequently, a Kalapalo listener has the ability to direct the flow of a narrator's speech into side channels of explication and elaboration. This aspect of the event helps the speaker to recall incidents and details that might otherwise have been omitted. The narrator's own mental images are thereby enhanced or contributed to by the listener, who is in effect a secondary performer.

At the end of the story, a listener sums up what was said, letting the narrator know not only that the listener has understood the point and drawn the correct inferences, but also that he or she agrees with the narrator's conclusion. In other words, among the Kalapalo (in marked contrast with our own more formal didactic strategies), the storyteller does not always directly state points that could explain an unclear event. Instead, the information is first provided by the storyteller through the quoted speech of characters in the narrative, and finally by the listener, who explicitly lets the storyteller know the explanatory elements are accepted by putting them together, like the pieces of a puzzle. The listener's understanding and acceptance of crucial information (especially that having an explanatory function, such as descriptions of characters' motives) offer a kind of affirmation and approval of the elements of the narrative as they emerge one by one, and ultimately of the narrative as a whole. This process of affirmation and approval characteristic of narrative validation may be a model for all Kalapalo dialogical relations. It may constitute, perhaps, an idealization of how Kalapalo expect interpersonal action to succeed.

Validation in Conversations and Greetings

Kalapalo generally anticipate that people who are speaking together will validate each other during the course of their conversation. In particular, what are affirmed and approved are the feelings that are the motivation or specific reasons for goals and plans, and sensory descriptions of events. In conversation (*tagitsunda*), even though there may not be thorough agreement among participants, verbal responsibility and, indeed, clarity requires a person to express particular reasons for a particular course of action, so that the reasons, at the very least, can be assessed and evaluated.

An important tool Kalapalo use to negotiate a common interpretative frame is to voice various grammatical particles that indicate the speaker's acceptance or disagreement with another person's statement. Operations of reasoning that are made explicit in this way include positive corroboration ("I agree that's right"), negative corroboration ("I agree that's wrong"), denial ("That's not right"), deduction ("I conclude"), and hypothesis ("I suppose"). These five operations are further based upon hearsay, firsthand, especially visual, evidence or generic (common-sense) evidence. Finally, the type of reasoning and the type of evidence can be tied to conclusions of certainty, doubt, or disbelief (which in some instances are also given temporal and aspectual qualities of purposiveness and connectedness with the past).

When Kalapalo speakers use expressions that show they are questioning, corroborating, deducing, disputing or speculating in varying degrees of certainty about any of the marked forms of evidence, they convey impressions about how the making of inferences contributes either to different points of view or to a single interpretation about an action, and how the making of inferences leads to particular conclusions.

If none of these forms of evidence occur, there is an ambiguous and illusory quality to what is being said. In any event, when Kalapalo hear speech that is not marked as either valid or invalid, they are placed in a psychological state of doubt, the intensity and nature of which is indicated by how they seek confirmation of their own understanding of what was just said.

These grammatical elements seem to appear at moments of heightened tension when people do not know if they share understandings of what is going on, in times of potential divisiveness, or when actual disputes are occurring, or seem imminent. They occur when a shared meaning is sought, or where it is being thwarted: at moments of initial contact between people, of poor insight, of resistance to an interpretation, of counter-affirmation, and of negotiation. They occur prominently in greetings, in the ritual declamations of hereditary leaders, and in the stilted speech of affines, on the one hand, as well as in sequences of dialogue where persuasion, disagreement, and sarcasm occur, on the other. In some of these occurrences, they are what tell us about feelings, subjectivity, isolation, and conflict. In others, they help to form the most intense bonds of solidarity of which the Kalapalo are capable. In all cases, claims are being made about shared interpretations of experience.

Goal validation, and experience verification, confirmation or corroboration are combined in various Kalapalo greeting and farewell dialogues. Somewhat formal expressions are used when people address visitors to their settlement. These include the particles *nika* (indicating the speaker is seeking confirmation of a deduction: "it's true, isn't it?"); *aka* (indicating one confirms another's visual evidence: "I see that's so"); and *taka* (indicating confirmation of someone's recent past deduction: "you're right to have thought that").

h) *adenika wegei dyadya:* "You are here, aren't you, Older Sister?"
   andeaka uge engiluiña weta: "As you see, I have come here to see you."

i) *amagokafigey:* "My relative, I see it is you."
   ah, tisugekegey: "Well, it is us, as you see."
   Eh he. inafofo heytsue: "Very well. Linger here awhile."

j) *Utelakigei:* "I'm leaving this place, as you see."
   Eh he, tekeapaketsange: "Very well, you must certainly leave if you wish."

k) *Andetaka tiñeta, eufidyuiña:* "Now that we've reached you, you can be sure we were looking for you."
   Ai atidyetaka ufitsa efekeni: "I thought you were looking for me, and you've finally shown me that you were."

Another interesting conventional use of *nika* occurs in a musical dialogue, where the bereaved address a dead person as if they hoped for a response; here, as with *anetu itagiñu*, extended vowels mark line segments:

l) *Yatsi, ufiñanonikaah,*
   ufiñanonikaah
   "Alas, it's true, isn't it, my older brother,
   it's true isn't it, my older brother?"

In less formal greetings, people make their goals explicit. These occur most commonly when people encounter one another along a path or other private region of the settlement:

m) *Unama eteta:* "Where are you going?"
   Tuwaka: "To get water."
   Eh he, tekefa: "All right, then go."

Or, as Kwatïngï was addressed by his young male relatives, the Uafagu Trees (lines 402–405, "Kwatïngï"):

n) *Ande uwkoto, nïgifeke:* "Here is our parent," he said.
   Andeketsange uge, ulimo: "I am indeed here, my child."
   Uwameitsa? nïgifeke: "What do you want?" (the Tree) asked him.
   Tïtomi eta tisingiluiña: "What is it that brings you to see us?"
   Eiñandsukainga itsomi: "I want you to be on (i.e., decorate) your sisters."
   Eh he, aingofegey: "Very well, that will be done."

Notice how in most of these examples, validation of a goal occurs through the remark *eh he* ("Very well" or "All right") and the modal "agreement" or "confirmation" action suffix *apa* ("as you wish," "as you say"). This is also, however, an interactive, metapragmatic validation of the ongoing dialogue.

Invalidation

Validation for the Kalapalo is a matter of willingness to share an imagined or dreamed configuration—a motive, plan, goal, sensory description, interpretation. To do otherwise, to disagree, or to refuse to validate, is not so much to deny the truth of the other person's vision (that is, to focus in some way on the logic of the argument) as it is to hesitate or even refuse to share that vision. Thus it becomes an interpersonal matter. However, the person who invalidates, or refuses to validate, may provide an alternative solution to a problem by offering evidence that did not enter into the other person's consideration before, or interpret something differently by suggesting that the person's feelings are misguided. All this is simply the way the Kalapalo express another point of view.

Different points of view in Kalapalo are indicated not only by different opinions (what people are referring to, and the reasons they give for doing so), but by the subtle differences in the certainty and directness with which speakers respond to each other. Polite disagreement often begins with a formulaic expression such as *eh he kingi* ("yes, you do" or, more literally, "usually I would agree"); *afitï kingi* ("no, you don't" or "usually I would disagree"); or *lanike ekinge* ("you shouldn't speak that way.") A different idea (especially concerning the goal of an action) is expressed politely with the "disjunctive" modal particle *fale* or its anaphoric form *mbale* (which qualify an activity as contrary to one previously described; I translate these as "but," "however," "this time," or "now"—as opposed to "then"). Less polite expressions of different ideas about action occur with the "contrastive" modal, *tale* (through which people declare they will do something different), or the "oppositive" modal, *male* (where there is a sense of frustration expressed at being resisted in one's goal). Two of these forms are in the next example, from a myth, in which a brother's barely suppressed anger and envy for his sister's husband's magical arrow are contrasted with the woman's passionate concern for her brother's safety. Her use of the expression *laitsani* (*lafa*, "like that"; *itsa*, equative copula "be"; *ni*, "punctate potential mood") tells him of the assured consequences if he steals the arrow. (In other stories, powerful characters use this expression as a curse, so that listeners realize the person referred to will be destroyed.) Used as in example o, with the negative directive *keñi* (having the sense of "don't do it"), this expression conveys a feeling of foreboding:

o) *undemale anïgï?:* "Where is it? (Why don't you give it to me?)"
   ko. laitsani kenimbale: "I don't know. Let it be, if you don't watch out it will harm you (if I did give it to you)."

A person's refusal to share a point of view can also be indicated by the more direct and informal expression *mazuu* ("you must be kidding"), which softens disagreement and seems to be most often used by children, or by adults in very relaxed circumstances. Other techniques are silence, which implies anger and disappointment, or the use of a "surprise" marker (*ki*). When voiced in a sharply rising intonation, this expression most directly and assertively lets someone know of the speaker's strong disapproval or disagreement with what was just said or done. The first and last sentences in example f and the first line in g are examples, as well as the following outbursts:

p) *unaki eta? etekefa:* "Why are you coming here? Go away!" (A mother to her daughter, who came out of puberty seclusion to warn her family of a visitor.)
   tïtomiki?: "You have no reason to want that!" (A woman in response to a man's suggestion that they "lie down together.")
   eh mbeki?: "That's what they did, did they?" (A disapproving response to someone's gossipy narrative.)

What about statements that a listener believes to be referentially and propositionally untrue, or intentionally deceptive? Sometimes, the listener responds very directly and labels these utterances "lies." However, this happens only among the closest of friends (where, as we've seen, these should be treated as jokes if the relationship is to continue as a friendship) or when the listener can place responsibility for the lie on people in distantly related households or on declared enemies, generally on "witches," a role that was created by Taugi, it will be remembered. When a difference of opinion is expressed, a household's routine can be disrupted surprisingly quickly. For, among the Kalapalo, the "truth" of the interpersonal relationship takes precedence over the propositional truth of the parties' statements. Another point of view is very disturbing to the Kalapalo because it threatens the basis of their society. When their goals are validated in a dialogue, the Kalapalo experience psychologically reassuring contact with the other person, their interpersonal ties are strengthened and expanded, and, ultimately, a way of life that all have agreed is worth living is perpetuated.

Under these circumstances, it is not surprising that differences in points of view tend to be downplayed, and that responsibility for unpopular judgments is shunted off onto members of other households or clear-cut enemies. Kalapalo who intend to convince their listeners, then, not only must point out the nature of their evidence, they also have to assert their honesty and sincerity, and clearly demonstrate the relationship that is the communicative context. They do this by using relationship terms of address, rather than names, and by asserting that they are "not lying." When a speaker uses the expression augïndafingï ("it isn't a deception"), by which Kalapalo mean to say, "I'm sincere," a striking response is elicited immediately. The listener's body becomes noticeably rigid and he or she gazes directly at the speaker. This is one of the rare instances (the others are during seduction and violent anger) when Kalapalo look each other directly in the eye. By saying "waugïndafingï" ("I'm not lying"), the speaker openly claims responsibility for the truth of what was just said. Hence, the strong, interested response.

Directly claiming responsibility for what one is saying is most apparent when there are accusations of witchcraft. To close relatives of the accused, the statements are gossipy lies. To others, people who are less close to the accused, they are accepted and validated judgments about motive and action. When such accusations are made, lines of affection (funita) and respect (ifutisu) tend to be drawn around the victim's family and the accused's family. People take sides if they can, according to where they live, and with whom. Of course, many people have their doubts. Involved with both factions, they are incapable of drawing lines strictly. This makes ostracism—local, and sometimes regional—rather than execution the more frequent strategy for dealing with accused witches. Here is a good example of how Kalapalo listeners depend upon their own understanding of the active involvement of other people in interpreting what is being said. Speaking can be understood only in the context of how it actually contributes to social reality.

I have used the words "ratification" and "validation" when writing of what Kalapalo hope to achieve in their dialogic discourse. Since, in Kalapalo speech, people try to overcome doubt, opposition, or reluctance, and share a common perspective on some interpretation, understanding, or goal, these words are appropriate. Similarly, I use the word "verification" when grammatical particles are used to authenticate or substantiate evidence or testimony or opinion. Both "validation" and "verification" are social processes involving the intersection of two or more points of view that need to be negotiated. In validation, negotiation is a simple matter of the parties maintaining an agreed-upon relationship; they do this by voicing conventional responses that imply affirmation and approval, as well as a shared imaginative intimacy. But in verification, the parties must provide considerably more information on their reasoning processes, on the nature of their evidence, and on the strength of their conclusions.

Validation, Verification, and Deception

Readers may well object to my using the English word "deception" to translate the Kalapalo *auginda*. Our English words for a target of deception suggest strongly that while the process is an extremely unpleasant one to undergo, blame for being deceived falls squarely on the target. One who is easily and repeatedly deceived is called a "dupe" or an "easy mark"; and one who repeatedly shows ignorance and stupidity is a "fool" or, again, a "dupe." ("Dupe" falls into that interesting class of "du—" words that includes "dumb," "dullard," "dull," "dummy," "dunce," "dolt.") For us, the target of a deception creates merriment for others ("laughingstock"); this may be why people writing about trickster stories so often think of them as "delightful." English speakers use words that also imply a target of deception readily succumbs to superior "force." Some old or uncommonly used words are "bubble," "pigeon," "jay," "pushover." There is a sense that the deceiver uses the dupe to accomplish the deceiver's own designs and protect his own interests ("puppet," "cat's-paw").

Literally and metaphorically, the deceiver is sly and deadly ("snake," "double-dealer," "Judas," "sharp"); is disguised in some way ("charlatan," "wolf in sheep's clothing," etc.); is hypocritical (in this case, the words are few and mostly allude to Biblical or literary figures); and is a compulsive storyteller ("mythomaniac," "liar," "spin-ner of yarns," and so forth).

These common-sense notions of deception of course affect the vari-ous definitions and functions of deception and lying proposed by linguists, speech-act theorists, and others who take the speaker of En-glish as a model for universal laws of language use. Some writers, like Bates and Schultz, consider conversation in the first place to be founded upon the successful following of Grice's Cooperative Prin-ciple, in the form of basic "conversational postulates" or "assump-tions which underlie conversation." "Truth" and "falsehood" are de-pendent upon appropriateness in most contexts, in other words, a propositional truth that can be widely generalized. Bates' sense of lying is not much different from that of Searle, who writes of fictive utterances, defined as propositionally untrue (that is, not subject to verification by experience), yet not intended as lies by the speaker. Lies are not only untrue, but (as L. Coleman and P. Kay point out) are intentionally uttered to deceive, being considered false by the speaker. Joking and lying thus are defined negatively as utterances that deviate from Grice's Cooperative Principle or in some other way violate con-versational postulates, even when these violations are anticipated and acceptable in a certain context. In all these studies, what is forgotten is that speakers of any language have values about how interpersonal re-lations can be developed and how they emerge through strategic interaction, the contextually located construction of reality. It is the interpersonal relationship between speakers that influences how and when "deception" is perceived, not, or not just, the logical features of the discourse.

Nowhere are the American values surrounding deception better il-lustrated than in Erving Goffman's *Frame Analysis*. This work treats de-ception, illusion, and self-deception as the consequences of different kinds of errors in orientation, "frame-related vulnerabilities" that are "problems" or "defects" to which the "misguided" and "eccentric" "succumb":

They are caused by limits placed on information about what is going on. If then, one thinks of *deception* as falsehood intendedly produced by persons not taken in by their own fabrications and one thinks of *illusions* as error re-sulting from a misconstruing that no one induced purposely and that is understandable in the circumstances, then one can think of *self-deception* (or delusion) as wrongheadedness actively aided, if not solely produced, by the head that is wrong. (p. 112)

A more far-reaching investigation of lying, drawing inspiration from religious philosophy and an evolutionary-adaptational perspec-tive, is found in Roy Rappaport's intriguing discussion of the sacred and what he calls "discursive sanctification." "Ultimate sacred postulates" help to create trust among people, Rappaport claims, and underscore the correctness of convention in an environment of "overwhelming alternative" and vulnerability to deception that the flexibility inherent in language-based thought inevitably creates. Here too, though, Rappaport clearly examines lying in terms of its negative implications for social functioning.

My preference is for thinking of "deception" in more comprehensive ways, recognizing, as the Kalapalo do, that our ability to "lie" creates opportunities and potencies, as well as deficits and weaknesses. Clearly, the English words "illusion," "fabrication," and "deception" (as well as "delusion," "slander," "lie," and "mistake") can each be used in restricted contexts to translate *augïnda*. But these translations operate at the risk of distorting the complexity of the senses conveyed by the Kalapalo word. *Augïnda* covers all these English terms, but also, as I have said, refers to action that imposes an alternative sense of reality upon some subject of speech. Our sense of "lying" revolves around our concern with propositional truth, and the violation of conversational "sincerity." For the Kalapalo, however, whether something someone says is "true" or "false" is far less interesting to them than that the statement "changes" or "hides" or "masks" something known or imagined, a matter that the listener assumes to be shared knowledge. Also, "deception" involves speech that, during the specification of motivated goals, is unvalidated. Here, what in our own view is perhaps strictly a matter of the speaker's intentions, the Kalapalo hold to be a consequence of the dialogical, interpersonal processes of speaking.

To use the word *augïnda* thus makes one focus less upon the propositional content of what is said (covering what to us might be instances of both "truth" and "falsehood") than upon the fact that a different point of view or experience of an activity is being shared and expressed in dialogical context. Different points of view are indicated in Kalapalo not only by different opinions (what people are referring to, and whether one person is "right" and another "wrong"), but by how speakers in a conversation respond to each other.

With all this in mind, we can now examine more directly how trickster speakers use language symbols to delude listeners into thinking that what is being said is sincere, and simultaneously to maintain distance from their listeners by emphasizing differences in values, especially about speech, and about validation and concealment. In Kalapalo stories about deception, considerable creative force results from conversational dialogue. Speaking freely and openly about themselves to others, characters name their feelings and assert the dynamic nature of their interpersonal relations through their various speech acts. These contextually located (and dialogically constructed) points of view are suggested by grammatical markers, described earlier in this chapter, that psychologically color speech-centered relations between people. Grammaticalization of feelings about evidence and validity also strongly suggests the values surrounding what is being said, ideas about procedure, and the implied consequences of a decision to act in a certain way. Thus, for example, ideas about a character's motive are expressed through that character's own statement of feelings concerning a situation or another agent, through responses to past or anticipated actions of others (as causes or effects of the speaker's own actions), and through references to authority—be it political, traditional, common sense, or even, in the case of hereditary leaders, one's own. This is how we come to understand doubt, dissimulation, negotiation, regret, assertion, defiance, validation, and assent not as isolated, independent feelings, but those whose meanings emerge from social enactments. In the Kalapalo stories about deception, this interrelated nature of feelings is just what contributes most strongly to a sense of polyphony, of opposed and irreconcilably different points of view.

These processes can be illustrated by several myths. In one, about a Dawn Person named Cuckoo, speech by human characters is contrasted with the utterances of Taugi. I present the original Kalapalo to make the importance of linguistic features as clear as possible. From this story, we learn about the importance of conversational ratification of action, the social and personal implications and consequences of that validation, some of the ways interpersonal relations are negotiated and validated, and why Taugi has to be considered an isolated actor who cannot be validated. It is especially interesting that this story, unlike most of the others Kalapalo tell about Taugi, is told not from the point of view of the trickster himself but from the perspective of a community of Dawn People who have to reconcile themselves to his deceptions.

Fitsagu the Cuckoo

Told by Kudyu at Aifa. July 4, 1982.

An analysis of the story appears on pages 268–275.

1 Now, do listen.
ah tsakefa.
    He was Cuckoo.
fitsagu eley.
    Cuckoo, you would know one if you saw it, wouldn't you?
fitsagu, tufutisanafa ekefe
    The one with the long tail.
igokogo igeyfungu itumitsugu
      He was Cuckoo.   5
fitsagu eley.
  Well, he had sat down.
umm, isakandïfïgï atani,
    He sat down.
isakandïfïgï.
    "Mother," he said,
ama nïgifeke,
    "Mother."
ama.
    "Yes?" she answered,   10
ai nïgifeke,
    "Yes?"
ai.
    "Listen now to what I am saying.
tsakefofo ukilï,
    Listen now to what I'm saying.
tsakefofo ukilï.
  I might go try for Uncle's daughter, even though it probably won't work out.
engufetsange talokimukaketsange awadyu indisïna utefota.
    At the Igifagafïtu settlement."   15
engufa Igifagafïtuna.
. . . .†
He was going there to be the husband of the daughter of the Igifagafïtu leader.
Igifagafïtu anetugu endisï ingisoi ege teta.
    He was asking his mother about her.
igia ikatafa legey tïtina.
      He wanted to go there.
etetomi.

---

†I omit a few lines in which I ask for (and receive from Kudyu) clarification that these were human beings.

Because Cuckoo wanted to go do service for his parents-in-law.
engïfa fitsagu tetomifa afatuwïi.
　　At Igifagafïtu.　　　　　　　　　　　　　　　　　　　20
　　Igifagafïtuna.
"It won't, you say?" his mother said.
en he kingi nïgifeke
　　　"It won't, you say?
　　　eh he kingi
　　Go if you wish,
　　etekepapa,
　　　　go then.
　　　　etekefa.
　　If your sister doesn't want you,　　　　　　　　　25
　　ñafetsïfa iñandsufeke etifuñetote,
　　　　you'll come back right away."
　　　　enïmingo
　　"All right," he answered.
　　eh he nïgifeke
　　　"I intend to do just that,
　　　sagagey witsani,
　　　　just that.
　　　　isagagy.
　　I'll do just that, I'll come back Mother,　　　　　30
　　sagageydyetafa wenïmingo ama.
　　　　Just that."
　　　　isagagey.

ʌ　Now, the next day at dawn,
ah mitote kogetsi,
　　　he went on.
　　　etelulefa.
Then,
lepene,
　　　"I'm going right now, Mother.　　　　　　　　35
　　　utelakigey ama.
　　　I'm going right now."
　　　utelakigey.
　　"All right, go then.
　　eh he tekesïfa.
　　　All right, go then,
　　　eh he teketsïfa.
　　　　go then.
　　　　teketsïfa.

If your uncle wants you to give up your sister,   40
ñafefa isogofekefa iñandsu etifuñenote,
    you will come right back."
    enïmingo.
"All right," he said,
eh he nïgifeke.
    "That's just what I'll have to do,
    sagageyfetsange witsani,
        that's just what I'll have to do," he said.
        sagageyfetsange witsani nïgifeke.
He went on after that.   45
etelumbe.
    So he went on,
    telïlefa,
    and he arrived that day.
    ande timbelu.

B "Kao!" Mbuh!
kao! mbuh!
    All the people of Igifagafïtu called out to him!
    ah Igifagafïtu otomo etukwenïgï.
        The people of Igifagafïtu Community.   50
        Igifagafïtu otomo.
He was going there to do service for his parents-in-law,
segatifa etetofo fatuwïi,
    to do service for his parents-in-law.
    fatuwïi.
"Why are you here?" they asked,
uwameitsa nïgifeke,
    as Cuckoo stood beside his uncle.
    ah tïdyogokainga.
"Uncle," he said.   55
awa, nïgifeke.
"Yes?" the other answered.
ai, nïgifeke.
"Now, as you see I am here.
ah, andeaka uwanïgï.
    I am certainly here.
    andeaka uwanïgï.
I had to come here to you because even though it might not work
out I want to try to be lazy,
wētaketsange igey talokimukefa engïnei witsomi,
    to be lazy."   60
    engïnei.
"It might not, you say?" he answered.
eh he kingi, nïgifeke.

That was Cuckoo.
fitsagu feley.
He was going there to do service for his parents-in-law,
fatuwïi eteta,
    to do service for his parents-in-law.
    fatuwïi.
"You say it might not?" his uncle said, 65
um! eh he kini nïgifeke,
    "You say it might not?"
    eh he kini.
"Look, your younger brother is here for you," he said.
engï, ngikefa, efisu enïgï eiña, nïgifeke.
    "To you alone,
    wegeykutsufa,
    to you alone."
    wegeykutsufa.
"Look what's happening to our daughter," he said to his wife. 70
ngikefofo ukindisï, nïgifeke tufïtsufeke.
    "Look what's happening to our daughter."
    ngikefofo ukindisï.
"That's just the way it should be, that's just the way it should be.
alatsï alatsï.
    Let him come do service for you if he wishes to be with our
    daughter.
    lapapa efatuwï etanitsïfa ukindisïna.
        Let him do that."
        la.
"All right." 75
eh he.
"Go ahead, as you wish."
ohsipapa
    Her father tied Cuckoo's hammock about her.
    idyatelïlefa isuponga isuwïfeke.
Above his daughter.
indisï ahtupona.
    There,
    inafa,
        there. 80
        ina.
So his wife slept beneath him then.
ofiñelefa ifitsu nïgï.
"All right, go ahead,
ogiña ogi,
    all right, go ahead.
    ogiña ogi.

Do make something to drink for your younger brother.
ah efisï imbake.
Make something to drink for your younger brother." 85
efisï imbake.
"All right," she answered.
eh he nïgifeke
Then she did make some cold manioc drink.
ah tilisiñe enïgïlefaifekelefa.
She made some cold manioc drink.
tilisiñe enïgï.
Kukuku, heh! Cuckoo gulped it all down while he sat there.
ku ku ku heh! tuakandimbele fïtsagu itsalefa.
While he sat there. 90
tuakandilefa.
On a seat.
tuakandi.
He was finished.
aifa.
"Here, drink some more."
ande timbake.
"All right," he said.
eh he nïgifeke.
"My young relative, drink this stuff that your sister just washed
her hands in. 95
untsi, ah iñandsu etiñatitsïgï iñambake.
This stuff your sister washed her hands in."
iñandsu etiñatitsïgï.
"All right," he said.
eh he nigifeke.
Kuku so he drank it up.
kuku elidyulefaifeke.
He drank it up,
elidyulefaifeke,
a big gourdful. 100
igeyfuna.
"All right, go ahead, make some of that cheap *solo* for your younger
brother.
ogiña ogi, ah efisiñafa solo engikitse,
Some *solo*."
solo.
He was talking about manioc bread.
kinefeke.
That's what a kind of manioc bread is called.
kine ititï aketsigey.

If it's poorly made—poorly made manioc bread— 105
fesiñifa, fesiñifa kine ikidyumbedya
 made from crudely made manioc starch,
 fesinifa timbuku,
  it's called *solo.*
  solo ititï.
That's what the Kanugidyafïtï people call it,
igatafoifa kanugidyafïtifeke,
 I mean the Kalapalo people.
 kalapalofekedyetsa.
Solo, 110
solo,
 solo.
 solo.
It's just like a dove's nest when it's made that way.
tafafotofïngïekugumbedya.
 That's what it's called.
 ititifegey.
Solo, that's its name,
solotsïfa itï,
 solo.
 solo. 115
When we have a lot of good starchy food,
ikinealefale igeyfungutalefale, tuiñanggi, ukwatani kine,
 we prepare *kine, kine.*
 ekinetsale, ekine.
  But *solo* is made from that other stuff.
  solotsalehale igeyfale.
   Solo.
   solo.
    That's just what's done. 120
    langoaketsigey.
"All right, go ahead. Make some *solo.*"
ogi ñafe solo engukitse.
Now, that meant his mother-in-law was preparing something special for him,
ah, engifa ifotisofofekefa ugu ikidyu,
 his mother-in-law.
 ifotisofofeke.
That was special food for Cuckoo,
fitsagu ugu igey,
 Cuckoo's special food. 125
 fitsagu ugu.

He was going about there as their son-in-law,
fatuwïïfegey etepïgï,
   their son-in-law.
   fatuwï.
It was ready
aifa.
"Mother," she said,
ama nïgï,
   "here it is.   130
   andefa nïgï.
   "Here it is."
   andefa nïgï.
"All right," she answered,
eh he nïgifeke.
"You'd as well make him some cheap *solo.*"
ah, talokitofoi solomuke iñambake.
   "All right," she said.
   eh he nïgifeke.
   He did continue to speak to her that way about what she was
   making.   135
   ah nïgimbelefaifeke.
Tuk, she set the bread down on top of his drinking bowl.
tuk, tïokugu uguponga,
   she set the bread down on top of his drinking bowl.
   tïokugu uguponga.

III A They say that was all that happened until,
uletsïgïtsedyetifa,
   it grew dark.
   afugutilïï.
In the darkness, when it was about the way it is now, he felt sort
of hot.   140
ñambetï, igeyfungufudya, itotungufungufudya.
"I never feel very well here,"
afïtïmbedyale anïgïla,
   that's what she did say to him, I'm told.
   ah nïgïtifeke.
   "I never feel very well here.
   afïtïmbedyale.
Because since it's like this, the smoke drifts back down
ulegotedyalefalegey gitsitse teta
   and it reddens our eyes,"   145
   tingundufisugisifeke,
      that's what she said to him.
      nïgï fegey ifeke.

It hurt their eyes,
ingugu afukenïgï ifeke,
 it hurt their eyes.
 ingugu afukenïgï.
Because of that Cuckoo's eyes turned red.
ulepefa fitsagu ingundu fisugui.
 While he was at Igifagafitu,
 igifagafitï atani,
  the smoke irritated their son-in-law's eyes.
  fatuwïi ingundutsipïgï gitsitsefeke.
 Before his eyes turned red, they were very clear,
 ingundu fisugu fegey, teh ingugu anïmi.
  he was clear-eyed.
  tautufisi.
  That's what happened to Cuckoo's eyes.
  fitsagu ingugu anïmi.
  Because of that.
  ulepefa.
While he was there doing service for his parents-in-law,
fatuwïi fatani,
  he lost the whites of his eyes,
  ingundutsipïgï,
  he lost the whites of his eyes.
  ingundutsipïgï.
  Her cousin,
  itsahenefeke,
  her cousin.
  itsahenefeke.
  The wife's brother.
  ifitsï fisuagifekefa.
   Because of the smoke he lost the whites of his eyes.
   ingundutsipïgï igitsitseki.
He asked her,
tifai,
 "Is this what made you all this way?"
 umaligey igeanikalefigey eiñalïko.
 "Yes, look at us,
 eh. ngikefa tisugey,
  look at us.
  ngikefa tisugey.
 As you see, this is how we are,
 igeyfunguaka tisugey,
  like this."
  igeyfungu.

"You are, are you?
eh he kingi.
You are, are you?"
eh he kingi.
Like this."
igeyfungu.
That was all.
aifa.

B "Tomorrow I must go see Mother and the others.
kogetsifetsange uteliïngofofo amañuko iña.
I'll tell her we're doing well together.
atëtëi utsatigi.
I'll tell her we're doing well together."
atëtëi utsatigi.
He wanted to relieve himself.
isikitomi fegey.
He wanted to relieve himself.
isikitomifa.
At his wife's settlement
tufitsu etute.
He went because of what had happened to them, since he wanted
to make thatching grass come out of himself.
uletitifegey eteta, isikitomifegey inefa.
That's how our houses came to be the way they are.
ulepefegey tiñïnga.
Thatch, thatch, thatch, I mean this stuff that covers our houses.
iñe, iñe, iñe igeytifa tiñïnga.
That stuff of his.
ulepefa.
Cuckoo's feces.
fitsagu itëpefa.
That's just what it was.
egeyaketsange.
Now look, as you know, when we clear away all the manioc stalks,
ingkepa, andenahila kwigi figey tiñiketa atifïgï,
the place we clear them from, where there once was some
forest,
tiñiketa atïfigï itsunipe,
that's where Cuckoo would relieve himself, he would relieve
himself.
isikingalïfa fitsagu ikingalï.
And from it thatching grass would grow up.
iñelefa atingalïlefa.

170

175

180

185

That's what it was.
lango eley.
The grass was his droppings. 190
iñe isitui.
But, anyway, because he wanted to do that he went to his mother,
uletomifalegey eteta tutiña alefale,
    to discuss it with her.
    tegikatigi.
He wanted to relieve himself.
isikitomifa.
He wanted to make a house.
une fitsomi.
    He wanted them to be able to build houses. 195
    iñungukoi itsomi.
    That was because the smoke kept hurting their eyes.
    ulefinefa gitsitsefekefa, inugu afukeniğifine.
That's how he was,
langofeley,
    that's how he was.
    langofeley.
      He was Cuckoo.
      fitsagu feley.
    He had gone to do service for his parents-in-law. 200
    fatuwïifegey teta.

C He arrived home.
etimbelï.
    "Look, my son's here.
    ingketi umukugu.
      He's here.
      ati.
    My dear son is here.
    atiti umukugu.
    Why, think of it, his sister didn't like him," she said, 205
    ah, ingkefa iñandsufeke etifuneniğï, niğifeke,
      his sister."
      iñandsufeke.
Tiki, he came inside.
tiki wenïgï.
    "Mother," he said,
    ama niğifeke,
    "As you can see, I am here to see you."
    andeaka uge engiluiña.
    "Yes, you are," she answered, 210
    eh he kingale.

"Nothing happend to you, did it?
uwafogima wegey?
   Nothing happened to you, did it?
   uwafogima wegey?
You were happy there, weren't you? You were happy there,
weren't you?"
angifogikafa fekite wegey?
"I was, Mother!
eh ama!
   Yes," he answered.   215
   eh nigifeke.
   "Your niece treats me very well,
   ah atutudyalefa afatifeke witëidyi,
      very well."
      atutui.
   "All right," she said.
   eh he nïgifeke.
"But, Mother,
engï ama,
   Uncle and the others don't live the way you do,   220
   eigeyfungumakina awadyukoi,
      the way you do.
      egeyfunu.
   You see how I look. Look at how I am."
   ingkenifa ukingike.
His mother looked at him.
tïti tingifeke.
   His eyes were all red!
   tingundekeneki!
      It was the smoke that had made his eyes red.   225
      ingugu atufisugitsïgïlefa gitsitsefeke.
"Did something strange happen to you then?"
um! uwakumale igey atifïgï?
   "Yes," he said.
   eh nïgifeke.
   "Yes, I found out this is what Uncle's settlement is like.
   igeyfungumakina awadyukoi etui.
      Like this.
      igeyfungu.
   That's why I must relieve myself,   230
   enïaketsange wikilïingo,
      I'm going to relieve myself."
      wikilïingo.
   "All right," she said.
   eh he nïgifeke.

"As you see, I've come to you. Because of what's happened to
them,
uleatiti aka weta,
    that's the reason why.
    uleatiti.
    To let you know about Uncle.   235
    awadyu ifatigi.
        To let you know about Uncle.
        awadyu ifatigi.
Yes, I found out this is what Uncle's settlement is like.
igeyfungutsïmakina awadyukoi.
    Like this."
    igeyfungu.
"Very well," she said.
eh he nïgifeke.

D So he left.   240
etelïlefa.
    He went away.
    etelïlefa.
To a cleared place,
atïtïgitagelefa,
    where he lay down with his wife,
    tïfïtsï ingati,
    where he lay down with his wife.
    tïfïtsï ingati.
"Let's go take care of our needs,   245
fainga ukige,
    let's go take care of our needs."
    faina ukige.
"All right," she answered.
eh he nïgifeke.
He looked around him.
ingipïgï itsaifeke.
    He was looking for a clearing.
    tigitafoliñï uifitsaifeke.
Well, because he needed a beautiful place,   250
ah engifo atani teh!
    he needed a sizable place,
    etsekegï ekugumbe,
    a place that was well-cleared.
    atïtï tepïgï tïgitafolinï tepïgï.

"I'll put it here.
ina fitsani.
I'll put it here."
ina fitsani.
He was standing right in the middle of it when he said that,   255
igitati ekugumbe igifikïgïna,
> so, that's where he relieved himself.
> *ah sikilï.*
When he was done,
aifa,
> he came back.
> *sinïgïlefa.*
He slept, he slept.
sïngïlï, sïngïlï,

IV After he had slept three days,   260
tilako sïngïpïgï,
> he went back there to see.
> *tïte ingiluiña.*
Over here, over here, over here, over here,
egefunde, egefunde, egefunde, egefunde, laikugu,
>> there were shoots all over the place, so many of them. They
>> were all over.
>> *tsïgifoti, laikugumbe.*
> Thatching grass grew there.
> *iñe atani.*
"Yes, I was right to do that.   265
hedyemaki,
> Yes, I was right to do that."
> *hedyemaki.*
So he came back.
isinïgïlefa.
> That was all.
> *aifa.*

V Then he slept, he slept,
lepe sïngïlï, sïngïlï,
> and when he went to look it was this high,   270
> *igefunde ingiluiña tïte,*
>> *bah* it had already started to grow,
>> *bah igeyfunde atïpïgï atani,*
>> it was almost three feet high, and it was still growing.
>> *igefunde, igefunde atilïfatalefa.*

"Yes, I was right to do that," he said.
hedyemaki, nïgifeke.
　"Yes, I was right to do that."
　hedyemaki.
　That's just the way it was.　　　　　　　　　　　　　　275
　langoaketsigey.
"Yes, I was right to do that."
hedyemaki.
"Now, listen to what I say," he said to his wife.
tsakefofo ukilï, tufïtsufeke.
　"I have just the thing our poor parents can use to protect us all.
　angiaketsange ukwotofekemukefa ukwetuwandetofoingo.
　　There's something here.
　　angi.
With that we will be living in a good place,　　　　　　280
igeyfiñe atïtïte ukwaningofiñe,
　　　with that.
　　　igeyfiñe.
　We will be living in a good place.
　atïtïte ukwaningofiñe.
Where we are now isn't anything like that at all.
tamigia kunalïko.
My own people have something different from this to live in, you know.
afïtïtaka igeyfungu tongofïngïtifa tisuge?
　　　Different.　　　　　　　　　　　　　　285
　　　afïtï.
　We people have shelter.
　ungalï tisugey.
　　Shelter."
　　ungalï.
That's what he said to his wife.
nïgififeke tufïtsufeke.
Then she told her father about it.
lepe tifatifeke tuwïiña.
　"Father," she said,　　　　　　　　　　　　290
　apa nïgifeke,
　　"Father."
　　apa.
"Yes?" he answered.
ai nïgifeke.
"We have our house."
angiaketsange kukïngï.
"What do you mean, 'We have our house'?"
tïmale kukïngï angi?

"'A house,' he just told me.   295
une tanaifeke.
'Your father himself should be the one to make it,'
owïfeketsïfa tufanïmingo,
    he just told me.
    tanaifeke.
        He just told me."
        tanaifeke.
    "Very well," her father said.
    eh he nïgifeke.
Then he went to see.   300
lepe ingiluiña tute.
    It was all over, wherever he happened to walk,
    ege aimbele etelufata,
    and there were no spiny parts on it at all, it was beautiful,
    teh! he he! ñalïma egey ifïgipitsu,
        there was nothing spiny on it.
        ñalï.
        Teh! heh heh! It was magnificent!
        teh! he he! ñalï ekugu!
    That was what Cuckoo had done for him.   305
    fitsagu atsatepïgï fegey.
That was the origin of what became thatching grass.
igeningo figeyingo, ulepe fegey iñefa.
    The very first, we've been told.
    iñïngo tifa.
        That.
        igeyfa.
            That was the origin of it.
            igeningo fegey.
    He intended to create that very thing.   31●
    igey fegey ingïitanïmi.

VI Do listen.
    etsakefa!
    Then after they had slept a long time they went to look at it.
    lepe akïngi sïngïpïgï atani ingiluiña tuteko.
        It was fully grown.
        apïpïgï atanilefa.
        Buh, EVERY bit of the cleared space was covered
        buh! utukufifiti ekugumbekudya!
            by the thatching grass!   31●
            iñembefa.

"Uncle," he went.
awa nïgifeke.
　　"Uncle.
　　awa.
　　Here is just the thing for you to use to cover your enclosure."
　　angiaketsange eũwa iputegofoingo efeke.
　　　　"Very well," he said.
　　　　eh he nïgifeke.
　　　　"Very well." 320
　　　　eh he.
"This is the thing to use.
igeyfiñefa.
　　This is the thing to use.
　　igeyfiñe.
　　　　This is the thing to use."
　　　　igeyfiñe.
But anyway, soon afterward
lepe apangangufïngïtalefale egey,
　　they cut their foundation posts, I'm told. 325
　　ñengikondotelïletïifeke.
He went to get them.
igey tuilulefaifeke.
　　He went to get them.
　　igey tuilulefa.
And he cut the rafters.
sikitsu tuilulefaifeke.
And he cut the rafter supports.
afundelïlefaifeke.
The house was ready! 330
aifa!
　　"It's all ready, Uncle," he said.
　　aifa nïgï awa nïgifeke,
　　　　"It's all ready."
　　　　aifa nïgï.
"All right, then!"
ohsifa!
　　"I want our parent to go pull it up.
　　ukwoto tetomi iñokiluiña.
　　　　I want our parent to go pull it up." 335
　　　　ukwoto tetomi.
　　"Very well," she said.
　　eh he nïgifeke.

"Father," she said.
apa nïgifeke.
  "Go pull it up, do you hear?
  omokitatïfa!
    Go pull it up!"
    omokita!
  "All right,"   340
  eh he.
    So he went to pull it up,
    ah, tïokifeke.
      and he pulled it up.
      iñokilïlefa.
Tugu, tugu, tugu,
Tugu, tugu, tugu,
    how beautiful!
    teh he he!
    That didn't have any spiny stems at all.   345
    ñalïma egey figifïdyo.
      None.
      ñalï.
Then they put it on the house,
lepe tufatifekeni,
    Teh, there weren't *any* of those things I was talking about,
  teh! ñalïmangu egeyfungu tsei,
    there weren't any spiny stems on it,
    tangope ñalïma figifïdyo.
      It didn't have any on itself,   350
      tangopena.
Teh, it was magnificent.
teh! heh heh, ñalï ekugu.
    They were finished.
    etïkilïko.

VII A Now do listen!
  etsakefa!
    It wasn't like that other place of theirs.
    tangope.
    "Well," I'm told he said.   355
  um! a nïgïtifeke.
    "It's all done!
    aifa atïkilï!

"Look at our house," he went.
ingkefa, nï
　"Look at it.
　ingkefa.
As you see, we're all ready here, once and for all,
kuapungukoaka igey,
　we're all ready.　　　　　　　　　　　　　　　　360
　kuapungu.
And we'll soon be inside here,
igeatsehale tiñanïgï,
　here."
　igea.

B　Then, well, someone told Taugi about it.
lepe, ah Taugi ina tikagi.
　　　Taugi.
　　　Taugina.
　　　He told Sun about it.　　　　　　　　　　　365
　　　Gitinambedya.
　　　　Sun.
　　　　Gitina.
"Say, I've just heard the leader of Igifagafitu has a house." They
said something like that to him.
ah, Igifagafïtï anetugu ungu nïgïtataifeke.
"Little brother," Taugi said to Aulukuma,
Ufi nïgifeke.
　　"Now, let's go right away to see this thing our grandmother's
　　made,
　　ah, kuñitafofo kunitsu atsatepïgï,
　　　that our grandfather's made.　　　　　　　　370
　　　kutaupïgï atsatepïgï.
　　　　Let's go see."
　　　　kuñita.
　　"All right."
　　eh he.
Mm mm mmmm! Now, they came as wind after that,
um um mmm! ah fitembe
　　they came there,
　　sinïnggo,
　　Taugi came.　　　　　　　　　　　　　　　　375
　　Taugi enïgï.
　　　Taugi.
　　　Taugi.

C   "Look at how these stems are growing out!"
ikefa ifïgikundigifa ah sinïgï!
> They saw there wasn't anything on them, they were beautiful!
> *teh heh heh, la anïmbiñe!*
> They were perfectly bare.
> *teh! heh heh! anïmbiñe.*
> They came closer.   380
> *tuendi.*
>> They peered down the length of the stems.
>> *timïkaifiko.*
teh heh, there weren't any spiny stems at all.
teh he ñalïmbe ifigifïdyoi.
Teh! heh heh! They were perfectly made!
teh! he he! kugumbekudye!
"Well, look at our grandfather's house, Little Brother,
um! ingkefofo kutaūpïgï ïngï ufi,
> look at it.   385
> *ingkefofo.*
It can't stay this way,
afitïdyale anïgïla,
> no.
> *afitï.*
Our grandfather won't stay this way.
tama igia taūpïgï inalï.
> He won't stay this way.
> *tamigia inalï.*
And the mortals won't be this way, even though they would
want to be,   390
igeya eykuapalefafigey afako,
if they went to protect themselves.
etuandefotalefa.
> Like this.
> *igeya agage.*
>> This.
>> *igeya.*
It won't stay like this any longer.
afitïaketsange igeya nïgïla.
> No.   395
> *afitï.*
It's too nice.
etefa igeya nalï.
If it should be like this, then the mortals' houses would be too
beautiful.
igeyakeñi afakofiliñïgï, atakofolï kulengapalefa.

Let our grandfather's house be that way.
lafa taūpïgï ïngï itsani.
  Let it be that way.
  lafa itsani.
    Let it be that way.   400
    lafa itsani.
Why does our grandfather's house have to be like this?
taikuma igia kutaūpïgï ïngï inali?
For them to be well made, the mortals should have to be strong
when they want to thatch their houses.
tapogi ule, afako filinïgïfeke, tugiga atani, tifekefa.
    When they want to do that."
    tifeke.
  "Very well," Aulukuma answered.
  eh he nïgifeke.
    "Very well."   405
    eh he.
"I wish he weren't like that all the time," his younger brother said.
fidyumbekufale! ifisï kilï.
  His younger brother spoke, Aulukuma spoke.
  ifisï kilï, Aulukuma kilï.
  "Why is he always like that?" I guess he said.
  fidyumbekufale! nïgïtifeke.
    "I wish he weren't like that all the time."
    fidyumbekufale!
"Let's go," Taugi said.
kigefa, nïgi,   410
    "Moh, let's go see our grandfather's clearing.
    moh taūpïgï ifatigofo kuñita.
      Our grandfather's clearing."
      kutaūpïgï ifatigofo.
He went to see the place where the others were pulling out the
grass.
ulefekefa iñokilïña tetofofeke.
MM MM MMM, he traveled as wind.
mm mm mm, etelï fite.
  The others didn't know,   415
  ñalïma funïmi,
    they didn't know.
    ñalïma funïmi.
Now, *mm mm mmmm.*
ah, mm mm mm.
  They were there.
  segati.

What they were pulling out still grew there.
igenga iñokipïgï itïpofongo atiga fegey.
Teh heh heh! There was more of it, even cleaner than before.   420
teh! he he! agetsïkï wate.
Because afterward, when he wanted to pull it out, *tïdï, tïdï,*
ule atehe iñokilïtifeke, tïdï, tïdï
    he slept, he slept, *bah!*
    isïngïlï sïngïlï, bah!
      and it grew up.
      atilïlefa.
That stuff of his.
ulepefegey.
The new sprouts kept growing up, and so there was new growth.   425
itïpofongo atilïfatalefa, itïpofongo atanilefa.
  Teh heh heh!
  teh heh heh!
    It was magnificent!
    añalï ekugu!
There weren't any spiny stems at all.
ñalïma ifigifïdyoi.
There weren't any yet at that place.
tangope ñalïmafofo.
"Let's do that to them.   430
etege inalï.
  Let our grandfather's enclosure be that way."
  latsa kutaũpïgï ïwa itsani.
"Let's go," he went.
kigefa nïgifeke.
  Mm mm mm, they circled around and came back,
  mm mm mm, itsetinefegey ogopidyï.
    as wind, to destroy it.
    fite feke tuelïïña.
To pull off the sheaths.   435
ipulïïña.
To pull the sheaths off the thatching grass stalks.
ipulïïña, iñepe ipulïïña.
Because he thought it was too beautiful to use as it was.
ulefiñe teh heh anïmbiñe.
MM MM MMM,
mm mm mm,
  ku ku ku ku tsu tsu tsu tsu,
  ku ku ku ku tsu tsu tsu tsu,
    so, they destroyed it all.   440
    ah tuelumbelefaifeke.

"Well, Taugi must have done that.
um! Taugifinambe.
  No one but Taugi.
  Taugi tuiñalïma.
    Only Taugi could have done that."
    Taugimbakegey.
He went on after that.
etelumbe.

D   Then after that had happened, even so he went back to where they
    were pulling it up.   445
lepetalelegey, lepembe togopisi, ñokitofoña.
  There he made the stems weak and soft.
  segati ifïgikamolïine.
  Then he threw the remains all around,
  lepe tufutsikundi ifeke,
    buuk,
    buuk,
      and so the stems became very spiny.
      lepefïñe fïgipidyoi.
Teh heh! It had been beautiful.   450
teh he! lafa atani.
      That's how it had been.
      lafa atani.
  But this time it came up the way it does now,
  langope fegey,
      this time it came up the way it does now.
      langope fegey.

E   Then the others went to their clearing to pull some out.
lepe tsupofongo ōkiluiña tuteko.
    "Look!" the grass was all covered with spiny stems.   455
ïïke! ah, fïgifïdyo atanilefa.
    "Well!" I guess he said,
um! anïgïtifeke,
      I mean the owner spoke.
      oto kilïtsïfa.
    "Well! Taugi must have done this.
um! Taugi finambe.
      Surely Taugi did this.
      Taugi mbakigey.
    But why did he have to do that to us?   460
tïmemale igea kwïïgate.
      Why did he have to do that to us?"
      tïemigia ukwïïte?

"All right," they pulled it up.
ohsi iñokilï.
>   *Tuguk! Tsiuk! Tsiuk!*
>   *tuguk! tsiuk! tsiuk!*
And so, look,
aimbefa ingke,
>   before when they pulled on it it came out fast,   465
>   *iñokigatïgïpenge,*
>>   but now *tsiuk, pok, tsiuk, pok.*
>>   *tsiuk, pok, tsiuk, pok.*
>>>   That's how it was this time.
>>>   *langopengine.*
They had to wipe off the spines, we've heard.
ifïdyipitsilïletifa ifekeni.
>   Well, that's the way it was.
>   *ah langope fegey.*
>   From that time on, the stems grew spiny the way they are now,
>   when we poor people go there,   470
>   *ulepeiñe fïgifïdyoi ikutifïgey, mukekutitsengatofoi,*
>>   when we go there.
>>   *titsengatofoi.*
Since then.
ulepefa.
It was Taugi who put the spines on.
Taugifekefa ifïgikundïfïgï.
That's how it happened.
alango fegey.
That's really all there is to that.   475
apïgïaketsange.

Notes to "Fitsagu the Cuckoo"

The hero of this story is associated metaphorically with the squirrel cuckoo (*Piaya sp.*), a bird that carefully builds its nest of coarse twigs.

Thatching a House With Grass, Aifa, 1979

Narrative Structures in "Fitsagu the Cuckoo"

This is a good story to illustrate my discourse-oriented methods of text analysis. The tale suggests alternative possibilities for how to abstract an underlying formal structure; it is composed mostly of quoted speech; and it nicely conveys a sense of the various techniques Kalapalo narrators use to delineate and connect together narrative segments of several orders of magnitude.

There are several ways to describe the narrative discourse structure of "Cuckoo." The first draws attention to an important segmentation device ubiquitous in Kalapalo narrative art: *references to the experiencing of time*. In general, such references are allusions to the planning or persistence of a character's goal-oriented action. In the story of Cuckoo, the narrator Kudyu makes five explicit references of this sort. Each seems to signal shifts in theme of one degree of importance or another. Counting an opening segment, six units result. These, together with the references to time that introduce each of them as apparently discrete narrative units, are listed in Table 3.1.

Within all six segments are references to sleeping, which seem to mark continuity in Cuckoo's psychological orientation to some existing state of affairs—from creating a plan to carrying it through. First, Cuckoo expresses his desire to marry and tells his mother he will depart the next day (I). After sleeping, he carries out this plan (II). Next, Cuckoo ponders his relatives' need for a real house. He tells his wife he must leave the next day to visit his mother. After sleeping, he goes to his mother for ratification of his plan to make their house possible (III). After saying he will depart the next day and sleeping once again, he decisively carries out the plan (IV). Along the way, reference is made several more times to sleeping, which suggests the plan is work-

Table 3.1. Narrative Segmentation According to References to Time

I. lines 1–31: begins with the opener *tsakefa*, which separates the performed narrative from ordinary conversation.

II. lines 32–137: begins with line
    "Now, the next day at dawn,"

III. lines 138–259: begins with lines
    "That was all that happened until,
        it grew dark."

IV. lines 260–268: begins with line
    "After he had slept three days,"

V. lines 269–310: begins with line
    "Then he slept, he slept,"

VI. lines 311–end: begins with lines
    "Listen.
    Then after they had slept a long time they went to look at it."

ing (for example, the grass keeps growing until it is mature enough to use, and this takes time) (V).

Table 3.2 lists references to time, to traveling, to the onset and completion of activities, and exhortations to a listener-responder to pay attention. These result in segmentation of the story, also shown in the table.

The last segment (VI) poses something of a problem, because in line 353 Kudyu again uses the expression *tsakefa* ("listen"), suggesting another narrative break. And indeed, although there is no reference to time following this line (as there is at the beginning of segment VI, in lines 311–312), there is such a major shift in narrative content that I feel justified in creating a seventh segment incorporating lines 353 through 475 (the conclusion). Segments IV and V are clearly less substantial than are the other segments, but I prefer to keep them separate as integral units of the same order as I, II, III, VI, and now VII; references to time and the introductory *tsakefa* are now used as joint markers of major segment breaks. Segment VII not only represents the introduction of a new character, it continues the narrative progression that is concerned with Cuckoo's goal-oriented action. The action in segment VII in fact modifies or transforms Cuckoo's expected goal into something different. Nonetheless, that goal still follows logically from what was described earlier, namely, Cuckoo's attitudes toward what he was trying to do. But before examining this point further, I continue with the narrative segmenting process.

Within three of the seven major segmental divisions are smaller ones that I have marked by capital letters (see Table 3.2). These divisions are suggested by Kudyu's references to *traveling*, another important segmenting technique in Kalapalo narrative discourse. When a character travels in these stories, there is a sense that he or she is crossing imaginative boundaries, as well as geographic ones. Traveling emphasizes the differences in the character's experiences occurring in discrete locales; not incidentally, distinctive linguistic styles are used in each place. Cuckoo, for example, moves back and forth between his mother, with whom he speaks casually and informally, and his in-laws, where conversations follow the very different patterns of speech between parents and their sons- or daughters-in-law. Each of the segments created by references to Cuckoo's travels connect his statements of goals with his activities, which eventually lead to fulfillment of his plan to give his in-laws a new kind of dwelling. And, similarly, Taugi's traveling in segment VII reinforces what he had decided to do about such a dwelling.[6] But these units are even more interesting because they key some distinctive changes in the character's contextually based point of view or shifts in "footing," to use an expression of Erving Goffman. (In other stories, travel-marked segments

Table 3.2. Segmentation by Features of Narrative Disclosure

I. lines 1–31 (the plan is described by Cuckoo and ratified by his mother)
    starts line 1
        Now, do listen
        ah tsakefa
    ends line 31:
        That's just what I'll do.
        isagagey
II. lines 32–137
    A. starts lines 32–33 (action toward goal initiated)
        Now, the next day at dawn,
        ah, mitote kogetsi
            he went on.
            etelulefa
        ends line 47
            and he arrived that day.
            ande timbelu
    B. starts line 48 (action toward goal completed)
        "Kao! Mbuh!
        kao! mbuh!
        ends line 137
            she set the bread down on top of his drinking bowl.
            Tïokugu uguponga
III. lines 138–258 (new problem described and solution proposed)
    A. starts lines 138–139 (wife describes problem and Cuckoo verifies)
        They say that was all that happened until.
        uletsïgïtsedyetifa,
            and it grew dark.
            afugutilïi
        ends line 172
            That was all.
            aifa.
    B. starts line 173 (Cuckoo's new plan begins)
        "Tomorrow I must go see Mother and the others.
        kogetsifetsange utelïingofofo amañuko ina.
        ends line 200
            He had gone to do service for his parents-in-law.
            fatuwïifegey teta.
    C. starts line 201 (Cuckoo seeks and receives verification of problem and
        ratification of plan by mother)
            He arrived home.
            etimbelï
        ends line 239
            "Very well," she said.
            eh he nïgifeke
    D. starts line 240 (goal-directed action begins)
            So he left.
            etelilefa.
        ends lines 257–258
            When he was done,
            aifa,
                he came back.
                sinïgïlefa.

IV.　lines 260–268 (persistence of goal-directed action)
　　　　starts line 260
　　　　　After he had slept three days,
　　　　　tilako sïngïpïgï,
　　　　ends line 268
　　　　　That was all.
　　　　　aifa.
V.　lines 269–310 (clarification of the motives for goal-directed action)
　　　　starts line 269
　　　　　Then he slept, he slept,
　　　　　lepe sïngïlï, sïngïlï,
　　　　ends line 310
　　　　　He intended to create that very thing.
　　　　　igey fegey ingïïtanïmi.
VI.　lines 311–352 (The house-building is proposed and ratified; new goal-oriented actions begin, are nearly completed)
　　　　starts line 311
　　　　　Listen
　　　　　etsakefa!
　　　　　　Then after they had slept a long time they went to look at it.
　　　　　　lepe akïngi sïngïpïgï atani ingiluiña tuteko.
　　　　ends lines 352
　　　　　They were finished.
　　　　　etïkilïko.
VII.　lines 353–475 (modification of final goal)
　　　A. starts line 353 (Cuckoo's premature declaration of accomplishment)
　　　　　Now do listen!
　　　　　ah tsakefa!
　　　　ends lines 361–362
　　　　　And we'll soon be inside here,
　　　　　igeatsehale tiñanïgï,
　　　　　　here."
　　　　　igea.
　　　B. starts line 363 (Taugi's unratified plan declared)
　　　　　Then, well, someone told Taugi about it.
　　　　　lepe, ah Taugi ina tikagi.
　　　　ends lines 373–376
　　　　　mm mm mmmm! Now, they came as wind after that, (speaker later clarifies who came)
　　　　　mm mm mmm! ah fïtembe . . .
　　　C. starts line 377 (action toward goal begins)
　　　　　"Look at how these stems are growing out!"
　　　　　ikefa ifïgikundïgïfa ah sinïgï!
　　　　ends line 444
　　　　　He went on after that.
　　　　　etelumbe.
　　　D. starts line 445 (completion of goal)
　　　　　Then after that had happened, even so he went back to where they were pulling it up.
　　　　　lepetalelegey, lepembetogopisi, ñokitofoña.
　　　　ends line 453
　　　　　this time it came up the way it does now.
　　　　　langope fegey.

Table 3.2. (continued)

E. starts line 454 (realization that goals have been modified)

Then the others went to their clearing to pull some out.

lepe tsupofongo ōkiluiña tuteko.

ends line 474

That's how it happened.

alango fegey.

End of story: line 475 (performance closure achieved)

That's really all there is to tell.

apïgïaketsange.

also underscore contrasts between the points of view of different characters.)

What makes Cuckoo an especially attractive character, as portrayed by Kudyu, is that he is an active, conscious person faced with necessities and purposes that force him to be ever-mindful of choices and consequences. His feelings are varied, ranging over uncertainty, commitment, self-assurance, and awareness of necessity or even duty. The latter develops from his successful marriage, established early in the story, which commits him to completing the exchange begun when he was allowed to live with his female cousin. Cuckoo's decision to make a new house is as much a consequence of his new son-in-law status as it is of the harm done to his eyes. Cuckoo's feelings are made most explicit in social contexts. These situations bring them to the surface, and allow them to be commented upon and responded to favorably by others. Supportive acquiescence from others seems needed initially because Cuckoo's earliest proposals are couched in terms of uncertainty and emphatic modesty. But, later on, having been confirmed by his relatives all along, Cuckoo becomes much too sure of himself, even though the support that is given him seems warranted since the relationship is proceeding well.

Shifts in Footing

The first kind of shift in footing has Cuckoo moving between the environment of his mother to the environment of his affines. There are three instances of this. The first is described in lines 33–47, when Cuckoo leaves home to seek a bride. In the second (line 201), Cuckoo returns home to seek confirmation of his desire to give his in-laws a new house. In the third (line 240), Cuckoo returns to his wife's family to accomplish his new goal of making thatch for them to use.

The different environments are of course made clear by what Kudyu tells us about where Cuckoo is at any given moment, and shifts in footing are suggested by the different ways of speaking Cuckoo and his relations use in each place. Among his affines, Cuckoo's speech is metaphoric and self-abnegating—that is, allusive and indirect. When Cuckoo and his hoped-for father-in-law are speaking to each other, for example, inversions figure prominently (lines 54–137); the discussion is actually more a marriage ritual than a conversation. When Cuckoo later has to convey some information to the man who is now his father-in-law, Cuckoo's wife serves as intermediary between her husband and her father because Cuckoo must respectfully avoid the older man.[7]

Contrasting with this stereotyped speech between in-laws are Cuckoo's conversations with his mother and his wife. These are entirely open, non-metaphorical, and direct.[8] But there is more than a simple contrast here between "formal" affinal ritual and "familiar" or "informal" conversations. Cuckoo experiences another interesting change during the progress of the story: his point of view is reinforced. Despite the several shifts in footing, this reinforcement is achieved through the assertion of a generally accepted authority—that of the community of relatives—that perpetuates exchange within the context of marriage relations. In the end, that authority acts convincingly to overcome Cuckoo's doubt and modest reluctance.

Validation in "Cuckoo"

In line 14, Cuckoo informs his mother of his desire to marry, but he is anxious and uncertain about being able to accomplish this. Cuckoo's modest doubt about his own worth as a husband (however stereotyped and expected it might be of a young man) is conveyed by his use of the expression *talokimukaketsange* (structurally, "without reason" + devalued mode + emphatic action mode, that is "the worthless, fruitless action that I must follow"). This statement is coupled with the continuous aspect/conditional mood marker *fota* ("might"). (The narrator's paraphrase, however, makes use of the intentional mode—"wants"—in line 18.) Despite this uncertainty, Cuckoo's mother validates his plan by the agreement phrase, *etekepapa*, "go if you wish." By contrast, Cuckoo is very assertive in line 30, when, in response to his mother's advice that he return immediately if his relatives don't accept him (a plausible expectation for Kalapalo suitors), he uses the punctate aspect/potential mood form *ingo* ("will right away"). He is even more assured when (in lines 173 and following) he tells his new wife that he needs to visit his mother: this time Cuckoo uses the emphatic declarative/punctate potential mood form *ketsange* + *ingo* ("must"). And, finally, Cuckoo confirms his own good judgment in lines 265–266 and 273–274. There is, in other words, a clear progression from Cuckoo's hesitation, modesty, and slight anxiety to an attitude of smooth confidence and self-assured anticipation of success. Toward the end, there is even an excess of confidence when, as the final segment begins, he assures his relatives (lines 359–362), "As you see we're all ready here, once and for all . . . we're all ready. And we'll soon be inside here, here." The progression from doubt to self-confidence, from slightly embarrassing desire to an expectation of fulfillment, seems to be a consequence of the unfailing validation that Cuckoo receives virtually every time he speaks to someone.

Cuckoo's inappropriate assurance about the future good life can be contrasted with how, somewhat later, Taugi speaks in lines 398–400. There, reference to the future by means of the continuous aspect/potential mood *ni* ("will continue") sets up this character as dominant, in the clearly important sense of controlling transformative power (*itseketu*) over the others. Taugi's transformative power reshapes Cuckoo's goals, and brings about an unanticipated conclusion to action that earlier seemed so certain of success.

"Lies About Himself": Taugi's Invalid Action

I turn now to what must have struck the reader as an obvious and neglected topic, the strange narrative disconformity between events involving Cuckoo and his family (segments I–VI) and those involving the trickster Taugi and his brother Aulukuma (VII). Taugi's speech and action seem to invert the formula laid out in Cuckoo's actions. His speech represents a point of view that is resisted, even irreconcilable with those around him. His actions are unratified and invalid, or even incapable of receiving validation. Although his brother Aulukuma apparently validates his plans, there is a muttered aside (lines 406–408) that tells us of his puzzlement about Taugi's compulsive behavior. Taugi's actions are therefore not developed through dialogue (as are Cuckoo's) but monologically in his mind—or, for Kalapalo, through the spell-laden musical mentation of the trickster's *itseketu*. (In other stories, we will see, people are musically enchanted by Taugi, instead of being convinced or even coerced through speech. At best, they only protest ineffectually to one another. At worst, they are destroyed outright.)

Related to the contrast between validation and non-validation is a social distinction. In the segments concerned primarily with Cuckoo's activities, there is a continuous chain of interaction in which one of the participants in each of the constituent segments also participates in the dialogue that follows that segment. But there is a disjunction between these segments and the last one, when the chain of interaction is broken. At the beginning of VII, an unidentified "someone" tells Taugi about the grass. There is no evidence that this person was a participant in the previous action involving Cuckoo and his relatives, and, to judge from other stories, most likely this "someone" was a marginal outsider who spied upon human existence (an Agouti, perhaps, digging in the trash mounds around the house, as in "Kafani-fani"). In other words, Taugi does not actively participate in Cuckoo's social network, but stands apart. This is much more than a "geographic" distance; it is more truly ecological in that Taugi's speech and actions can't actually be validated at all because he exists outside the sphere of human social life. More cosmological than personal, the portrayal of Taugi has eternal implications for all human beings. Whereas the validation of Cuckoo's actions perpetuates a situation of solidarity that is characterized by exchange, Taugi's action is not only about invalid action, but about the opposite of exchange: it is one-sided, senseless destruction that doesn't even benefit the destroyer. And, yet, we have to remember that Taugi is a trickster. While his actions can't be validated, there is an ambiguity to them that we see in the consequences he attributes to them. Thatching grass is no longer easy to work with, but the very fact that it is now an unpleasant and difficult material to work with makes human beings stronger, since they are forced by necessity to work harder. It is in such hidden consequences that Taugi's trickster character achieves its most optimistic form of expression.

A second story, "Nakika," transforms the basic elements of "Cuckoo": an effort to marry, a gift given in exchange, conversational speech in which validation is sought, a contrast between a collective effort and one that is excessively subjective. Juxtaposed in the story of Nakika are the failed trickster Taugi (helped by his younger brother Aulukuma) and the target of his deception, the sybarite Nakika. Whereas Cuckoo modestly and with some hesitation seeks to marry and to contribute his hard labor to the household of his relatives, Taugi and Aulukuma disguise themselves so as to seduce the lusty Nakika, because they crave his magnificent house of red and blue macaw-tail feathers (trimmed with black vulture feathers below, where thatching tends to get ragged and dirty). Cuckoo turns his feces into thatching grass after some effort; Taugi and Aulukuma ask Bee to bring his poisonous pollen cache to Nakika, pretending it is the material for making delicious piqui soup.

Much of the story is told from Taugi's point of view, but, as in "Cuckoo," there is a shift at the end to the entirely different point of view of Nakika. Whereas the dialogues in "Cuckoo" develop a deepening sense of validation, validation is never achieved in the dialogues between Nakika and Taugi. Action is always diverted, hindered, or at best only partially fulfilled. In "Nakika," dialogues are almost always confrontational, except at the very beginning and end, with nothing but destruction achieved. Almost from the start, the narrative progress is blocked by so many half-penetrated deceptions that it seems inevitable the trick will fail. In fact, there are too many clues, and in the end Taugi and Aulukuma are found out.

During the second part of the story, Nakika admits to the shamans he calls to cure him that he was seduced by the beauty of the women. They seemed "all right" to him. Still, he is saved from being poisoned to death because he "knew all about them," that is, he suspected things weren't really as "right" as they seemed. Nakika, while pretending to go along with his "wives," in fact begins to be wary of them, and eventually saves himself from being poisoned to death. However, he is temporarily overcome by lust for the two "women," and by his desire for the rich fruit soup, which kills the rest of his people. Taugi's trick works, if only temporarily, because he successfully overstimulates Nakika's love of luxury to the point that Nakika doesn't really think about what might be going on.

Nakika

Told by Ulutsi at Aifa. July 7, 1982.
Bracketed sentences are remarks and questions I asked as the what-sayer.

A house he had made, how beautiful! It wasn't thatched, though.
  He had made it with macaws' tail feathers.
  And the layers beneath them were made with the tail feathers of
harpy eagles.
  And hawk-eagle tail feathers.
  Teh! Those who saw it said the whole thing was a magnificent red!   5
    It was perfect, those who saw it said.
  That was why someone began to feel envy.
Anyway, here along the lower edge of the house was something else,
vultures' feathers,
    vultures' feathers.
  And here, close to the ground as well.   10
    Here, and here.
  That was because they could throw off the rain.
    They threw off the rain.
    Threw off the rain.
      Vultures.   15
  Now, the house never got touched, the house never got touched
    by the rain.
Because of that someone was on the point of feeling envy.
    Taugi began to envy him.
  "Well! You," he said to his younger brother.   20
    "Aulukuma," he said.
    "Let's go see our grandfather," he said,
    "Our grandfather."
  "All right.
    All right, let's go."   25
  So they came to him to stir his desire.
  So that he would have to marry them.
  He would.
  He would have to marry them.
    The Nakika leader would marry them.   30
  "Let them all remain as they are.
    Let them all remain as they are."
Then they slept, they slept for five days.
  They had a grandfather who was Ātapa Bee, think of it. Ātapa
Bee.
    Ātapa Bee.   35
    Who was a kind of honey maker. [Yes. I know about it.]
    You do? Yes.

He was accustomed to pack his pollen caches into storage silos,
like these.
  And so he had a very tall one packed with piqui. [Oh, yes?]
    Yes.
"Grandfather," he said, Taugi spoke. "Grandfather," he said.
"Right after Aulukuma and I have slept five days, you will hurry
over.
  Bring it to us."
"All right.
  All right."
Then the two went on after that.
  The older sister went on, beautifully adorned with her pubic
ornament.
    Teh, how beautiful she was, those who saw her said.
  And the younger sister . . . the younger sister's breasts were *iñu*
shells, *iñu* shells. Made from *iñu* shells.
    Yes.
As I was saying, the younger sister's breasts were *iñu*, I'm told.
How beautiful were her necklaces, hanging full between her
breasts.
  Now, her older brother's breasts were *oīke* shells.
    Oīke shells.
    Yes.
"Let's go," he said.
  "Let's go."
They took along their seats to lay beneath them on the ground.
The kind made of split palm shoots.
  Their seats.
Their long hair fell down to here.
  their beautiful long hair.
The younger sister's hair was very long, falling below her waist.
They had both turned into women.
  Those men.
Then *tititi*, early in the day they walked into the settlement.
"Waah, kooh, kooh. Here come his brides.
Here come his brides," they called out.
"Why, here come Nakika's brides.
They're almost here.
Here come Nakika's brides!" they called out.
  "Very well."
Then *tititi* they walked over to him.
"Why, I see you are certainly here, my relatives, my sisters," he
went.
  "I see you are certainly here, my relatives."

"We two are certainly here, our younger sister and I, 75
   we two.
Yes, we two, our younger sister and I.
   We two."
"Very well," he went.
   "Very well," he went. 80
"Now I shall marry you both."
"Now our younger sister and I have come to you.
   Our younger sister and I."
So the younger sister slept beneath him, while the older sister slept
by his side.
   Yes. 85
Teh! They both were very beautiful.
   Yes.
They stayed there . . . [*interruption*]

Listen.
   They stayed there, and they slept, they slept, 90
      and after they had slept two nights,
   "Let's all go to get manioc, let's all go," Nakika said.
   "All right, let's go as you say," they answered.
      He wanted to do that so he could touch them.
   He wanted to make love to them. 95
"No," the older sister said.
   "No," she said.
"We're not well at all, my younger sister and I.
      We're not well.
   We're not well this time." 100
   "All right.
      All right."
"We'll have to sleep five more days.
After we have slept five days, our grandfather will come to us,"
she said.
   "All right," he answered. 105

Then they slept, they slept, they slept for five days.
   Next their grandfather approached, carrying his silo on his back.
      But they were still unable to prepare food.
      But they were still unable to prepare food.
      But they were still unable to prepare food. 110
      But they were still unable to prepare food.
      [*interruption*] [All right. Go on.]

Listen.
When the sun was over here he came,
    their grandfathers the Bees came carrying the silos.   115
    "Kao kao kao," the others cheered. They walked in.
        Moh, they carried some huge things on their backs.
            Fermented piqui.
                Fermented piqui.
        Those were Bee's pollen caches.   120
He had preserved his pollen caches, until the silos stood very tall.
    That was what Taugi had wanted him to carry to them.
But anyway he arrived, and came to them, to where his
grandchildren stood.
    "Here they are. Take this one. Take this one. Take this one.
    Take this one. . . ."   125
"Grandfather," Nakika said.
    "Yes?" he answered.
"Why, I see that it's really you."
    "Yes, it's really me."
    "Your grandchildren wanted to marry me.   130
        They wanted to marry me."
"Very well. As you see, that's why I've come."
    Even so, they were still unable to prepare food.
    Even so, they were still unable to prepare food.
    They were menstruating.   135
    That's why they were still unable to prepare food.

Then they stayed there, and the next day they prepared their drinks.
    "Tomorrow we'll be ready. That's because we'll be able to prepare
    it then." (They were men who were actually talking that way.)
    "Tomorrow we'll be ready, our younger sister and I. We can't
    prepare any food right now," she said.
    "Tomorrow we'll be ready to give it to your followers. We'll be able
    to prepare our grandfather's gift," I'm told she said.   140
        "We want to."
    "All right," Nakika answered.
        "All right," he answered.
Then the next day they were ready.
    Taugi got ready to make it.   145
    "All right now, let's prepare it," he said, "For our grandfathers."
    So they prepared some cold manioc soup.
Then they prepared some,
    they prepared some cold manioc soup.
    They prepared what Atapa Bee had carried to them.   150
        While their grandfathers sat waiting.
        Their grandfathers sat waiting. [Nakika?]

Nakika? No. His wives were doing that. His wife. His wife. Taugi
and his brother. [Oh. Taugi and his brother.]
Next they mixed it all up,
   and then, when the sun was here it was ready.
But they didn't drink any.
   They didn't sip any of it, none.
   They had to be careful not to do that,
   since it was poisonous.
   Yes.
Then, they were ready.
So they brought it out, they brought more out, they brought more
out, they brought more out.
Next, "Share this.
   Share this among your followers."
   "All right!"
Then Nakika did it, he shared it. *Tah*, that stuff the others had made
for him looked just like delicious piqui soup.
     Like piqui soup. [Piqui soup?]
     Yes.
   So there was no reason that he should not have shared it, there
was no reason that he should not have shared it.
   There was no reason that he should not have shared it, and he
shared it, until it was all used up.
The older sister offered some to Nakika in a gourd spoon.
   "Won't you try some of this?"
   To her husband.
   "Won't you try some now?"
   "All right, but I'm going to wait for a while," he said.
     "I'll wait a bit longer," he said.
     He knew all about it.
   "I'm going to wait for a while," he said.
     "I won't forget to drink some."
When the first portion was finished,
   the older sister passed around more of it.
By now the sun was here, it was late afternoon.
   The sun was almost gone.
"Drink some now," she said.
   "Drink some," she said.
   The older sister drew some out for him, *puuk*.
Then while she held it up to him, he sipped just a little while she
held it up to his mouth. He swallowed what he had just sipped.
     Yes.
   He only swallowed two little sips.
     Yes.

155

160

165

170

175

180

185

190

That was all. Following that, the people in one of the houses started
to vomit, and those in another house were vomiting, those in
another house were vomiting, those in another house were
vomiting.
> *Bu, bu, bu, bu* they were all dying because of what Nakika's
> wives had given them.
In the other houses *buh*, they were all dying because of what Nakika's
wives had given them.
> As for that other person—Nakika—"We're not going to make it at
> all!" he said.
> "What happened to us?" he asked.
> "Why, Nakika's wives have poisoned us," they all said.
>> "They've poisoned us.
>> They've poisoned us."
> The two heard what he was saying about them.
So, when it was pitch dark, they left after they had heard what he
had said.
> "You," the older sister said.
> "Nakika," she said.
> "I must go now," she said.
> "I must go now," she said.
> "We've been shamed for good.
>> Our younger sister and I.
>> For good."
So, people in one house were all dead, and those in another house
were all dead,
> and those in another house were all dead,
> It had happened to everyone, those who saw it said.
> They were all dead after Taugi did that to them.
> He had poisoned them all with that stuff.
>> With Ātapa's pollen caches.
>> Ātapa.
> He had killed them all.
That was all. The two went off after that. They had killed them all.
> People in one house were all dead, another household were all
> dead, another household were all dead, another household were
> all dead, another household were all dead, another household
> were all dead. The two had gone away because they had all died.
> And as for Nakika, he also had taken some of it when she offered
> it to him.
>> He was poisoned by it.
>> He was poisoned.
> Just a little, not very badly.
> He had drunk just a little.
> That was all.

195

200

205

210

215

220

Then,
   "Please come here," he said. 225
   "Please come here," he said.
   His grandfathers.
   His grandfathers.
   To his grandfathers.
The tiny fish called Tefuku. And Figutungu, that tiny one who lives
in the oxbow lakes and the grasslands lakes, the tiniest one. 230
   That one.
   And Ñekïgi.
   He as well.
   And Fugoi.
   Fugoi. 235
That was all. Look, he had four grandfathers.
   "Come on, come on, let's all go see our grandchildren," they said.
   "Let's go see them right now."
   "All right, let's go!"
   And so they came there. 240
   They all appeared after that . . . and they stood beside him.
"All right now," and they began to examine Nakika's people.
   They went around doing that.
   They began to examine Nakika's people.
   "What is all this, Grandson?" they asked. 245
   "Well, we're like this because they did something to us.
   Only my relatives could have done it.
      Only my relatives could have done it."
   "Even so, how did they manage to get away with it?
   Even so, how did they manage to get away with it?" 250
   "It was too much for us. Although I knew what they were trying
to do to us.
   Even though I knew what they were trying to do to us."
"We should do something now!"
   The first one was curing them.
   That was Tefuku. 255
   He was curing them.
Next the tiniest one of all, the tiniest chiclid.
   Figutungu did it.
And the one who followed him was Nekïgi.
   And there was even another one. 260
And then, that one who followed him was Fugoi.
They all cured those other people,
   the people of one house, and another house, and another house
   . . . So that they all got better, they turned to life. *Mbiih*, all that
   had happened before was done away with!

They were all cured.
    They were all cured, they were alive.   265
        Yes.
        They were all better after that.
"It's over, isn't it?" Nakika said.
    "Yes, it is."
    "Yes, I knew about them.   270
        I knew about them.
    Only I should have known better.
        I should have known better.
            I should have known better.
That only happened because I agreed when they seemed all right
to me, they seemed to be women," he said.   275
        That's what I'm told he said.
The others left after all that,
        and they went away.
That's all, that's just what happened.

The stories of "Cuckoo" and "Nakika" illustrate a commonplace about Kalapalo narratives. Most quoted speech in these stories is dialogue discourse, in which two people talk to each other.[10] Indeed, like many people, the Kalapalo understand speech in general to be preeminently dialogical. But, within this dialogue discourse, there is often an emergent collective monologue, a sharing of a single point of view. The power and authority of the social whole, in other words, is seen to exist by virtue of ratification, validation, and reference to traditional and commonly agreed-upon authority. Dialogue of this distinctive kind assists in creating a coherent, shared understanding of the content of what is being discussed. It also brings about a shared understanding and explicit acceptance of explanatory or didactic messages and particular points of view and interpretations. The narrative progression in "Cuckoo" leads in the direction of community solidarity and mutual confidence. Conversations effect a successful tie between two families, expanding the domain of interpersonal ties and increasing their force. All this is resisted and subverted by "Lies About Himself."

Invalidation thus poses some real dangers, since for the Kalapalo the continuation of their particular way of life depends utterly upon validation. So, in "Mïti," the next story, as in "Nakika," invalidation of domestic decisions has disastrous consequences. Just as Taugi occasionally violently deceives characters who mock and resist his selfish desires (not just Nakika, but also the Currasows, Lizards, and Ducks in "Origin of Fire," for example) so does a rejected suitor make a horrible example of poor Mïti.

Miti

Told by Kambe at Aifa. March 1, 1979.
Notes appear on page 292.

This is about Miti,
    someone's wife's sister.
The younger sister was married.
    She herself,
      the older sister, was unmarried.   5
He kept desiring her.
    But she rejected him,
      he was rejected.
        Their husband was rejected.
"No." She didn't want him.   10
    "No, I don't want to."
      She didn't want him.
And so he went sometime later to an oxbow lake.
    Approaching that place he came across some snake's eggs,
      snake's eggs were what he noticed.   15
There he wrapped them up *pu pu pu pu.*
    He roasted them for her food.
      She was going to eat them.
        They were for his wife's sister.

When the sun was in the western sky he arrived home.   20
    After he had finished doing that, he came home carrying the fish
he had caught on his back inside a basket.
    He had wrapped up . . . he had wrapped up . . .
      he had wrapped up the snake's eggs.
After he finished doing that he returned.
    He carried the snake's eggs which he'd wrapped up earlier.   25
      Those of a snake monster.
"Give this to your older sister," he said to his wife,
    "There were some fish eggs there I wrapped up."
      "All right."
They were in his carrying basket by the storage platform,
    where he had set down his carrying basket.   30
      He had put it down.
"Go ahead," he gave it to his wife.
    "Here's something for her to eat."
      "All right."
        He had wrapped them up very carefully.   35

Then she ate them.
　　She must have eaten them up quickly, that woman.
　　　　She was single, without a husband.
　　　　　　She had no husband.
　　　　The younger sister did have a husband, though. 　　　40
　　　　　　But that other one had no husband.
　　Finally those things I spoke of went into her stomach.
　　　　Then within her stomach they cracked open.
　　　　　　What had happened inside there to make them crack open?
　　　　Something very large *boh!* started to grow inside her stomach. 　　　45
　　　　She was hugely pregnant like this, while her body grew much
　　　　thinner.
　　　　　　She became even thinner even though it had only been there
　　　　　　a short while.
　　　　Not long after she had eaten the eggs there was something in
　　　　her stomach.
　　　　　　A coiled-up snake.
　　　　Boh! It was this size, huge. 　　　50
　　　　That thing was very long.
　　　　　　Inside her stomach.
　　　　　　　　"Why must your delivery be so late?"
　　She would go to get wood,
　　　　to get bark she would go. 　　　55
　　　　　　She would go to get the covering of a tree.
　　When she would go to get bark, as she would pull it off,
　　　　boh! she would fall down.
　　She would arrive home with the bark after that happened.
　　Then right away she would go to get water. 　　　60
　　She now realized something was wrong with her stomach.
　　She went about bruised,
　　　　bruised.
　　"A snake must be causing this.
　　　　This is nothing at all like our children. 　　　65
　　　　　　It's a snake."
　　　　　　　　Mïti was her name.

She went again to get wood.
　　She must have gone another time to get wood,
　　　　and she finally almost pulled a piece away,
　　　　　　the covering of *fala*. 　　　70
　　"Mother, I will make it come off," someone said.
　　　　The thing that was inside her stomach said that!
　　　　　　The thing that was inside her stomach spoke to her.
　　　　　　　　"I will make it come off, Mother." 　　　75

"(This thing is speaking to me!)
   Very well, go get it, if you wish," she said to it.
      That was how she spoke to what was inside her stomach.
She came to the tree,
   duuu and crouched beneath the tree with her legs apart.   80
Bok, she sat down beneath the tree,
      bok.
Then *tsutsutsu* it broke the waters.
   Inside her that began to happen.
The snake did that,   85
   and it started to go up the tree *popopopo.*
High up, it was doing that,
   it went to the top of the tree.
Chiuk! It tore off the bark.
   Bom! it threw it down.   90
      Chiuk! Bom!
It was pulling it off,
   it was pulling off its mother's firewood.
      It was pulling off the bark. *Chiuk! Bom!*
It had finished.   95
   A part of it was still inside her while it was doing that.
Then it returned inside *ti ti ti.*
   It returned inside.
It coiled up as it must have done before *paupaupau,*
   it coiled up inside her stomach.   100
She rose and tied up the bark.
   She realized now what was wrong inside her stomach.
"There's nothing human at all about this creature inside me,
   it's not human."
She came home right away.   105
   Bom! She arrived.
      She threw down *bom* what the snake had pulled off for
      her.
         For its mother, *bok!*
She slept right after that,
   she slept.   110
      She now realized what was wrong with her stomach.
"Is there anything at all I can do? I don't know!"
   She woke up.
"Go get some water," her younger sister said, so she went to
the water's edge.
   There she remained, sadly.   115
She now realized what was wrong with her stomach.
   "What's going to happen to me?" she asked herself.

So listen.
"I'll go get some palm fruit," she said to her younger sister,
"I'll go get some palm fruit," she said.   120
"All right, go if you wish," the other said.
"You must come back soon."
"Yes, I'm leaving right now."
She went to Angafuku, where there were some burity palms.
Because she went to look for a tall one,   125
    that kind of palm, with bunches of fruit hanging from it.
We eat its fruit.
    Fruit hanging down from such a one as that.
        A very tall palm.
"Might you pull this one down for me?" she asked,   130
    "Will you pick this for me?"
"I want to get it, Mother, I want to get it."
    Once again what was inside her stomach said that.
"Very well, go if you wish," she said.
    She was glad the snake wanted to pick the fruit.   135
She had a large oyster shell, the kind called *aue.*
    She held one of those close to her.
        Aue, the very sharp one.
            Tsik, like that.
She went beneath the tree.   140
Ti ti ti once again she did that, and its head came out.
Po po po after it did that it went up the tree.
    It went far up to the top of the tree.
It went to the top of that tree, to the top of the burity palm.
    All of it had come out, *mbisuk!*   145
        No longer was any left inside her.
            It had come out completely *mbisuk!*
                There it was.
"Here's some," it said.
It cut down the fruit.   150
Tuluk! it came back.
That's all there is!"
After saying that, it crawled back down.
While it was doing that she slashed at it, *tsiuk!*
    she slashed at what she had held inside her,   155
        she slashed at the snake.
Tsiuk, dzidzidzi.
    Tsiuk! Tsiuk! Tsiuk! as it came from far above where it had
    been,
        bom! it died.

Then she piled it up. 160
 Pok! Pok! Three piles.
 Three.
 Piled high were the different lengths,
  what had been inside her stomach.
 Pok! she went to where its head lay and picked it up. 165
  Pïpïpï she whirled it above her head.
   "Here comes the food of Mortals!"
 It was going to be our food,
  what she had just done that to became the electric eel.
 Tum! she threw it into the water. 170
  "Go be the food of my people."
 Because of what she did we eat it.
  That thing's its head.
She had made three large piles, *pok pok pok.*
 She broke off some *kedyite.* 175
  She used the branches of *kedyite* she had broken off to cover
  them, *pok.*
When she came home,
 her stomach was very small,
  as she came home.
 The burity fruit was on her head. 180
 Undiki, she came inside.
 "Look!" her younger sister said.
  "Look!" she said.
 "Oh! She's flat!
  What happened to it?" she asked, 185
   "What became of it?"
    It took a long time for the other to tell her what had
    happened.
 Her mother came to her to listen.
  "Mother," she went,
   "What was inside me was certainly not human," she said, 190
   "not human."
    "No, it wasn't," her mother answered.
  "That thing inside me was really a snake," she said to her
  mother.
   Her mother sat listening.
   Mïti still had that same thing with which she had been
   able to cut it up. 195

Following that she stayed there.
 The snake no longer came outside as it had done before.
Then while she stayed there the new moon rose,
  her moon rose.

Then she went away.   200
    "Now I will see what's beginning to happen there."
She went away to look,
    to what she had cut up.
    One had begun to molder, another had begun to molder, and
    the third had begun to molder.
        This was their body hair,   205
            they were already becoming human.

She stayed there longer,
            until three of her months had passed.
    She went again to see.
        One pile, another pile, another pile was there,   210
            of human beings.
    Those same people were Kayapo Indians.*
        Those same people were Kayapo,
            they were Kayapo.
    They were,   215
        they themselves.
            They were Mïti's womb contents.
    Those Fierce People came into being that way,
        unlike we people.
    The mother of the snake,   220
        Mïti is their mother.
    Some were tall.
        Others that she had cut were short.
    Like this were the ones she kept doing that to,
        long ones.   225
    Like this were the ones she had done that to,
        the cut-off ones.
            They were short.
                Imhmm! There were so many of them!

By touching her relative's food when she had been doing all that,   230
    she polluted them.
        She polluted them.
            She polluted them when the snake was inside her
            stomach.
    Her uncle, his brothers,
        their mother's brothers,   235
            the men,
                they would come to their sister's house and hit her
                stomach.
                    It was covered with bruises.

Only one of the brothers told them,
"Don't do this to our sister," he said to them.   240
"We don't know why our sister is like this."
She was bruised all over.
"Mother," she said,
"Mother, *boh ah,* there are so many Fierce People!
Have my dear uncles make their arrows,   245
have my dear uncles make their arrows."
"All right," she answered.
"Ask your brother's children to make their arrows."
They began to make them,
on the following day, and the following day, the following day,   250
those were very long ones.
They also made bows,
their bows.
Tsu tsu.
When that was finished, they made bow cords.   255
Then they put them on, *bok bok.*
She gave them to her children,
all of them.
Bahhah to all of that great group!

"Mother," she went,   260
"They will remain as they are now, my dear uncles, because they
were the ones who slapped my stomach,"
tok! when her stomach was still full.
"The others are fierce."
"All right, you must have them kill your uncles, have them kill
your uncles.
Except just one."   265
"All right," she said.
Very early it happened.
"Uh!" the fierce ones shouted out as they did that.
They shot everyone,
those of the snake did that.   270
They shot everyone, *tïk! tïk! tïk!*
Mbisuk! they were all dead.
Only one of her uncles and only the mother remained.
There they stayed.

Notes to "Mïti"
line
212   "Kayapo Indians": a Ge-speaking people the Kalapalo consider
           "Fierce People."

Chapter 4

Illusionists Modern and Ancient

At the height of the dry season, during the time the Kalapalo call Funggegi ("Rufous-Sided Heron," after the stars known to us as "Orion's Belt"), the Kalapalo must do the heavy and tediously repetitive work of harvesting manioc and clearing new fields. Their labors are only barely relieved by the fishing trips they occasionally take to the oxbow lakes that line the eastern side of the Culuene River. The days are very hot, and most people try to stay indoors as much as possible. On one such scorching afternoon, Kudyu shaved off all the hair growing just above his forehead, imitating a Suya man—a Fierce Person (*angikogo*)—whose photograph he had seen recently in a magazine. Kudyu, like many Kalapalo, has bad teeth, and some of these had just been pulled by a dentist from São Paulo who makes annual trips to the Upper Xingu. With his upper front teeth newly missing, Kudyu did look very strange. While some of the small children who always gather in his house were playing in the shaded doorway, he sneaked around from the back and suddenly peered at them from behind the house wall. The children shrieked and ran inside. This kind and generous person whom they so trusted had suddenly become a frighteningly weird apparition. But for Kudyu's wife and older sons, this sort of thing was to be expected of him, and they laughed at how easily he had grasped the delightful possibilities of the magazine photographs that had been passed around the week before.

Late one afternoon, after his trip to a nearby Brazilian Air Force base, the soft-spoken shaman Kwatagi came into the plaza in full paratrooper's get-up: orange jumpsuit, one of those triangular hats worn by soldiers, and heavy black rubber boots with lots of clips and clamps (these were part of the reason he traded some good bows and arrows for the outfit, he told me later, since he could use the bits of

Kwatagi

metal as tools when the boots wore out). His hair was newly cut army style, that is, too short and irregular for more reserved Kalapalo tastes. Kwatagi is a tall man, and the costume worked well. An old woman who was sitting in front of her house on the opposite side of the settlement called out to her household: "A Brazilian soldier is coming over to see us!" Her young granddaughter began crying, but everyone else who was watching laughed and cheered at the success of Kwatagi's disguise.

When I returned to the Kalapalo settlement of Aifa after a very long absence, four friends who met me at the airstrip helped me carry the things I had brought back to the community. For a half-hour, we walked from the canoe landing carrying the awkward parcels as best we could on our heads and shoulders. My excitement grew as the path led us past one familiar old tree after another and then across a gully where, for some reason—perhaps the many exposed tree roots or something I had heard about the place before I ever set foot there— I had always anticipated seeing a snake. When we could see the tops of the houses taking shape over the trees like enormous haystacks, my four companions excitedly told me to cover my head with a scarf, and to put on my sunglasses and my jacket. "You'll be Maria," they said. Maria was the Brazilian wife of one of their relatives, expected just then from Brasilia. Solemnly, they led me into their settlement, as if I were on some serious and unknown business. But as we walked in, heralded by the men's calls that always announce a visitor's entrance, I passed by a house where a familiar figure stood anxiously in the doorway. Turning to face me, Kuaku needed no more than a glance to see that it was I. Suddenly relaxing and smiling in a knowing way, she said in a matter-of-fact voice, "Oh, it's Elena returned to us again." We heard my name mentioned with surprise inside the house, and people next door passing the news between hammocks: "It's not Maria. It's Elena." The men who were with me grinned; their joke had been successful, and what's more, they felt they had deceived the entire settlement.

As mythological tricksters make sport with their enemies, so in these ways do people attempt to deceive one another. This kind of Kalapalo humor deliberately provokes anxiety or even dread. Many Kalapalo jokes consist of people trying, inappropriately, to create such feelings in one another. Such jokes are in the main visual, usually instigated by men, and depend upon disguise and the matter-of-fact demeanor. Kwatagi and Kudyu are only two of the many Kalapalo men who persist in teasing the rest of the community, trying to deceive and mildly alarm people whom they consider especially naive and trusting. These people all too easily misperceive the situation in which the joke occurs.

Erotic Tricksters

This characteristic joking, dependent on disguise and motivating anxiety, occurs as well in more private, erotic contexts. In fact, heightened eroticism seems related to a "trickster" form of sexuality, characteristic of Kalapalo, in which things never are what they seem. Kalapalo try to conceal their love affairs, even though lovers frequently couple close to where a spouse might be asleep or working nearby inside a house or in a field. So, most love affairs, while furtive, are tacitly recognized. At night, an "alligator" (a man sneaking around to visit a lover) easily can mistake a visitor lying in his lover's hammock for the woman herself. I once heard such a visitor allowing himself to be groped until the inevitable embarrassing discovery was made. The frustrated lover, rather than being angry, walked back to the group of men seated in the central plaza and, in a voice loud enough for those of us in the houses to hear, quickly told them what had happened. Loud cheers and giggly laughter followed: one alligator had discovered another.

Kalapalo Combs

It is customary for Kalapalo men to make combs for their lovers and—as a special gesture of affection—for their wives. The owners usually keep these beautifully made objects hidden away, wrapped in pieces of cloth to prevent soiling; the newer ones are most often taken out when the women groom themselves in private behind their houses. Although they are important grooming tools that help to thin the women's thick, snarly hair and to catch the lice eggs with which everyone is infested, Kalapalo combs are also objects of erotic contemplation. What's more, they are striking representations of what to the Kalapalo is the importance of illusion and deception in lovemaking.

The ambiguities that surround love affairs are most brilliantly expressed in the comb patterns themselves, patterns that are also woven into women's carrying baskets. The cotton materials used in weaving the combs allow for a play of light, texture, and shape, so that when the combs are held in different ways they seem to move, revealing hidden forms and contrasts between light and dark shapes. A design called "the arrows of Akwakanga" uses light to create contrasts of this kind when the comb is held up to the sun. Held horizontally or toward the ground, the contrast between the brown of the palm materials and the white thread—also a textural contrast—is the reverse of what appeared when the comb was held up to the light. A "diamond-in-square" pattern is a moiré weave that shifts from diamond-shaped representations of vulvas to an innocuous striped checkerboard. Yet another pattern works by "mirror-imaging," one side being the reverse of the other.

There is a particularly fine comb (called *akugifutofo,* "the agouti's image") that men often make for their brides early in the marriage. The name refers to the carved rodent images at each of the four ends of the comb's crosspieces. These are made from pieces of hardwood, rather than the usual palm slats, and are covered by basketry plaitwork. Agouti appears in the stories of "Kafanifani" and "The Original Piqui" as a sneak and a spy, a furtive character who lurks around the garbage dumps behind the house, where women pass on their way to the fields and latrine areas—and to assignations. In a position to know other people's secrets, Agouti often betrays women to their husbands. By carving the animal on this gift to a young wife, the maker advises discretion and creates a playful warning: "Be careful, there are agoutis all around (and I may be one of them)."

Teasing Each Other About Women

Along with their seemingly constant preoccupation with love affairs, men also enjoy teasing and punning, which heightens their speech and makes it especially interesting. Puns on people's names—allegedly forgotten for a moment—are one such "illusion" in speech.

Ifadyu was probably the most persistent Kalapalo punster I knew. One morning he came to the house of his father, Kambe, and remained standing in the doorway, gossiping about another family. When the subject of a certain woman came up, he pretended to forget her name: "Uh, uh, what's-her-name, uh, *pagina* ('toasted manioc flour')." His older sister laughingly told him the woman's correct name: *Tagima*. Ifadyu seemed to "forget" this woman's name quite often. I once heard him pretending to try to recall it, saying, "*süigïpe eku, eku. Sagima, eku, Tagima* ("her teeth, what's-her-name, what's-her-name, *Tagima*")."

Occasionally, I would hear men (and less often, very old women) tell mildly bizarre stories about love affairs that made both the story and the storytelling something of a joke. Sometimes, a man tells such a story about himself to an intimate friend (an *ato*), fantasy and incident becoming impossibly interlaced until the listener cuts him off with a skeptical sneer.

Kamina, Kwatagi, and I were seated one hot afternoon in an ephemeral patch of shade beside an oxbow lake called Kagayaña, where about twenty men were making a bamboo weir for a fish-poisoning expedition. We were trying to relax the best we could in the half-hour or so that seemed acceptable for my two companions to take a break from working in the scratchy, insect-ridden thickets. And as we shifted about, trying to find some comfortable spot to sit on the hard, blisteringly hot ground, Kamina abruptly began teasing his friend and trying to amuse me with a ridiculous tale about a love affair that may or may not have occurred in their youth:

Listen. I will tell you about what this person here used to do a long time ago at Wagifïtï. (me: "ah"; Kwatagi: smiles.)
He had a lover he used to visit over and over. (K, realizing he's about to be teased: "No, I didn't.")
A secluded maiden. (me: "Really, you saw her?"; K: "He's lying!").
Yes, I remember she was a mother of his. (me: "I see"; K, still grinning: "He's lying, worthless one, he's lying!")
"Mother," he used to call to her. "Mother, open the door for me." (Laughter from both of us.)
She was covered all over with a fungus infection. (me: "How disgusting"; K, laughing: "Oh, what he's saying!")
So she used to paint her entire body with red paint all the time, to cover her skin infection. (me: "She painted herself with red paint"; K: "That's the worst so far!")
To hide the fungus. (me: "ah"; K, laughing, gives up: "That's enough.")
She was his lover, his mother. I'm sure because I was there. (K, still laughing: "*That* is a *lie*, Elena.")

Like narrative proper (*akiñatunda*), these teasing sorts of stories (*tegutsunda*) require a listener-responder. Often, the only listener is the person being teased (though there are quite commonly people eavesdropping, as in the story "Women Kill Jaguar Sorcerers," where the entire setting provides an ominous contrast with the men's fun). The listener is expected to protest laughingly the outrageous content of the story, line by line. But, more usually, yelps of outrage are nicely juxtaposed with the bland, naive-sounding comments of another friendly but apparently "neutral" listener, to whom the story is directly told. All the people involved are friends, their intimacy growing in these very situations of relaxed joking, which usually occur during times of shared hard work.

Tegutsunda plays on the values of more formal storytelling. *Akiñatunda* generally is believed to instruct as well as to entertain, preserving traditional knowledge and particular memories and interpretations for future listeners. Ephemeral jokes, *tegutsunda*, parody those functions: the storyteller claims a historical interest for ludicrously unbelievable love affairs. And, while the relationship between narrator and what-sayer typically is one that effects a shared understanding of the story, that between teaser and teased is just the opposite: one in which points of view, and especially memories, are in deliberate conflict.

The Disgusting Dawn People

Anyone who has read even casually in older collections of Native American mythologies has almost certainly come across stories about people or animals whose excessive bodily appetites cause them to engage in foolish and absurd adventure. These adventures violate the reciprocity and solidarity that among the Kalapalo are maintained through conversational validation, as I have shown. Such stories are often explicitly about deception and tricks, and some (like the Winnebago Trickster and Navaho Coyote) involve specially designated sacred "trickster" characters distinguished by their apparently unstructured selves and oddly motivated buffoonery. Because they so often involve frank and even obscene references to bodily processes, our anthropological awareness of their significance has been sorely limited by a tradition of our own, partly prudish, partly prideful: that of leaving out of the great collections of Native American stories and jokes those that toy with genital and anal events. As a consequence, we have hardly advanced in our understanding of this vast body of narrative tradition since the beginning of this century, when Alice Fletcher complained to Franz Boas about the "stable-boy humor" of some indulgently obscene stories published by Alfred Kroeber.[1]

The Kalapalo call these "stories of Disgusting Dawn People." *Kïtsï angifolo* are the "disgusting, witless Dawn People" who stupidly pervert normal human feeling and suffer ridiculously in the end from their incompetent loss of self-control. Like us, Kalapalo associate obscenity with vulgarity and inelegance. Their obscene stories concern people who misdirect their desire onto inappropriate objects: childless, they lovingly raise toads and worms as if they were human offspring; having no lovers, they have intercourse with snakes, dogs, or such phallic objects as lumps of resin or knots of wood. Palms, seedlings of piqui trees, dung beetles, and other peculiar objects provoke erotic longings because, in the minds of disgusting Dawn People, they evoke fantasies of human lovers. Disgusting Dawn People are caught in absurd lies when they fail to cover up previous peccadilloes, and they suffer and even die in a particularly ridiculous manner when their physical passions get the better of them.

Unlike other Kalapalo *akiña*, which take much longer to tell, a narrator quickly runs through several of these utterly improbable tales, and people take turns telling them to one another. Tellers and listeners start the session with a certain degree of polite reserve, created by the soothing, relatively innocuous tales with which speakers begin. The increasingly ridiculous stories gradually weaken this control and become a joking test of the participants' ability to preserve their public composure. The humor lies in engendering in a listener the very feeling—lust, nausea, or greedy passion for a certain food—that is being ridiculed in the story. A man might suddenly have an erection during the course of one of the erotic tales, or a woman might visibly retch at the thought of the food Dung Beetle Woman serves her husband or the image of the repulsive Toad Children fed by their human mother. These people have succumbed to the seductive game of the Disgusting Dawn People stories and must suffer the hilarity of the rest of the party. In turn, they have a good chance of taking gentle revenge when next the roles of teller and listener are reversed.

While these narratives are very much like the classic Trickster tales in their portrayal of "selfish buffoonery," and their emphasis on the necessity of control of one's physical appetites for the preservation of social harmony, they are much less moralizing tales than they are narrative jokes. Unlike narrators of the stories I presented in earlier chapters, people who tell disgusting Dawn People stories do not frame the speech of their characters with the evidential particle *ti*, "they say," "I'm told," or "tradition says." I think this is because while the stories are "traditional," they are considered "fictive" or even "made up," much like the teasing and joking among men I discussed earlier in this chapter. And like those jokes, stories of disgusting Dawn People have a reduced narrative format which is in part replaced by detailed *scenes* in which the mechanics of strange passions are evoked as in theatrical tableaux. This makes it easy for the stories to be used by tellers to play a gentle trick on their listeners; they are a source of great fun for the Kalapalo, for the very feelings that are mocked are forever the substance of community-wide gossip. They are directly concerned with the absurdity of human life, suggesting to the Kalapalo that it is possible to laugh, even uproariously, while something utterly horrid or repulsive is occurring. In the disgusting Dawn People stories, feelings of worry about social competence, and the absurd problems people have controlling their physical passions, are the object of a good deal of mythological parody.

The first stories in this chapter were told to me one afternoon as I was sitting in the house of Nikumalu and her husband, Kwatagi. I had been playing a tape of music for them, after which Kwatagi—lying in his hammock with his youngest son, a boy of about five—asked me if I had heard the story "Woodknot Lover." When I answered no, he said he would tell it to me. When he finished his story, the couple's three unmarried daughters, who had been listening nearby with their mother as they prepared the day's manioc soup, urged him to continue. Kwatagi cheerfully kept talking until his son's squirming impatience put an end to the stories.

Stories Told by Kwatagi at Aifa. July 8, 1979
Notes appear on page 307.

I. She Hit Her Lover with Her Manioc Turner

Listen,
    continuing with one about a manioc turner,
        a manioc turner.

Late in the afternoon when there was no one else in the house,
        no one else in the house,
            a husband was there.
                His wife had gone to the manioc field,
                    so no one else was in the house.
        Then he came to the house next door.
            Someone was beginning to make manioc bread.
                "Lie down with me."
                "Wait a moment, I'm about to make some manioc bread."
                "I see. Come on right now, lie down with me."
                "Wait a moment," she said,
                    "Wait."
                "That's enough, come here right now, come on right now
                and lie down with me."
                "Wait a moment," she said,
                    "I want to make some manioc bread."
            Then he got up.
                "Come on right now and lie down with me."
            She was annoyed,
                and she jumped up still holding her manioc turner.
            Boh! she accidentally hit him here,
                on his forehead.
            Titi, blood came and he left when that happened,
                he went away to his own house,
                    and he stayed there.

    Then his wife approached carrying manioc on her head.
        "Take off my basket."
            "All right."
        Then he got up.
            A pole for bracing the house wall was nearby.
        Tok! he bumped into it.
            "Hey, I just bumped into this!"

As he came toward her after that *maah!*,
  his blood really flowed down from his having done that,
    while he put down her basket.
  His wife washed it off with water,
    she washed it off.
"I'll go bathe now."
  His wife went,
    she went *tititi*.
Her lover went to meet her.
    They were together.
  "What's the matter with that guy?" he asked.
  "I don't know. He seems to be lying to me about his having just
  banged his forehead on the big house pole."
  "That other guy's wife did that to him when she hit him with a
  manioc bread turner," he told her,
    "That's how it really happened."
Then she came back to him.
  "Someone just told me that other guy's wife just hit you with
  her manioc bread turner."
  "Who told you?"
  "Yes, you came to her."

Listen.

II. A Lover Killed by Her Pet

Someone was making manioc bread again.
  "Come on right now and lie down with me."
    "Wait a moment."
  Suddenly he had an erection,
    he had an erection.
  Her pet bird was perched above him,
    her pet bird.
  "Come on right now and lie down with me,
    lie down with me."
  "Wait a moment,
    I want to make some manioc bread."
  "Come on now and lie down with me," he told her.
    "Come on now," he told her,
      come on!"
        "Wait!"

He fell asleep still doing as before,
  he fell asleep as aroused as before.
Watch out!
  Watch out!
Because while that was happening,
  tchew! her pet came down,
    tsik! to kill it while he was sleeping.
Tsiu, tsiu, tsiu, it ate it up,
  while the man lay asleep.
It ate his penis, *tsiu, tsiu, tsiu,*
  right down to the bone!
Pupupu it flew away.
  Buh, its throat was filled.
    So the man died.

Then she came to lie down.
  "All right, now I can lie down with you."
    Well, he was already stiffened,
      he had stiffened.

Listen, they were Dawn People.

III. Snake Lover

Something was done with *fū* the two-headed snake.
  Someone did something with a snake.
    A person without a husband.
This woman here doesn't have a husband.
  Tagima doesn't have a husband at all.
    That woman also had no husband.
By her side, underneath a piece of giant reed she kept a *fū*.
  She would paint herself to do something with it,
    at dawn she would paint herself.
  She painted her forehead to do something with it.
Then she would go to the manioc fields.
Then she would go afterward to the water,
  then she would go there.
Afterward she would scrape the manioc while the other was
inside the giant reed,
  underneath her seat.
Then while she was occupied with scraping manioc she would make
love to the *fū*.

Crazy, she always made love to it while she was doing that.
Tititi she made love to it while she was doing that,
 she pressed down on it in the way I described.
Her brother's wife noticed it.
 Her brother's wife noticed it while she was lying in her
 hammock.
 Afterward the woman carried it beneath her hammock.
Then she went away once again.
 The woman almost made love to it again but after her brother's
 wife saw it she beat it to death.
 The woman was in the manioc fields when the other beat it to
 death *tuk!* on its head and it died,
 her *fu* died.

Then the woman arrived home.
 She scraped the manioc roots after she came back,
 she was scraping the manioc roots, *si, si.*
It was dead because of what the other woman had done.
She looked at it.
 It was already stiff,
 because of what the other woman had done.
"How my pubic ornament is hurting me, oi, oi,"
 how she wept, because she loved it!
 The one who had beaten it was in the manioc fields.
She arrived home,
 the woman's brother's wife arrived home.
"What's the matter with you?" she asked,
 "What's the matter with you, now? What?
 Does it have something to do with your teeth hurting?
You're really crying because I beat that *fū* to death, that one you
kept underneath you.
 I was the one who beat the *fu* to death," she told her.
Buh, the other said nothing,
 she fell silent.
 "Very well."
 And so she stopped crying.

IV. Toad Child

Then, "All right now."
 Someone was cooking hot manioc soup.
 Why, her child was a *kagifugu,* a giant toad!
 She kept one this size in that way,
 a big giant toad.

I don't know why it wore necklaces,
    the giant toad's necklaces.
Buh hah! it had on many necklaces!
    Shell disk necklaces.
Its arm bands,
    its ankle wrappings,
        what ankle wrappings it had!
            That was how she dressed the giant toad.
When hot manioc soup was ready,
    "Now I'll scoop off some foam for my dear little one."
    Its mother scooped off some foam for it,
        when the soup was ready to drink.
Then she would go outside to give that stuff to the toad to lick,
    from a little spoon used for licking up the foam.
She kept going to it for that reason.
    When it was done, she wiped its lips,
        and then its parent would drink some.

Because she kept doing that her husband's sister followed her.
    Her husband's sister followed her.
        There it was, with its quivering throat.
At that place she clubbed it while it was doing that,
    and it died right away when she did that,
        it died.

The next day the woman came to see it.
    It was no longer alive,
        it was dead because her sister-in-law had killed it.
"Oi, oi," she wept,
    its parent wept.
        She came back.
"What's the matter with her?" someone asked.
    "She's that way because yesterday I happened to have clubbed a
giant toad."
        The other was weeping,
            boh, she fell silent.

Listen. She was a childless Dawn Person.

V. Alligatoring

Listen.
A Dawn Person went alligatoring,
       to his uncle's place.
    "I'll go next door," he said to his wife.
      He came alligatoring there.
    Inside the doorway was piqui fruit piled up between sticks,
      piqui in a pile.
  "My young relative," the older man told him,
      "You mustn't do as I once did."
    "What happened, Uncle?" he asked.
    "Once I went alligatoring,
      alligatoring,
        and I must have almost reached there," he told him.
    "Just inside the doorway was a pile of piqui that I crashed into
as I came toward her.
    Tik! bokoh!
      How it all fell down, *hoh hoh!*
    Everyone inside woke up when that happened
      and I ran outside."

And another time,
  "My young relative," he said.
    "You must beware of doing as I once did."
  "What happened, Uncle?" the other said.
    "I went alligatoring as before,
      I went to do that.
    Right inside the doorway was a pile of boiled piqui.
    As I went on, *gitik, tsobobo, bïtsïki!* I was really covered with that
stuff!
      The piqui was all over me."
    "Oh, what did *he* just do?"
    Then I ran away.

Listen. They were Dawn People.
  Yes, listen!

"My young relative,
    you must beware of doing as I once did,
      as I was."
  "What happened, Uncle?" he said.

"I must have gone alligatoring.
   Then once again outside the house,
      outside the house over there just by the doorway out here
         a child had just relieved itself.
            The child had relieved itself in the entrance.
               The child had done that and its shit was there.
   'A child has just relieved itself here,' someone called.
      The mother came to throw it away when that was said.
   Onto my back!
      Onto my back, *pïtsïk!*"
He ducked down and went away after that.
   He went into the water to wash himself.

Then once again,
      he came again to his uncle.
   "My young relative," the other said.
   "Beware of doing as I once did."
   "What happened, Uncle?" he said.
   "I must have gone alligatoring," he said.
      "Right outside the house were wasps,
         wasps, *tsadauk!*
      Ouch, one stung me really hard on my face,
         so I ran away!"

Listen.

Notes to "Snake Lover"

The snake called *fü* in Kalapalo is the *cobra das duas cabecas* ("snake with two heads") in Brazilian Portuguese; since its tail closely resembles its head. It is a fairly common, pinkish reptile, which is often uncovered during excavations in the soil around the settlement. Toothless and utterly harmless, I have seen men teasing women by suddenly flinging them about.

Notes to Alligatoring Stories

The term "alligatoring" is used by the Kalapalo to refer to the practice of men sneaking around to visit their lovers' houses, just as "alligators" (caimans) move between different territories controlled by females.

A second set of stories was told to me by another old man, Kākaku of Dyagamï, who lived for many years with the Kalapalo. In this set, there is a conflict between wife and mother-in-law (or, in the last story, between husband and wife), revolving around a rude and inappropriate complaint. This conflict shows what happens when people refuse to validate each other and thus fail to carry forward the reciprocity necessary for successful social relations. The wife's activities in favor of her husband's relatives result in miraculous gifts for her new family. Unfortunately for her, her efforts are invalidated by her mother-in-law. Consequently, the reciprocity so crucial for developing an affinal bond is not reinforced by validation. Rather, it is deliberately thwarted by a disgusted reaction against the magical gifts.

Kākaku

I. Burity Palm Woman

"I wish this one were my wife," someone said,
        about a burity palm.
  Teh! it was a beautiful one,
        very tall and straight.
      "I wish this was my wife," someone said.
        A man spoke.
            Then he went away to his settlement.

At dusk—it was almost sunset—
  she came to him and stood outside,
        she stood outside.
      "Here I am," she said.
      "Who are you?" he said.
  He told his mother about her.
      "I'm not sure she's human.
        'Here I am, "Be my wife," you said to me.'"
      "Go get your sister," his mother said,
        "Go get your sister."
  He came to her.
      There she was *teh!* Burity Woman was a beauty!
        Burity.
      He brought her into the house,
        he took her inside.
She remained there beneath him.
  She remained there for a long time.
    She remained there for a very long time.
      A long time.

The hammock belonging to her mother-in-law was old and torn,
        it was an ugly thing.
  "Dear child," she said to her son.
    "Dear child, I would like your sister to knot my hammock.
    Have your sister knot my hammock."
        "All right," he said.
      "Make mother's hammock."
        "Very well."

Then she tore it apart and burned it until it was reduced to ashes.
   His mother came to him right away.
   "Has your sister made my hammock?"
   "No, she's just burned it."
   "How can you two make it that way?
      I now say to you,
         a hammock can't be made that way.
            Really, I can't understand why you two just put it on
            the fire."
She was really angry then.
   When she said that, she hurt her daughter-in-law's feelings.
   "Why did you two just burn it?
      For what purpose?"
Then Burity took the ashes and put them inside a gourd
container,
         inside a gourd.
   She moistened them *tik tik,*
      and they dripped down through a hole to the ground.
         Just as salt is made,
            it dripped down that way.

When the sun was high,
   she packed the ashes into her nostrils, *tik, tik,*
         she packed them into her nostrils.
   Ti ti ti ti she drew it out,
      she drew out
         a hammock.
   Di di di di di one like this kind came also,
      a broad banded hammock.
And once again as before she packed it into her nostrils again,
   and *ti ti ti ti ti ti,* one like this, a hammock with closely placed
   bands.
   Again *ti ti ti ti* an all-cotton hammock,
      one like this.
   "Look," *ti ti ti ti, ti ti ti ti ti* she said to her husband,
      "Look.
   Does your mother—she who is angry with me—see this?
   In our case, this is how we make them.
      In our case, this is how we make them.
         This is how we ourselves, this is how we make them."
   "Mother, here's your hammock."
   "Yes, indeed, it *has* been made!
      My hammock is done!"
         She was very happy,
            the one who was angry with her daughter-in-law.

Right away *teh,* she tied the beautiful hammock up.
   Teh heh, it was a magnificent one!
Then the woman gave one to each of his relatives.
   His brothers were given some more which she made the same
   way,
      and then her husband's hammock.

Then when it was growing dark at dusk,
   "I will go right now," she said.
      "I must leave you.
      I will leave you.
      Unfortunately, my own shame never stops, no.
      Since the time I heard our parent's anger against me.
         No, she will remain that way."
   "Don't go!"
   "No, I will go now."

Then when it became dark
   right away she did it,
      she went away.
      "She will remain as she is."
      "Don't go!"
Then she left,
      she went to her own place.
She went on,
      she went on and when she had gone far he saw that she had
      become the burity palm she had been before.

II. Water Hyacinth Woman

Teh, a water hyacinth whose leaves were beautifully rounded.
   "I wish this one were my wife," a person from the Dawn Time
   said.
      "I wish this one were my wife."
Then when it was becoming dark she came to him,
      she came to him.
   "Mother," he said,
      "Someone's here."
   "Go look right away."
He went to her and just as the other one had done,
   Water Hyacinth was a woman also, as happened before.
      Water Hyacinth Woman.

"Bring your sister inside, bring her inside."
    She came inside then,
        and she remained there,
            she remained there beneath him.
When finally some fish were brought to her,
        she boiled them.
    She peed,
        but her mother-in-law didn't see her.
            She probably peed right into it.
    Next she mixed it into the fish, *tik*
        and it became salty.
    And once again as before,
        she boiled some fish.
    Then she peed
        and it became salty.
    All the others ate it after she did that to it,
        they ate all of it up.
    "Well, this is nicely salted fish."
        They liked the way it tasted.

She kept doing that for a long time,
    when her mother-in-law saw her urinate.
        "How disgusting!" she said.
        "How disgusting, this is what we've all been eating," the
woman said to him.
        "Yes, this thing of hers is what we've both eaten. How
disgusting!
        You must let her be, your sister will always be this way.
        You must let her be.
        You must send your sister away, send her away.
        Really, it's disgusting that we both ate this sort of thing, how
disgusting!"
"I will leave right now," to her husband,
        "I will leave right now.
    My parent rejects me because she's disgusted with me.
        My parent rejects me because she's disgusted with me."

At dusk, "I'm leaving right now,"
    her husband kept doing as before,
        holding on to her.
        Nothing happened,
            she left.
                She was Water Hyacinth Woman.

Listen.

III. Piqui Man

Listen, piqui as well.
  Yes, even piqui.
  "I wish you were my husband," a woman told one of them as well.
    "I wish you were my husband."
  She was looking at a beautiful red piqui shoot *teh heh!*
    So clean, erect.
  Then he came to her.
    "Here I am,
      'I wish you were my husband,' you were the one who told
      me that."
    Following that he came inside.
  Then he stayed there and eventually she made some cold manioc
  drink for him.
    Then he went to where there was a burl on the piqui tree.
    Next he chopped at it *tsik tsik* until it opened *chiuk.*
    Pïtsapïtsapïtsa he took something out of the trunk to mix into
    what she had made for him earlier.
      He mixed it into the manioc drink.
    "Mix this in with it."
      "All right."
  Another time when she made some cold manioc drink for him,
    he went and afterward set some piqui pulp down outside,
      tsiuk
        and she mixed it in.
From that time on for a long, long time,
  for a really long time over and again he did that.
    "It's disgusting to have this done," someone said.
      His mother-in-law spoke as had the other one.
    "He's doing something disgusting.
      Our bowls are always greasy," she said to her daughter.
    "Our bowls are always greasy. He's been doing this too often.
      It's disgusting what he does."
  Because of that,
    "I'll go right now, I will go.
      Our parent just can't stop being disgusted by me,
        our parent finds me disgusting."
  When it became dusk,
    "You shouldn't go," his wife said,
      but he had already gone away.

IV. The Dung Beetle Wife

Feulugi the Dung Beetle became a Dawn Person's wife.
    Dung Beetle.
    "I wish you were my wife!"
Then again,
    she came to him,
      to him.
    "Here I am. Here.
      'I wish you were my wife' was what you said to me."
      As happened before she was brought inside.
    Afterward he went to live with her relatives.
    To Dung Beetle Woman's home.
      The man went to Dung Beetle Woman.
    Then she made some cold manioc drink for him and mixed
something into it.
      She went to get feces to use for that purpose.
    She made his cold manioc drink for him and she mixed it in.
      It became dark when she did that.
    "What could that rotten smell be?" he said to himself.
      Then he drank it.
    "What could that rotten smell be?"
Once again she went,
    and then she mixed it in.
    It was dark.
      She kept doing that with feces.
"Dear child," her mother said to her daughter.
    "Please ask your younger brother to get some split piqui."
      She wanted piqui that had already split open on the tree to
mix into what she had made.
      "Please ask your younger brother to get some split piqui."
Then she came to him,
    she came to her husband,
    "Go get Mother's split piqui."
    "Very well," he said.
Then he came to the trees,
    looking for some.
    He only found feces there,
      nothing more,
        so he came back.
She came to him.
    "There isn't any," he said.
    "I couldn't find anything.
    I only found feces when I was looking for that other thing.
      Feces was what I found."

"Hi hi," she laughed.
"That's just the thing we collect."
"Ugh! How disgusting!
Was that really what I've been drinking?
I must go right away if I did that, I'll go now!
I'll really go!"
When it became dark he left.
"Now I am certainly going."
"Don't go, I'm really very sad."
He went as she said that.
Because he had been the drinker of feces.

Notes to "Burity Palm Woman"

The erect, tall trunk of this palm (*Mauritia vinifera*) suggests the height considered desirable in a woman. Burity palm fronds are the source of fiber used in making hammocks and cords. The joke of this story lies in the fact that instead of laboriously processing palm fiber into string to be knotted with cotton thread, Burity Woman is able to make beautiful new hammocks for all her affines simply by stuffing the burned ingredients into her nostrils, and then withdrawing the finished hammocks.

Notes to "Piqui Man"

The red shoots suggest beautiful red paint, and the sturdy growth of a young man, as well as an erect penis. But the technique of making the drink evokes cannibalism.

Notes to "Dung Beetle Wife"

During the dry season, various species of dung beetles can be encountered in the latrine areas that surround the Kalapalo settlement. Piqui trees are often found there, too, hence the association between those plants and dung beetles.

These stories are hardly restricted to old men. At the settlement of Tanguro one afternoon, after a long day of transcribing and translating some of the more somber stories I had collected during the previous month, I was putting away my equipment and was about to take a swim in the river. Ugaki, who had been hard at work over her manioc all day, listening to me play the tapes, came over and surprised me with this story about Kwakwagï, the Potoo Bird:

Kwakwagï
Told by Ugaki at Tanguro. July 19, 1982

Listen. This is about Kwakwagï, the Potoo Bird.
"Your mouth looks like a vulva," someone said to him, to Kwakwagï.
   He felt deeply embarrassed.
"It doesn't." "Yes, it does."
"Who shall I ask?"
"I'll go to the Pestles. They will know.
   Because the women raise them up close to their bodies, they
   might know."
      So he went to the Pestles.
"Someone said to me, 'Your mouth is like a vulva,'" he said to them.
"Is that so? We don't know. Go to the Cooking Pots.
   Because the women stand above them, they might know."
      "All right," he said.
         So he went there.
"Someone said to me, 'Your mouth is like a vulva,'" he said to them,
to the Cooking Pots.
"Is that so? We don't know. Go to Penis. Because he penetrates the
vulva, he might know."
      "All right," he said.
         So he went to Penis.
"Someone said to me, 'Your mouth is like a vulva.'"
"Is that so? I don't know.
Go to Mawa, the Giant Trees.
Only they know,
   because the women have to cross over them after they've fallen
   across the path."
      "Very well."
         So he went there.
"Someone said to me, 'Your mouth looks like a vulva.'"
"Yes. That's right. Everything about it.
   Your lips, your stretched-out appearance, that red tongue of yours
   inside. Your mouth is exactly like a vulva."
      "Very well."
So then Kwakwagï went away. He was very sad.
   Because his mouth looked like a vulva.

"How dumb," say it.

Chapter 5

Afasa: The Impossible Imitation

The cannibal forest monster Afasa is one of the more important and interesting of the powerful beings (*itseke*) the Kalapalo associate with serious illness, and upon whom they sometimes call to effect a cure. If a very sick person dreams of Afasa, or a shaman in narcotic trance learns that Afasa has captured the victim's *akua* ("interactive self"), a ritual representation of that powerful being takes place. It is thought that this musical and visual enactment of Afasa's own peculiarities will beguile the *itseke* and persuade them to return the *akua* and thereby assist in returning the victim to health and well-being.

Afasas are gourd-headed monsters. The shamans make Afasa masks that are at once beautiful and horrible. Very large, round gourds are carefully selected, cleaned, and painted with red, white, and black stripes. Bulbous eyes are formed of pieces of oyster shell, while from the mouth protrude grotesque, spiky teeth taken from dogfish. Afasas' woven palm-leaf ears also protrude, as do their large, bridge-less noses (characteristic, it will be remembered, of all powerful beings) and their beetling eyebrows—all modeled of black beeswax.

The masks are made in groups of three, to represent a family: the old man (*ndosafi*), the old woman (*tagonggo*), and their one or two "old" children (*tsuitsui*), who are usually played by young men in the curing rituals. Three men wear these masks and cover their bodies with burity-palm skirts. Carrying staffs, they slowly hobble along from the ceremonial house in the center of the settlement to the house of the sick person, where the shamans and virtually everyone in the settlement await their entrance. In this context, the three Afasas are old, grandparental sorts of powerful beings who call their human supplicants *witi* ("my grandchild"). When an Afasa speaks in stories, it is as if the voice comes from inside the gourd: deep and resonant, with extended vowels. True, the voice is humorous, but, like the physical characteristics of the mask, it is distorted and excessive in a blown-up sort of way, like one would expect a "gourd head" to sound.

There is a special relationship between Afasa and small children. During a curing, women and children stand crowded together across from the interior performance space of the household, the younger children anticipating with some fright the appearance of this monster whom they have most likely never seen before. The impression on the children was tremendous during the performance I saw in 1979. The more nervous and insecure cried openly, turning their heads from the singing figures, while even the more confident ones stared silently, inching closer to their mothers. The few Kalapalo children who had persistently misbehaved during the previous past months were deliberately approached by the Afasa group; this move only increased the uproar. Only after approaching the children did the performers turn their attention to the patient. They sang and danced before her, and then they were sent off by the shamans. Later in the day and for the next week or so—until every man and finally boy who wished to had a chance to perform—the Afasa group walked around the house circle, visiting each residence in turn, demanding food from the women. As is always the case with masked performances, this was an opportunity for men, suitably disguised, to tease their female relations, and to scrutinize houses they might not otherwise have been able to enter as freely. The Afasa ritual is one of the few occasions when young boys have a chance to practice doing these things.

Afasa thus paradoxically combines attributes both of elders and of small children, both as an image and during the experience of ritual performance. In the serious curing rituals, Afasa is an elder (physically as an older person and metaphorically as a grandparent) to the human community, but then eventually he is tried out as a role by young boys. He is one of the few powerful beings who can be imitated and ridiculed by small children, who are encouraged to sing those of his songs that are quoted in myths. In stories about people's encounters with Afasa, the monster also bears exaggeratedly childish attributes, particularly an extreme naiveté and a willingness to believe everything that is told him. While Afasa are murderously angry when they are victimized, they are also puzzled and hurt. Afasa consequently appears somewhat awkward and stupid, and is easily tricked despite his incontrovertibly violent nature.

I taped the Afasa stories as Agakuni told them to his brother-in-law and me late one afternoon in the doorway of his crowded house. As it was getting dark, Agakuni spoke quickly, animatedly alternating between the deep, booming voice of Afasa and the normal sounds of the human beings with whom the monster comes into contact. I present them in the exact order in which Agakuni told them. The sequence is apparently significant because there is a difference between the format of the first two and the formats of the last four. The stories that open Agakuni's Afasa narrative constitute a related pair, concern some very basic attitudes the Kalapalo have about Afasa, and describe the horror of encounters with him. While living deep in the forest, Afasa has the unpleasant habit of hanging around human habitations, trying to make friends with people. Thus, while in some ways an absurd and even ridiculous monster, Afasa is dangerous, and therefore escape from him must be quick and effective. As we see in the following stories, those who come too close to Afasa gradually lose all human feeling, until they become Afasa himself.

Agakuni (facing camera)

Afasa's Bones

I

"Wato."
    It was a Dawn Person who was speaking, tradition says.
      (At the Beginning they said *"wato"* to one another.
        Now everyone says *"amigo,"*
          like the Christians.   5
           Originally, I'm sure it was *"wato."*)
"Wato," he called to the other,
    "Wato. Friend."
      "What?" the other said.
    "Let's go to that place way over there,   10
     I want to look around that place way over there."
    "All right, we'll go if you wish."
    They each went their way.
At dusk,
    "Friend," he said.   15
      "What?"
It was dusk. "We'll go to that place way over there."
     "Where?"
    "That place way over there where we planned to shoot parrots."
     "We'll certainly go if you wish."   20
    "When shall we go?" "Tomorrow, tomorrow we'll leave for sure."
    "All right."
The next day,
    "Friend, let's go now."
      "Let's go."   25
      They went away.

Before dawn,
     ti ti ti they walked away.
When the sun was here they came to a house,
     just like the one at our plantation.   30
    "Let's stay here for a while,"
     so they tied up their hammocks,
       inside the house I mean.
Stored there were balls of dried manioc mash,
     bah ah! a great pile of it,   35
      and manioc starch.
 "Let's go shoot parrots."
    They went to shoot parrots.

Bah ah aaah, they kept piling and piling them up,
   those they had shot with their arrows.   40
Then they skinned and cut them open.
   They ate some.
Then at dusk when a very little light remained,
   they came back.
   "Hoh hoooh," someone grunted.   45
   On the path someone was about to come.
   "Oh!" one said.
   "Oh! Friend!"
   "What?"
   "Listen, who could that be doing that?"   50
   "Where?" the other said.
   "Listen this time."
   "Hoh hoooh!"
   "Oh! Afasa! Afasa!"
   (That's a giant, a powerful being.)   55
   Buh! His legs are huge!
   His head, his huge body, his teeth, his arms—every part of
   him was enormous!
He came after that, "Hoh hoooh!"
   "Friend, he must be right there!"
   "What will we do?"   60
   "We'll hide ourselves."
There was a platform nearby,
   the manioc storage platform.
As he approached, they scattered their fire, *tsiki, tsiki.*
He came "UUUU."   65
   They kept silent.
   How could he possibly let himself be killed?
   Boh! But in the end that was what finally happened.
   "After a while he'll stop, Afasa will stop."
   That was all.   70

One of them had wanted to pee for some time,
   all through the night that's how he felt.
At dawn, when *kāka* the laughing hawk called, he said,
   "Friend!"
   "What?"   75
   "I have to pee!"
   "No, Friend, it will have to be this way.
      Don't leave yet!"
   "No, Friend, I have to pee!"
   "No, he's still outside!   80
   Go pee over there against the wall just this one time."

"No, I think it's disgusting to do that inside here,
  it's disgusting," he said.
    They continued to sit there.
"Ouch, it's painful! Ouch, Friend!" he said,   85
  "I've got to pee right now!"
  "No, pee here!"
  "No, I'll go outside, outside,"
    "No, Friend, he's still out there, he's stayed there, he's still
    out there!"
But then it was too much for him.   90
  Finally, "Friend, I'm going."
  "All right."
    He was angry,
      angry with the other one.
  "Go, if you wish, go on,"   95
    so the other climbed down from where they were up above,
      from on top of the platform.
  He came to the front of the house and opened the door slightly.
  Tok! As he went outside, as he went outside . . .
    boh! he was grabbed by the monster after all, *buduk!*   100
  "Aaa aah, Friend, he's eating me, he's eating me!"
  "Look, look now, 'He's still there,' I know I just said that to you,
    'He's still there,' I told you," his friend said.
Then, "Come here, Friend, come here, Friend!"
    How could his friend possibly go and be killed by Afasa?   105
  "Come here, Friend, come here!"
  The monster ate him, his teeth went *kuk, kuk,*
    so the other died.
      He was eaten after that,
        tsuk! tsuk! went his bones.   110
Bok the other man crept down while Afasa was doing that.
  "Hoh hoh hoh!" Afasa said as the other man left his hiding
  place.
    "He's still there," the other man said to himself.
  Afasa went [sings]: "Inside my canoe, like that look for him.
    Inside my flute."   115
    By now his song was far away.
The friend went outside to look, *tikii.*
  "I'll go see."
  Afasa was still going away,
    going away singing: 120
    "Inside my canoe, like that, look for him.
    Inside my canoe, like that, look for him.
    Inside my flute, ho hooh,"
      he never stopped crying out.

Then *bububu* Afasa was beside that place,   125
    beside the house once more *bububu* coming toward him.
    Afasa began looking around there.
"He's still walking around here,
    he hasn't stopped walking around here,
        I'm sure he's still walking around here," the other told
            himself.   130
The monster kept going away on the path as before,
    he kept singing as he had been doing before.
        Teh it was a well-made path!
    Going, going, going farther . . .
        he went ve-ry far until . . .   135
            it curved, it was bending,
                he went away singing all the while.
    "Yes, he has finally gone away once and for all."
Tututu the man climbed down.
        "I'll go now."   140
    He untied his hammock.
        There was the trail he had made.
Titititi, he left quickly.
    He kept his eyes on Afasa's footprints.
    He went on, and in case the other was still around,   145
        he ran for a very long way.
"Kaah, kaah!" he cried out to the mother of his friend.
        There were people there, *bah hah* so many of them!
    "Kaah kaah. No, no, not at all. Certainly we will all wail!"
"What happened to him!"   150
    (He has no name
        I don't know it, no name.
    He was a Dawn Person,
        that man I'm speaking of.
            No name.)   155
He came,
        titi tikii he entered the house.
    "My friend is certainly no longer alive, he is no longer alive!"
    "Ah, ah, ah!"
        his brother,   160
        his mother,
        his wife began to cry.
            Everyone was crying.
    "What happened to him!"
    "Afasa ate him, Afasa."   165
    "Where?"
    "Right by his house."

"Let's go burn him up!"
"All right!"
Then they all mourned, lots of people.   170
    "We'll have to do something about this."

They slept, they slept,
    while arrows were being made,
        many of them, which were going to be used to kill Afasa.
        The arrows were finished.   175
    "That's enough, tomorrow we will leave.
        Tomorrow it will happen,
            tomorrow."
                "All right."
The next day, very early in the morning,   180
    "Let's go now."
        This time there weren't just a few people,
            there were many of them.
    "Let's go now," they said,
        "to that place."   185
    "Where is it?" they asked.
        "Far away, far away.
        We'll search for him,
            his tracks are there."
        Boh hoh! His tracks were huge!   190
            Like this, look. . . .
When the sun was here, they came to a creek,
        alongside water,
            they came to the water.
    Then they walked around searching for Afasa,   195
        searching for his house.
    "Dom! dom!" they found it.
        He was sleeping.
            Way up inside a huge tree that had fallen.
    "Dom!" he was snoring inside the tree.   200
        This was Afasa's house.
    "Here he is, all right now," they said.
        They piled up wood around the rotted log,
            ku ku ku, so much wood!
    "We should do something about this now," they said.   205
        With fire they lit what had been piled around the log,
            with fire they did that.
            The others didn't hear them.
                They were asleep far inside the log.
        From inside the log,   210
            "Dom! dom! dom!" the people heard the snoring.

Afasa's children were there, there were so many children!
"All right now," the people said.
A great deal of wood was burning now.
The fire went inside the log.   215
    Smoke did the same.
        It went all the way up the log.
Finally, the others began to flee, to flee from the smoke.
    "Ouch, ouch! Old Woman, Old Woman!"
        "What?" she said.   220
        They were coming out.
    "Old Woman, we've really had it, we've really had it!" he said.
    "Wake up, wake up!
        Our grandchildren are burning us up!" he told her.
Fire was piled up so they couldn't get out.   225
    The smoke was coming toward them.
        "Eii!" they screamed.
        "Old Woman!"
Then slowly it grew,
        the fire grew.   230
And finally, just as they had done before,
    "Old Woman! I'm sure we are done for now, we're done for!"
"Pee! Pee!"
Tchew, Tchew, he tried to douse the fire.
    Tsududu, his wife peed.   235
        Nothing happened.
Her husband peed once more.
    Their poor little offspring did the same,
        but nothing happened.
"Fart, fart!"   240
    He farted,
        he farted,
    and *booh!* the fire grew up.
His wife farted also.
    Booh!   245
Once again she did that and the fire really grew up when she
did that!
    Then the husband again.
His little children grew silent,
    his little children.
        I mean they all died, *mbuh.*   250
        Their mother. . . .
"We should do something now!"
    Just then that happened to their father . . . their mother.
        I mean, she died.
            Her husband was still there by himself.   255

"I'm done for, I'm done for," he declared.
"Come, my relatives," he called to his brothers.
    Afasa's settlement is far, far away.
"Come. Come, my relatives.
    Avenge us, avenge us," he said.   260
        "Remember us, remember us," he said.
            "Remember what happened to us," he said.
Then again, soon after, he said that he was finished, after what
the people had done to him.
        I mean, he was finished, after what they had done to him.
    "Too bad he had to be that way."   265
Then they went inside their houses,
    and they stayed there.
That's all.

II

There were some friends,
    still others this time,
        others.
    "Friend."
(There were so many Dawn People who were friends,   5
    so many who were like that!)
"Friend," someone said.
    "What?"
"Let's go look at Afasa's bones."
    "Let's go as you say!"   10
They didn't tell their other friends.
    They went to that same place.
Then *boh* his bones.
    Bah scattered about!
    Teh how white!   15
    Boh hoh how huge they were!
"Look, his bones.
    What can be done with them, what?"
        "I don't know."
He picked some up,   20
    small ones.
He began to whittle one, *tsiu, tsiu.*
    and again another one, *tsiu, tsiu.*
Then he put one here, in the hole in his ear lobe, *tsidik!*
Mboh! the friend was still in his own form.   25
    But when he put the bones in his ears, *mboh*
        his friend couldn't see him!

"Oh, Friend, where are you, where are you?
    Where are you?"
The friend took them out *tsiki, mboh!*   30
    He had become his usual self.
"Oh, Friend, how nice!" he said.
    "This is something good," he said.
    "Is it?" the other said.
"Yes, Friend, how nice!   35
    Doing that might have some use.
        Go ahead, try it."
    "What shall I do with them?"
    "Put them in your ears.
        Go ahead, try it."   40
"What shall I do with them?"
    "Put them in your ears."
        "All right, as you say."
            The other man made some.
Tsiuk, tsiuk, they were cut.   45
        Tsiduk! Like that, little ones.
    "You should try and put them on!"
He put one on, *kiduk.* The other side, *kiduk.*
    Boh.
And he became invisible!   50
"Oh, Friend, Friend!"
    "What?"
The other called to his friend.
    "Friend, where are you, where are you?"
His friend saw him as he was,   55
    but as for the other man, he couldn't see him.
        His friend was seeing *him,* though.
            "Friend, where are you?"
Then he pulled them out. *Tsik, mboh!*
    "Friend, how nice!"   60
    "Yes, it is," he went,
        "this is going to be very useful."
    "All right, as you say,"
        he made some more.
Tsiuk tsiuk he cut them.   65
    The other man made some of his own.
Tsiuk, tsiuk, he cut some up.
        Tsiduk! Like that, little ones.
    "You should try and put them on!"

He put one on, *kiduk!*   70
   Boh! He became invisible!
   "Oh, Friend, Friend!"
     "What?"
The other called to his friend.
     "Friend, where are you, where are you?"   75
The friend saw him as he was, but as for the other man, he
couldn't see him.
     His friend was seeing *him,* though.
       "Friend, where are you?"
Then the other pulled them out. *Tsik, mboh!*
   "Friend, how nice!"   80
   "Yes, it is," he went,
     "it's going to be very useful."
"Some of our people, some of our people are going to fish at
that place way over there.
We'll soon eat."
   "All right, let's go."   85
     "All right," he answered.
       "All right, let's go."
Then they went into their houses,
   and they stayed inside their houses.
The fishermen slept a few days,   90
   but the others were still as they were.
The others still kept to their houses.
   They slept three days.
     That was over.
"Hu, hu, hu," the people called out in greeting to the fishermen.   95
   "Hu, hu, hu."
   Boh haah, their fish catch was huge!
The fishermen all came home to their wives.
   "Friend!"
     "What?"   100
   "Friend!"
     "What?"
   "I want us to go where the fish are being carried outside, over
there."
Then inside the ceremonial house they put the plugs in their ears,
kidi, kidi, mboh!
   They couldn't be seen!   105
     Each friend saw the other, however.
They went on,
   and they came to the plaza.
   People were walking around near them but they weren't seen,
     not at all.   110

Ummbok. They sat down close to the fish.
  "We'll eat soon."
Some people were walking around there.
  Bah haah!
    A whole crowd of people were eating.   115
      They didn't see the friends at all,
        no.
They sat down,
  kuh kuk, they broke off pieces of fish,
    and they ate.   120
They tore off pieces of manioc bread.
  Kaw kaw kaw they chewed it up.
After they had filled themselves,
  "Let's go, Friend.
    We'll take one of these fish with us."   125
Another was taken,
  Boh a big one,
    and they went away.
      They carried the fish behind a house.
There *tsiki, tsiki,*   130
  they removed their earplugs.
    And so once again they were like people.
  "Let's go, Friend."
  "Let's go."
    To another house.   135
      In one house lived one friend,
        the other friend was next door.
His wife said,
  "Where does this come from? From where?"
  "What's-his-name gave it to me."   140
    "All right."
      So they were all eating it.
        That was over.
The same time next day some more fishermen returned,
  fishermen.   145
    "Friend!"
    "What?"
    "Huu huu!" once again the people greeted them.
      "Bah ahaah, they have a huge catch!" someone said.
One of the two came inside.   150
  "Friend, let's go! Let's eat!"
    "Let's go!"

They ca-ame, to that same place.
   Tik, tik, they entered unseen.
   They unwrapped the baskets of fish,   155
      kidi kidi kidi.
         Boh! boh! They carried some away.
A person came,
      someone else came.
      "Oh! Where could it have gone to?" he said.   160
      "Listen. Where has it gone to?"
      "I don't know."
      "Who could have taken it away?"
      "Who knows?"
         "Who could have taken it away?"   165
   The others were right there, no one knew anything about it
   at all.
         "Who could have taken it away?"
         "Who knows?"
They couldn't be seen, I'm told, when they did that.
There were only three fish left,   170
   since they had carried off most of them when they did that.
And they boiled what they had taken away, *ku ku ku.*
They sat around while one of their wives boiled the fish.
Once again some people went fishing.
   They did the same thing again.   175
      That was all.

So, it became a long time afterward.
   At dawn, he was ready.
      "Friend."
      "What?"   180
   "Come over here to me."
   He was in the plaza.
   "I want us to go over there."
      "All right."
There they were in the plaza,   185
   seated.
They sat down together and talked.
They talked, they talked, they talked.
Then a manioc drying rack,
   a manioc drying rack called *faka,*   190
      that kind of thing.
         (You probably haven't seen a *faka,* Elena.)

Ti ti ti someone unrolled it.
  A woman unrolled it.
    This thing is for drying manioc starch high above the
      ground.
Then, *tak, bok,* she was crumbling the starch onto the rack,
  a woman was.
  Tik, tik, bent over she went,
    crumbling it.
      Tik tik tik tik.
As she finished, she backed up toward them.
    The woman was almost finished.
"Friend!" he said.
  "I'll try to take her while she's doing that, I'll try to take her."
  "No, Friend, no.
    If you go and take her, you'll be transformed, you'll become a
    wild thing."
    "No, Friend, even so I will go."
  "Go as you say, go as you say," the other answered.
    "I'm certainly going."
Ngïruk ngïruk, boh,
    she was crumbling the starch.
He went as he said he would,
    ti ti ti until he was beside her.
While she was just about finishing up, the man came from behind
inside her vulva to take her.
  His penis was going inside her vulva,
    and he did it to her.
He took her,
    and finally
      that foolish one came.
  As he ejaculated, something was happening.
    "Hoo hooooh!" He became Afasa!
  Afasa!
    He became Afasa!
"EEOOH!"
  "Umah! Who's that?" the woman said.
    "Who's doing that?"
  "EEOOH, hoh, hoh!" he ran away after he did that to her,
    and he went on . . . to the forest.
    That man had become Afasa.
  "Look, he became something evil.
    'Beware of touching her, something awful will happen
    afterward,'
      I certainly spoke that way to you just now."

Now his friend was frightened.
   "Let it be,"
      and he threw one away.   235
         He threw the other one away.
   "Lest I become like him.
      Doing what he did, that would happen."
The other went farther on after all that had happened to him,
      toward the forest.   240
     Now he himself was Afasa,
        he himself, the human being.

Listen.
   It's over. There just isn't any more at all.

Other stories are concerned with quite different relations between human beings and Afasa. Agakuni told these following the first two, which introduced his character. The later stories clearly imply the impossibility of any satisfactory bond of "likeness" between the monster and human beings; therefore, they logically follow from the earlier ones. They are usually told after the earlier stories, or even independently of them (judging by how I heard them from other storytellers).

I. Afasa Wants to Have His Hair Painted

Notes appear on page 348.

Listen.
"Friend!" "What?"
  Is that right? No, he went,
    he went into the middle of a field,
      into the middle of a field.
"Well, Grandson." "What?"   5
  "What happened to *you?*"
    He had painted his hair,
      I'm talking about a man who had done that.
"Whatever happened to you, what happened?"   10
"I cut my hair, that's what happened.
  I cut my hair."
"Very well. Do me just like you,
  like you."
"But really, you can't be like me, no.   15
  You might die after you painted your hair like me," the man
  told him.
"No, no. Do me like you, like you."
"No, really it can't be me.
  No," he told him.
    Boh, Afasa's teeth were huge!   20
"No, if I were to paint you,
  really, you'd be almost dead from that.
    Really, you'd be almost dead,
      almost dead."
"Never mind, even so."   25
"All right, if you wish," the other said.
  "Do it."
"Very well, all right then, if you want to.
  You must be sure not to say, 'Ouch, ouch,' because it's very
  painful."
    The man was lying to him.   30
      "All right, as you wish," he said.
Finally he did that with his knife,
  finally he did that.
  No, he didn't have a knife.
    I meant to say he did it with a piranha jaw.   35
    They didn't yet know about knives.
    He used a piranha jaw.
Tsuk, tsuk, tsuk, finally he did that.

"Ouch! So that's really how it is, is it?"
"Stop it, don't say that,   40
    stop it.
        This is really painful, it's painful."
"All right, go ahead," Afasa answered.
    Tsuk! Tsuk!
"Ouch, so it *was* really painful, wasn't it," Afasa observed.   45
"I told you to stop saying that,
    this is very painful,
        painful."
            "All right."
Tsuk tsuk tsuk tsuk tsuk.   50
    He stood motionless.
        The man really worked on him!
Then fi . . . *tiki.* It was all ready, his scalp had been done this way,
cut all around.
Then the man pulled at it this way, *kï kï kï,*
    he loosened it all!   55
"Does it hurt?"
"It doesn't."
"Keep perfectly still then."
Here, right over his face *SHUUMBUKAH!*
Buh! as the man ran away Afasa grabbed at him.   60
    Tuh! the man sped away from him!
Afasa's scalp, all his hair was *mbok* covering his face.
    That was what had happened to him, *mbok.*
As the man ran off, Afasa almost grabbed him.
"You certainly kept lying to me all that time, you certainly kept
lying to me all that time!"   65
After he had done all that,
    tok the man ran away.
There Afasa remained after that had been done to him.
    He wept, while his scalp was here *mbok,*
        covering his face.   70

Listen, a short one.

II. A Stingray on Afasa's Face

He himself again,
    Afasa again.
        And a person as well.
"Let's go, Friend," someone said,
    right outside another man's house.   5

"Friend," he said.
    "What?"
"Tomorrow let's take out the fish from our *utu* traps,
    our *utu* traps."
    "We'll certainly go as you say."
"At the beginning of the day you must come to me,
    at the beginning of the day we'll go."
        "All right."
But while that was going on, Afasa was listening to them talking,
    Afasa was.
        He was walking around outside the house while the other
        man stood there.
So then they stayed there.
    That was all.

"Kwakagaako," the rooster crowed.
    "Friend . . . Friend . . . Friend."
        That was Afasa speaking!
The man wasn't there,
    he slept.
        The friend was still asleep.
"Friend, Friend!"
    "What?" the man inside the house said.
"Come on!"
    That was really Afasa speaking!
        "Come on!"
            "All right," the man said.
He packed up his arrows
    and took along his manioc bread and his bit of fire, saying
    "Let's go, Friend."
"Come on!"
    "All right."
        It was night, and he couldn't see who it was at all.
            "Let's go."
Ti ti ti ti ti to that place I spoke of,
    to the traps.
    "We'll leave the fire." They made a fire.
        Pu pu pu, and so it grew up.
    "Let's go."
        To draw the fish from the traps,
            to empty the traps.
                Mbah haah, there were so many fish!
Kululu, kululu, these were strung on a vine.

The man went to the last of the traps.
In one, a stingray flapped about *tchew, tchew, tchew.*
"Friend," he said, "here's a stingray!"
"Bring it to me, let's see it," Afasa said.
He never turned toward the man,   50
   he never showed his face to him,
      not at all.
The other would have seen his teeth.
   Moh! his teeth!
The real friend didn't know anything about what had happened.   55
   When it was daylight and the roosters crowed, "Friend!"
      This time it was the person speaking, that's who I mean.
         He kept calling to him: "Friend!"
"He left a long time ago," the man's wife told him,
   " 'Friend,' someone said to him in a strange way."   60
"But who was that strange person who came before me, who
came?"
   "I don't know. 'Friend, Friend,' someone said to him in a
   strange way."
"Oh. But I'm still here, still here.
   Well, let them go to them there."
      The other man wasn't going to go.   65
         He went away.

Then the others left the fish traps and they came back to their fire,
   to their fire.
Bok, beside the fire.
"Friend, let's grill some of these fish."   70
   "All right."
He sat with his back turned,
   Afasa's back was turned.
The friend also sat that way.
Like this, like this. They sat with their backs to each other.   75
   He was grilling some fish for them to eat.
Just about then,
   "It's done." When he told Afasa that,
      Afasa was about to eat only what the man had been cooking,
         Afasa planned to eat only that.   80
            He only wanted to eat the fish, just fish.
               The man had kept them on the fire until everything
               was roasted.
"Friend," he said, "Won't you show me your face now? Show me
your face," the man said.
   "Won't you show me your face?"

The other showed his face just a little.   85
  There were his teeth!
  "My friend didn't come to see me, it was that Afasa!" the man
  said to himself.
"Friend."
  He wanted to grill the stingray.
"Friend."   90
  "What?"
"Let's grill the stingray."
  "Grill it if you'd like."
Bok, he put it on the fire with a stick thrust through to its anus.
  Kururu like that.   95
  After, he was going to cover Afasa's entire face with the
  stingray.
He held some fish up like this, behind his back.
  "Eat, Friend, eat."
  He had finished stringing his fish catch on a vine, *ku ku ku.*
  A vine this long,   100
    which he put away inside his net bag.
  He packed up his arrows *pu pu pu* and *tïk*
    placed his bow close beside him.
It was all roasted.
  The stingray was covered with painful coals.   105
And so *bok*, the man picked it up right away and held it out
behind him,
  in order to cover Afasa's face with the stingray.
"Friend," he said.
  "What?"
"Turn your face toward me this time."   110
  "All right," Afasa answered.
As he began to show his face, the man threw it at him.
  Buhtsïk!
  Tsïktsïktsïk, Afasa rubbed his face,
    tsïk tsïk tsïk!   115
    Afasa tried to grab him when he did that to him.
  "Ouch! Friend! Why-did-you-want-to-do-this-to-me? Friend!
  Why-did-you-want-to-do-this-to-me?"
Pupu tïtïtïtï!
  The man ran away.
    Tutututututu.   120
  "Ouch, ouch, ouch!" Afasa was saying that because of the fire.
He began to pick off the stuff that had been thrown on him,
  there were lots of painful burns on his face,
    the stingray really hurt when the man threw it on him.

Then the man ran on,   125
  he ran away,
    he was running.
  He ran until he was far away,
    far.
  "Where am I going to go, where am I going to go?   130
  Poor me! Poor me!" he said to himself.
By now, Afasa was feeling better.
  His face had already healed.
  Tsïkitsïki he wiped it off with water, and he looked around him.
  "Where is he, where?" he said,   135
    "Where is that worthless one? Where?
    I want to eat that worthless one."
      The man was already far away.
  "I want to grill that man."
    "*Uuoh! Uuoh!*" Afasa cried out as he raced after him.   140
      He didn't see anything.
Finally he began to sing:
  "Where could my friend be?
  A stingray, a stingray, my friend threw on my face."
While the friend came to a certain place,   145
  Afasa was getting there.
"Here he is," *pïpïpïpï*
  and the friend was running,
    the friend was running,
      as Afasa came closer, closer, closer.   150
        He stopped.
When Afasa was very close to him,
  "Here he is," Afasa said.
    "Now he's done for, he's done for!" he went.
    "I want to eat him, I want to eat him," he went.   155
Then *pu pu pu* the man ran to an *iku* tree.
  Pu pu pu the friend climbed up on it,
    onto the *iku* tree.
  There was a lot of *iku* sap there,
    tak very sticky *iku* sap.   160
With it *tsïk* the man smeared himself around his eyes *duuu*,
  around his eyes *duuu*.
  Boh! his eyes looked huge after he did that,
    just like *kwakwagï* the long-tailed potoo bird.
  "*Kwakwakwa!*" he went.   165
  "*Kwakwakwa!*"
    Afasa saw him.

"Huuoh! Huuoh! Huuoh!
     What's this strange thing here?" and he ran away.
          because he was afraid of it.   170
"This must be *adyafi* the potoo!"
When he left the man came down the tree. He sped away!
     Once again as before the other came there,
          Afasa came there.
Pu pu pu on top of the tree again as the other came close to him
once more.   175
     "Kwa . . . ", Afasa looked around.
     There was the man with charcoal smeared around his eyes.
     Afasa looked around him once more.
          "Kwa kwa kwa!"
"Oh no, oh no!" he went away once and for all after that!   180
For the last time *tututu* the man ran to his house,
     his house was nearby.
          He stopped running.
     "Huuoh!" he called to the others,
          "Huuoh!"   185
Tiki, he came inside.
     "I don't have anything at all," he told his wife.
          "No fish."
               "All right," she answered.
     "Over there are three little ones."   190
          "Very well."
His wife built up the fire.
     His friend was also there,
          I mean the other man was also there.
     "Friend!"   195
          "What?"
     "What made you leave without me?
          Why?"
     "Friend, it seemed as if you came to pick me up,
          but I really wasn't safe there at all, not safe."   200
     "What happened to you?"
     "Afasa very nearly ate me up, Afasa did."
          "Oh really?"
     "Yes," he answered. "I'm sure he was about to eat me, but I
covered his face with a stingray.
     Then he ran after me and I'm sure he almost grabbed me."   205
     "Must you die because of what happened?
     Where is he now?"
     "I don't know—he went some other way after I did that to him.
          I don't know, he went away."

"But why are your eyes painted like that?"

"But why are your eyes painted like that?"   210
    "To make him frightened of me.
    Each time I called *'Kwakwa,' tututu* he would run away."

Listen. It's over.

III. The Stinging Caterpillar

Some Dawn People went,
    Dyagamï people went,
        around the Matipu territory.
            That's where they were living.
        Now, they were of the Beginning,   5
            Dyagamï people of the Beginning.
                They went to scoop up fish with their *kusu* baskets and
                kundu traps.
        "Let's try and catch a few fish at that place over there."
            "All right," the other said.
They hadn't been at it for very long,   10
    when *tuuu* Afasa also began to move about there.
Buh, buh, buh why, he also began to throw his *kundu* trap.
        Afasa was throwing his *kundu* traps there.
    "Oh!" one of the men said. "Who could *that* be doing that over
    there?"
    "Gïdoo, gïdoo."   15
    "Afasa!" the other said.
    "Temeteme fukadyi!"
        Afasa sang.
            Tsididi pïk, tsididi pïk.
    "Temeteme fukadyi!"   20
            Tsididi pïk, tsididi pïk.
                Why, he sang and sang while he threw his *kundu* trap!
        "That's Afasa doing that," the man said,
            "that's Afasa doing that."
        "What shall we do to him?"   25
        "I don't know, what's the best thing?"
        "I don't know."
They used *taidyoko*, a stinging caterpillar, *taidyoko*.
    You haven't seen *taidyoko*, have you?
        Ouch! It bites us.   30
    "I'll rub his ass with a *taidyoko*."
        "All right," the other said.
            To do that, the first man went to pick a *taidyoko* from off a
            tree, using a stick folded in half.

Then *puk* when he had it securely held, *tititi* he ran back.
"I'll go now."   35
"All right."
So he went *tititititititititi*
very close to where Afasa had begun to throw his *kundu*.
Tsuk tsuk Afasa kept on moving about.
The man began to rub Afasa's ass with the *taidyoko*,   40
tuuh!
And again he did it.
Tuuuh beneath the water!
"Ouch, ouch!" Afasa said.
"That must be an *utusi* bug, that must be *utusi!*   45
Where is it, where is it?" and he went on again.
He went on again,
"*Temeteme fudyaki,*"
tsididi pïk, tsididi pïk,
why, he kept on,   50
tsididi pïk, tsididi pïk.
Why, he kept on,
he went on again.
And once more, "Ouch, ouch! Where is it, that must be *utusi,* that
must be *utusi.*"
He still hadn't seen the man, who had run away.   55
And once more,
and once more,
and once more,
and once more.
The man stopped and came back.   60
"I'll go now," Afasa said to himself.
"I'll go now,"
and so he left.
Afasa strung his fish catch on a vine and went away.

Listen, a short one.

IV. Afasa and the Maiden

It was at dusk—no—dawn.
All the people had gone to the manioc fields.
Her mother had gone,
her father had gone.
The maiden—a woman—the maiden was alone.   5
Tiki, someone came into the house.
Tiki, he came in and glanced around.

Then he went into her seclusion chamber, one like this one here.
    Her enclosure, *tiki.* He went in, *tiki.*
    "Oh," he said, "Oh.   10
    What has been done here?"
She looked up at him.
    Umah, it was Afasa speaking!
    Boh his teeth were huge!
    It was Afasa speaking!   15
    "Why are *you* here?" she asked.
    "Why are *you* here?"
    "Never mind, I didn't come to you for any special reason."
    "All right," she answered.
He was staring at her.   20
    Her calves *buh* were huge,
        and *teh he* she was beautifully pale.
    Her hair as well *teh he* was beautiful,
        because she no longer cut her bangs and it fell across her face.
            That's all.   25
    "How was this done? How was this thing done?"
    Her calves.
    "This is what's been done to my calves." *
    "I see. Do me like you, I want to be just like you.
        I want my calves to be like yours, I want it."   30
    "Beware of wanting that done."
    "Never mind.
        I want to be like you."
    "No, be careful.
        It's really painful to do that."   35
    "I see," he replied.
        He stood there staring at them.
    "Come on. I want to be like you."
        "It's really painful to do that."
    "Never mind, even so I want to be like you.   40
        Even so do me,
            do me."
    "All right, as you wish!"
        A bow cord.
    "You mustn't complain of the pain because I'll put this on very
tightly,   45
        very tightly."
            "All right."
    "You're not to say, 'Ouch, ouch!'"
        "All right."

Then she removed the bow cord, *tïk,*   50
    and she unwound it.
"All right now," she said to him.
"Go ahead!"
She tied his ankles together very tightly.
    She wrapped the bow cord around one side *pu pu pu* and around
    the other.   55
        She finished.
    "Look, it's really happening."
      His blood was pulsing painfully after she did that to him,
        tïk tïk his blood was pulsing painfully.
    "So it's really like this, is it?"   60
    "Shall I do it under your knees?"
    "Don't say that!"
    "*Teh,* you'll become really beautiful that way,
      so beautiful *teh he!*"
When she finished he got up and tried in vain to walk.   65
    Very slowly,
      and he just about collapsed.
    While he was doing that she began to run away,
      the maiden went outside,
        tututu next door.   70
    "Hey!" she said,
      "Afasa's here!"
      "Where?"
      "Here.
        'Do me just like you,' that's the strange thing he just told me.   75
        'Do me just like you,' he told me," she told them.
    "He's here, I've left him tied up!"
    "Come on, let's go see him!"
The others came, the people came there.
    Everyone came there to see him.   80
    There he was still tied up,
      lying on the ground.
        He was still there, just as she had left him.
Puu, they all stood around staring at him.
    "That's him!" they said.   85
    "Good, he's done for, he's done for!"
Everyone, all the people came inside,
    they came inside to see him.
    He didn't run away at all.
    They tied his hands behind his back *pupupu* and tied up his legs,
pupupu.   90
    He had to stay right there.

Then *kawkawkaw* he tried to remove the rope from his wrists,
  but nothing happened.
"All right, now," the people said.
They clubbed him after that,   95
  they clubbed him and they buried him.

Why, listen.

V. Afasa Tries to Get Painted with Genipapa and Is Burned Up
by Fire

Another one again,
  Afasa again.
Teh, some people had painted themselves beautifully with genipapa
juice.
  They applied their genipapa with their fingers *tïtïtï,*
    teh heh heh very beautifully indeed!   5
  And they painted their hair with red urucu paint,
      their hair.
        Some men did.
  "Why are you here?" one of them asked him.
    "No particular reason."   10
    "I see."
      (It was someplace far away, outside the settlement.)
    "Why are you here?"
    "No particular reason," Afasa said.
  "How nice.   15
    How do you do that?
      How is that done?"
    "This is my genipapa design,
    my genipapa design," the man answered.
  "How nice, how nice!" he told him, Afasa said.   20
      "And what is this thing here?"
    "That's *mïngi* I've put on.
    We paint our hair with *mïngi,*
      mïngi.
        Ouch! It's dangerous to paint with it."   25
  "Never mind, I want to be like you, like you."
  "All right, but let's not do it just yet."
  The man studied him.
    "Just as you wish, I'll try to make a genipapa design on you,
      I'll try to make a genipapa design on you."   30

"All right."
"I was made this way by going into a fire,
    into a fire."
The man began to burn the field he had cleared.*
        He began to burn his field,   35
            Tsikïtsikï tsikïtsikï
            He began to burn his field.
                It hadn't reached Afasa,
                    who was still waiting while all that was being
                    done.
        "Ouch!"   40
        "You're supposed to go into the fire.
But then if you let the fire come to you.
    when you return you'll be *teh heh heh*,
        very beautiful! Just like me!"
        "All right, I want to be like you."   45
        "All right, you'll be just the same."
            "All right."
    "Go way over there,
        where the field is burning,
            to the clearing."   50
When the sun was here,
    "Go ahead now if you wish.
    Be sure not to run away,
        don't run away."
            "All right."   55
    "You're not to say, 'Ouch! Ouch!' no.
You'll become black,
    you'll be just like this paint.
If you were to run away because of the pain,
    you wouldn't become black."   60
        The man lied to him.
    "Go ahead. I'm ready. Go ahead!"
The man took him there, to the burning place,
    in the middle of the field.
    "Stay here, you mustn't worry about it,"   65
        and so he came back.
    "All right now,"
and finally, as before, he lit more fire *tsïk tsïk tsïk.*
And finally the fire came *tsïk tsïk tsïk, ndïïï,*
        it encircled the field.   70
        And having done that, *mm mm mm* then it grew up.
    "Do we really have to do it this way? Do we really have to do it
this way?"
        Afasa asked him.

"No, no, no! Don't worry!" the Dawn Person was saying.
"Be very, very careful, don't run away."   75
The fire came right up to him *mm mm*.
"Do we really have to do it this way?"
Afasa ran into the fire!
Boh! he blew up!
He died after that happened,   80
he shriveled up.

Listen. Another short one.

Note to "Afasa and the Maiden"
line
28   The maiden in puberty seclusion tightly binds her ankles and the
        area just below her knees, after which a relative periodically scrapes
        her lower limbs with a bloodletting tool. The result—grossly dis-
        tended calves—is greatly admired. For a monster like Afasa to wish
        this done to him is absurd.

Note to "Afasa Tries to Get Painted . . ."
line
34   "burned the field he had cleared": as in slash-and-burn agriculture,
        practiced by the Kalapalo.

As we have seen, much of the action of these stories centers around Afasa's attempts to "be human," in particular, to engage in activities and have experiences that people who are close friends tend to share. In "Stingray," Agakuni remarks in lines 77 and following that Afasa planned to eat only fish, not his human companion. He kept his face hidden because, as we are told earlier, in lines 49–53, the man would have seen his enormous teeth. In this story, Afasa wants to enjoy human companionship, represented by an activity often shared by close friends, that is, by men who call each other 'wato'. But the man, realizing he is about to dine with a monster, and anticipating rightly or wrongly that it will be he whom Afasa eventually devours, does the only thing possible. He saves himself through trickery. Similarly, in the stories "Afasa Wants to Have His Hair Painted" and "Afasa and the Maiden," the monster is undone by his wish to "be like" a human being. Insisting that he be treated like a person is a kind of "deanimation" for Afasa, a weakening of his *itseke* status. In contrast, the men who play around with Afasa's bones become "hyper-animated," acquiring the powers of *itseke* and one even turns into the monster himself. This is another, inverted, kind of imitation, also an impossible one.

Afasa's deanimation suggests how Taugi, the most creatively dangerous of powerful beings, can be tricked by considerably inferior characters. The reader may remember that in the story of "Kafanifani," for example, Taugi "fails to use his power," as his friend Agouti reminds him, and thus is deceived by his wives and his cousin. Taugi in effect deanimates himself by behaving in an "ordinary" (that is, "not powerful") way. Afasa, trying to effect an impossible transformation, also forgets himself, temporarily suppressing his violent, cannibalistic nature. Of course, his would-be friends do not forget what he is, so the conclusion of each of these episodes is inevitable.

Afasa is tricked through deception; that much is obvious. Yet these deceptions seem characteristically human, very different from those we have seen already in the stories about Taugi and Aulukuma. In general, we can say that the humans who overcome Afasa do so by deceiving him verbally in a special way, namely, by playing upon Afasa's own self-deception. Afasa attempts to create a shared understanding or perspective with his human companions, to "be like them" not just by virtue of a haircut or a design painted on his body or beautifully distended calves, but by adopting a very human feeling— friendship—that involves sharing many intimate experiences. This is just what the human beings cannot do with a monster, an outsider who is, moreover, visibly cannibalistic. Afasa, however, is too persistent to be ignored. So, to deceive him, people need to pretend validation. Finally agreeing to what Afasa wishes, they persuade him that his particular goal can be achieved only in a particular way, a way that, unknown to Afasa, is their means of harming him. Clearly, they are insecure in what they say to Afasa since they have to pretend to agree to help him. More importantly, from the Kalapalo perspective on conversational functioning, they violate the expectation that conversations will consist of attempts at verification, ratification, or validation. Their pretense in the conversations with Afasa denies the usual understanding of conversation as a context in which shared goals can be effected; this is the locus of the deceptive action. Here again, we see how invalid speech—both Afasa's inappropriate request and its deceptive validation—is treated as antisocial.

Chapter 6

In Favor of Deceit

It should be clear to the reader by now that Kalapalo stories about deceit are especially concerned with people's action qualified by feelings: about how enacted emotions give meaning to particular contexts, relationships, and goals, and thereby create several discrete points of view. The contrasts in points of view that we have seen include male/female and older brother/younger brother, and interactional contrasts between *itseke* ("powerful beings") and people, including monster/human being, transformer/human being, and enabler/human being.

These points of view arise from the way enactments of emotion are described. Especially important are the distinctive representations of interpersonal strategies associated with subjective goals. The stories are extended commentaries on particular processes of awareness, not strictly of "self," but of the mutuality of selves, of a sense of personal difference that nonetheless moves toward negotiation and comprehension, often aiming toward reconciliation. Resolution is not always achieved, it is true. More often, discrete points of view remain forever distinct and apart from each other. The evidence of deception is of primary importance in developing this awareness of mutuality and personal distinctiveness. The conclusion is that the Kalapalo understand deception to be a fundamental mode of insight and understanding in human thought.

In a Kalapalo story, the narrator gives straightforward descriptions of emotions, but, as I have taken care to emphasize, a character's quoted speech is even more important for conveying this emotional flavor. Characters are generally introduced by their saying what it is they want to do. Usually, they want to do something that is going to affect *someone*, and a declaration to this effect always seems to need a hearer, a person who will agree and validate the feeling, or disagree and invalidate. Through such conversations, we are able to understand what it is like for a Kalapalo—or a character imagined by a Kalapalo storyteller—to feel in a certain way about a particular situation. The conversations also demonstrate what a Kalapalo might do about such a feeling, and how he or she might evaluate different responses. We gain insight into motives, decisions to act, and other consequences of the feeling. In this way, we can see how people enact the psychological processes in which feelings lead to motives or reasons, motives to decisions to act, and actions to consequences. And, we see them enacted within an implicit, evaluative commentary. The Kalapalo psychodynamic should not be defined in terms of propulsive forces, then. Rather, it is a verbalized representation of the operations of thinking, a model of thinking as action.

Not all Kalapalo myths describe this process in the same way. Some stories about Taugi devote more time to motive and planning, while others, about Afasa, emphasize the details of procedure. Those about Disgusting Dawn People focus upon the peculiar feelings and consequences of compulsive action. Collectively, then, these stories describe the experiences of deceit from several different points of view: that of the successful trickster, of the trickster who is thwarted, of the dupe or target of a deception, and of the person who succeeds in penetrating and blocking deception.

Elements of Deceit

In all the different stories about deception, overstimulated emotions seem to rule over these psychodynamic processes. In contrast to the acceptable display of *ifutisu*—that controlled manner of speaking and moving that people expect of one another in everyday life—trickster-like situations are initiated and conclude with socially disruptive, personally violent, and interpretively subjective events. The psychodynamic narrative makes clear not only what these feelings are, but also delineates the consequences of acting greedily, gluttonously, or with undue anger or misplaced lust.

As good deceptions overstimulate emotion, so overstimulated emotions motivate and assist deception by weakening the intellect. People listening to the stories about Disgusting Dawn People often are made to realize that their emotions have been overstimulated in ridiculous ways, considering the situation—an informal, relaxed session of unplanned-for storytelling. The same holds true for teasing stories and for the various visual jokes Kalapalo play on each other, which tend to provoke inappropriately excessive or misplaced feelings, usually lust or worry, sometimes both at once.

Concealment is another important component in the Kalapalo notion of deceit, and the one most closely tied to reference in speech. Making secret certain things about identity is necessary if tricks are to excite inappropriate emotions, or, on the other hand, to allay suspicions. Taugi especially violates the usual expectation that people represent themselves to be who they are. He deceives people about who he is by a false appearance, and, in speech, by the use of deceptive forms of address and an absence of markers of evidence. Truly Taugi "lies about himself." His human counterparts in the Afasa stories lie about intentions and the consequences of procedure: the action occurs after they seem to agree to a particular goal proposed by Afasa, who does not find out what is really intended until it is too late. Disgusting Dawn People are secretive about their activities in general, but their compulsion to perform these activities eventually draws curious relatives to observe them more closely. The narrator of such stories lies about frame and context. In other words, the narrator pretends to be "just" telling another story about the distant past, but actually deceives the listener, and gets the listener to respond in a ridiculous way.

Hence, the relations between tricksters and their marks are power relations, unequal at the outset. This state of affairs is reversed as conversational and visual ploys together charm the more powerful into becoming dupes. Some characters who are initially set up as far more powerful than the eventually successful deceivers (including some putative tricksters themselves) only fail when they act stupidly or unthinkingly or carelessly. This happens when they ignore clues (as Taugi does in "Kafanifani," or Nakika does in his story), or outright warnings (as do the two friends in the first two Afasa stories, or Afasa himself in the other tales). Sometimes, like Taugi in "Nakika," they are simply overconfident about the weakness of their adversaries. (The men in "Women Kill Jaguar Sorcerers" or "Miti" are other examples of overconfidence. These episodes suggest the usual expectations men have about their superior powers of force.) Tricksters also fail when they meet beings of equal or greater powers of insight. This always seems to happen to Afasa, and frequently to Taugi, as in the stories about his encounters with Kutsafugu, Nakika, Mbambangisu, and Yanama.

Finally, Kalapalo deceit cannot be validated in conversation. The interactive sense of deceit in all these Kalapalo stories has a crucial discourse component: the trickster refrains from sincere (or any) validation or ratification of the dupe's goals. In conversations with Taugi, characters in these stories do not always cooperate, and they do not always share interpretive conventions about validation. It is hardly ever the case that someone truly accepts what Taugi says, although he or she may appear to do so. People know he is a liar because of what he has done before, and because of how he appears to them. Only when he is deliberately encompassed by a particular social domain and people ask him to help them is he validated (as in "The Original Piqui" or "Tukusi," or any of the stories in which action is initiated by the Ani Women).

Taugi works hard to thwart people's skepticism about him. Like other powerful beings, he charms people with compelling mono-logical spells into doing things they would not otherwise do. He is unique, however, in being able to exist in more than one place at once, which he often does to confuse people. Most important, the absence of evidential-validation particles in his speech makes what he says vague and difficult to evaluate, so that a different view of speaking it-self and of experience more generally seems to guide his thoughts. Other characters are thereby given a variety of clues to his identity and correctly conclude, as Cuckoo does: "It must have been Taugi. Only Taugi could have done this."

In the Afasa stories, men and women confront a monster who attempts the impossible: he tries to imitate them, to become "like them." What makes this imitation impossible is the humans' refusal to validate Afasa's intentions, or their efforts to validate them falsely by concealing the consequences of a procedure they suggest. Their re-fusal to validate underscores the inherent separation between the per-son and the monster and the impossibility of effective communication between them. Negotiation, if it is tried at all, never brings about understanding between them.

Powerful beings in their interactional "monster" role are one thing; powerful beings as enablers are quite another. Some contacts with en-abling powers are fortunate and beneficial to people, leading to the acquisition of techniques, including spells, that make human beings (especially *fuati* or shamans) enablers themselves. Thus Taugi receives some praise from the Kalapalo for showing people how to cook corn and piqui, although I think they imply that if he hadn't made these discoveries, someone else would have. (After all, before Taugi ex-plained it to them, the only thing the Cicadas *hadn't* tried for process-ing piqui was water.) Powerful beings as transformers perhaps repre-sent an extreme or overvalidated discourse, since they are beguilers, musical spell-blowers.

In the Disgusting Ancestor stories, the validation offered by a what-sayer is undermined by the speaker's intent *not* to share a point of view with the listener, while pretending to create a shared imaginative intimacy. In a similar way, disgust and scorn follow the revelation of the peculiar habits of a Disgusting Dawn Person or of the spouse, such as Piqui Man or Burity Palm Woman, who has been drawn from the world of living beings. The characters who are just not human enough to share a common way of life with human beings; their behavior does not elicit affirmation and approval from the people among whom they try to live.

A positive tolerance of illusionary consciousness and deceptive action is implied by these female characters and by men like Kutsafugu and Kangangatï (helped by Kwatïngï) who successfully persist in working toward their goals, despite repeated attempts by others to deceive and even destroy them. Afasa's persistence leads to failure, it is true, though this may have to do with the fact that he is too trusting or literal-minded, while the people whom he meets are properly skeptical. Humans are able to succeed because of this very skepticism, which makes them especially sensitive to the clues that key deceptions. Unlike Afasa, the people he meets can easily penetrate pretense while falsely appearing to succumb to an illusion. In Kalapalo practice, deceit is softened because real-life people respond in similar fashion, anticipating, accepting, and even welcoming being tricked. When Kalapalos' original plans are thwarted, or when the outcome is not what they hoped for, they exhibit a certain detachment. Openly bitter resignation seems absent among these people. Even in the most oppressive situations, they help each other to put back on a public face that is calm and content. In the myths, when dupes are tricked, they do not accept alternative outcomes to their goals very willingly. Some, Afasa, for instance, gleefully use this opportunity to attempt revenge, as do the Dawn People in "Women Kill Jaguar Sorcerers" and "Mïti." Taugi, the master trickster of them all, seems willing to give up when his own deceptions fail, claiming shame or embarrassment as an excuse to withdraw. In contrast, Afasa becomes angry and vengeful when he discovers that he has been duped, and Disgusting Dawn People are deeply embarrassed when their secrets are exposed.

From another, perhaps more negative, point of view, characters have to be ready to respond to tricks at any time, and are skeptical, uncertain, and dissatisfied with what appears on the surface. Both in the stories and in the Kalapalo settlements, there is an ever-present concern with the need for concealment and verbal dissimulation, and with the probability that differences might occur between what people say and what they really feel. This contributes toward the skepticism Kalapalo direct against authorities and even against the most forbidding of the powerful beings, who are not beyond being openly condemned and ridiculed. It also leads to repeated demonstrations that absolute truths are reversible. The Kalapalo fabricator, acutely aware of absurdity, is thus a friend of paradox and contradiction. But, all these aspects of illusion are treated by the Kalapalo as if they were naturally, almost inevitably, even usefully, part of the human condition, not just exotic peculiarities of mythological characters who live in a confused and ridiculous past.

"Illusion" thus achieves its greatest substance by contributing to ways of thinking about how human beings experience and learn to comprehend and create a set of meanings about the sensory world, and how these understandings in turn are shaped by the distinctively human ability to invent, to communicate, indeed, to experience at all, through language. Ultimately, then, the concern with illusion contributes directly to the kinds of emotions enacted by Kalapalo illusionists and by the people we come across both in traditional Kalapalo narratives and in contemporary Kalapalo communities.

Perhaps it is too facile to link the Kalapalo fascination with deception to their self-enforced sociality, their emphasis upon *ifutisu* values, the very closely focused scrutiny with which they observe one another, the difficulties their domestic architecture affords for maintaining privacy or securing personal secrets, and the very closeness of their manner of living. The preoccupation with deception in Kalapalo culture contributes strongly to the feeling that performances are best community efforts, to the dislike some have of being observed alone and "on stage," to their somewhat obsessive search for privacy, and to their constant concern with concealment and subterfuge. The very varieties of deception commented on in Kalapalo oral traditions are quite frequently apparent in their personal lives, tradition and the contemporary each modeling themselves on the other.

There is yet another side to this concern with deception. It is impossible to think of deception as consistently troublesome or arduous. First, it is probably the greatest source of Kalapalo humor, the substance of considerable irony and self-mockery, and the basis of Kalapalo creativity in speech. Second, favoring and even welcoming deception—recognizing that it is inseparable from being human—is important to the successful maintenance of Kalapalo life. This is because deception helps Kalapalo circumvent institutional order and intimidating roles and relationships; it encourages skepticism of anything purported to be fixed, rule-bounded, dogmatic, and coercive; and, thus, it allows resistance to the status quo. At the same time, the mythological favoring of deceit suggests a variety of ways to resist conformity, showing Kalapalo there are ways of laughing at themselves when they most need to appear to be adhering scrupulously to the moral order.

Most anthropologists have been accustomed to working with an idea of fixed psychic structure, generalized over all situations and goals. That there are so many difficulties involved in generalizing about tricksters has long been fascinating and perplexing. However, if the idea of fixed psychic structure is questioned (and some psychologists have questioned it), then the contradictions in the patterns of a trickster's action need not be viewed as anomalous or paradoxical. In fact, to the Kalapalo, those characters whose action is stable and falls into a general pattern, whose goals and modes of orientation to them seem not to vary, are regarded as excessively compulsive and inflexible, and, ultimately, as failures of imagination. Pragmatic creativity and flexibility, the ability to conceive of more than a single kind of relation with other people, and the ability to fashion or invent a variety of thoughts about one's capacity as an agent, is, on the other hand, entirely human. These skills, after all, are learned by most people everywhere as they come to understand how to experiment strategically and tactically with personal experience.

Finally, what may appear to some to be an ambiguous sense of flux and of indeterminacy in trickster stories can be understood more positively as a kind of stroboscopic sense of multiple possibilities. This vision fixes in a didactic, narrative frame the complex transiency of experience and the sense of many different experiential worlds existing side by side.

Appendix

Kalapalo Astronomy

When the Kalapalo observe the stars and their movements, they focus upon one of two distinct regions of the sky: either the southern horizon or the zenith of *Ifuinga,* "The River," that is, the Milky Way. These people are accustomed to rising very early, about three or four o'clock in the morning, at the time of crepuscular light, a time they call *mitote.* The appearance of a particular star or star group on the southern horizon at *mitote* indicates the beginning of a new calendrical or temporal unit, one that is associated with meteorological conditions and the human activities they precribe. Most of these divisions occur during the rainy season, which extends roughly from September through April. As the story of Sagangguegï describes, seasonality is a consequence of things Taugi once did. For example, when the "hands of Duck" appear on the southwestern horizon, the Kalapalo say the rainy season (*sisoanïgï*) will be coming soon, and begin to prepare for the ritual performances they hold during the refreshing days of first rainfall, around the end of September. Duck is the sign of "an abundance of manioc," a staple that is needed in large amounts to feed visitors at ceremonies. This is because Duck was given water by Taugi. Similarly, *Motmot,* present on the horizon during November and December, is the sign of the piqui harvest, when people move through their extensive orchards gathering the fallen fruit. *Embisa* is the sign of the migrations of fish called *kwatagi* (*curimata* in Portuguese) that occur during January and February, which is also a time of depleted manioc stores and heavy rains (Taugi filled up a large gourd for Embisa). Storage Platform appears toward the end of the rainy season, in March or April, while *Ema* ("who received only enough water from Taugi to splash her face") indicates the sporadic and brief rainshowers that occur during the dry season, particularly in late June or early July. Thus, even these celestial phenomena were created in a context of trickery.

There are other stars and star groups that are of interest to the Kalapalo, but these are not used for calendrical purposes. Most of them are clustered about the Milky Way, the celestial river, and tend to be human-like characters such as the Jaguar (Nitsuegï, whom Aulukuma threw onto the sky), and closely associated with mythological events involving Taugi or Kafanifani. These are most often observed late at night by men, who are generally outside in the plaza at that time.

Kalapalo Star Chart

The Kalapalo names and their English translations are followed by stellar designations.

1a. Kofongo, "Duck": Procyon and Canopus

1b. *Kofongo isakafongo ingatïfigï*, "Duck's hands rising up ahead": Castor and Pollox

2. Akwakanga: Archerner and Ankaa in Phoenix

3. Ndïtï: "Motmot"
    a. alive, eating *aga* bees: Corvus
    b. attacked by *aga* bees: Crater
    c. scattered bones: tail of Hydra and Alphard

4. Embisa, also called *ngufisugiñe*, "the red-eyed one": Antares in Scorpio

5. Tō, "Ema" (Pleiades)

6. Ngukokiñe, "the wide-eyed one": Sirius

7. Funggegi, "Rufous-Sided Heron": Orion's belt

8. Tute, "Hawk"
    a. *nagipoñe*, "the pierced-nose one" (decorated like a Fierce Person with macaw-tail feathers through his nose): Altair with beta and gamma Aquila
    b. *tukwengitagïgï*, "decorated like us" (with feathers through his ears): Fomalhaut with Al Na'ir (alpha Grus) and beta Grus

9. Embisa efugu, "Embisa's canoe": elongated dust cloud below Antares

10. Tōfufisugu, "Ema's redness": includes Aldebaran, Capella, Bellatrix, Betelgeuse, El Nath, possibly also Arcturus, and lesser stars located among them.

11. Ogo, "storage platform": Great Square of Pegasus (Alpheratx, Scheat, Albenib, Markab)

12. Kutsu atangagï, "Ornate Hawk-Eagle's double flutes":
    a. alpha, beta Musca
    b. beta Crux and oc4755 in Crux

13. Taugi kusugu, "Taugi's fishing basket": Kaus Australis in Sagittarius and Shaula in Scorpius (hanging cord), through iota, theta, nu, upsilon and rho Scorpius (body of basket)

14. Ituga añagï, "Kingfisher's Path" (resembles the zig-zag flight of kingfishers): Phecda, Megrz, Aliath, Alcor, Mizar, Alkaid in Ursa Major

15. Agañagi, "Path of Dangerous Bees": Crux (seen as bees' circular flight outside hive)

16. Aga, "Nest of Dangerous Bees": Coalsack (a dust cloud that appears to the naked eye as a large black shape in the Milky Way)

17. Kafanifani: beta Hydra and psi Hydra

18. a) Ikege the Jaguar pounding on b) Idyali the Tapir with c) Ongogu the Tiger Heron and d) Asa the Deer looking on

19. Taugi lumbegïpe, "remains of Taugi's salt ashes": Greater Magallanic Cloud

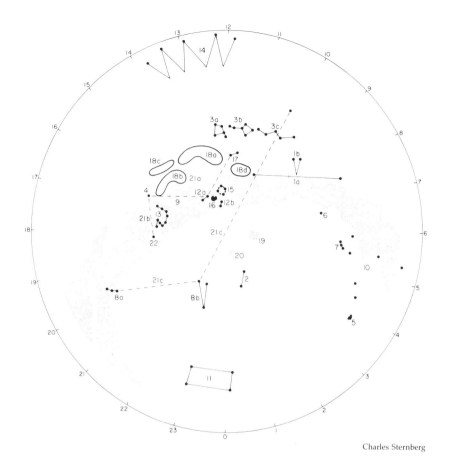

Charles Sternberg

20. Kusengi agafï titsïpe, "remains of Kusengi's tossed-out salt": Lesser Magallanic Cloud

21. Talondeñï, "fishing barriers":
   a. from #4 to #12 to #17
   b. from #4 across Ifuinga, "The River" (the Milky Way) to #22
   c. from Cetus to #8b to #8a

22. Kutsafugu: Vega

Notes To Chapters

Chapter 1

1. Boas addressed the trickster problem at some length using comparative materials, in his introduction to James Tait's collection of Thompson River Indian stories (1898).

In his famous book *The Trickster: A Study in American Indian Mythology,* Radin proposed that Trickster is among the most ancient of figures in North American mythology, combining an original image of a "nondescript person obsessed by hunger, by an uncontrollable urge to wander, and by sexuality" (p. 165) with intrusive culture-hero aspects (p. 165). He understood the divinity of Trickster to be a secondary reworking of the character by tribal intellectuals. Trickster functioned as "an archaic *speculum mentis*"; his character was an attempt to come to terms with psychological inconsistencies and the need to resolve them in the context of practical activities.

Despite the considerable interpretive potential of a concern with Trickster shared by Kerenyi, the historian of religion, Jung, the psychologist, and Radin, the ethnographer (all interested in the thematic, functional, and developmental aspects of mythology), the collaboration in this still-popular book was a failure. The Boasian anthropologist, set on ethnographic description in historical context, inevitably had to come to terms with materials the analyst ignored. For Jung, trickster images in North American myths had to be explained with respect to a universally posited psychology, and especially in terms of his particular etiology of the human mind. Consequently, the book is less a collaboration than a series of independent essays, and Radin's attempts to use psychological interpretation seem irresolute in comparison with his historical and ethnographic analyses.

2. More contemporary, comparative work includes that of Barbara Babcock-Abrahams, 1975; T. O. Beidelman (1980); Michael P. Carrol, 1984; Denise Paulme, 1976, 1977; and Robert D. Pelton, 1980. E. E. Evans-Pritchard (1967) views trickster tales told by the Azande as essentially "meaningless" entertainment appealing in the main because they describe actions people would like to perform, but which are forbidden to them, a view expanded and devel-

oped by Brian Street (1972). The Africanist Denise Paulme (1976) took the approach of more traditional folklorists by classifying Trickster tale sequences according to the most prominent themes or events in the stories. Thus, for example, she describes three types of trickster tales in which Trickster ". . . is seen to fail for want of taking stock of his strength before undertaking a task which surpasses it" (1977:64). She finds similarities between these tricksters and Lévi-Strauss's "bungling host" in North American mythology.

In one of his more bizarre reductive statements, Claude Lévi-Strauss claims that Salish Coyote stories explain "the origin of commercial exchange" (1981:283). Elsewhere in the same work, the trickster is reduced to a "bungling host" (the title was introduced by Boas in 1916). This theme emphasizes the characters' atavism (tricksters in Lévi-Strauss's view try to revive ancient forms of behavior) but hinders understanding of most other activities in which tricksters engage. Neither creative deceptions nor the evil associated with them is discussed:

". . . for most American tribes, (the trickster) had a highly sacred character, in spite of its farcical and scatological elements. It is easy to understand why this should be so, if the misadventures of the bungling host are a series of symmetrical inversions of the exploits of the demiurge. The latter changed animate or inanimate beings from what they were into what they were henceforth to be. The trickster, on the contrary, acting as bungling host to a whole series of creatures, tries to imitate them as they still were in mythic times, but can no longer be. He thus attempts to extend to different species, and to perpetuate in time, aberrant types of behavior or manners, and consequently behaves *as if* privileges, exceptions, or anomalies could become the rule, unlike the demiurge, whose function is to put an end to peculiarities, and to promulgate rules universally applicable to every species or category" (pp. 384–385).

Dell Hymes uses his closely focused discourse methods on a Salish "bungling host" story to demonstrate how a narrator makes Coyote a morally isolated character, "separated from reciprocity" (1984).

Barbara Babcock-Abrahams provides an exceptionally critical review of theories proposed about tricksters from the time of the earliest American anthropologists. Judging that scholars have confused the causes of the trickster images and activities, and that they have either explained away or reduced to mechanical functions of mythology the paradoxical, ambiguous, and contradictory aspects of this character, she focuses upon ". . . the paradox that that which is socially marginal is symbolically central and predominant." Her reanalysis of the Winnebago texts published by Radin concludes with an orientation toward the cross-cultural meanings of marginality, inversion, and multiplicity in trickster images (1975). T. O. Beidelman protested against this and other comparative approaches, claiming there are no grounds for justifying the concept "trickster" as a cross-cultural category. Nonetheless, in that author's opinion, whatever the characteristics of any particular "trickster," his social functions are what give him meaning.

To my knowledge, the only contemporary study of South American trickster stories is that of Howe and Sherzer (1985). They discuss the relationship of some traditional Kuna stories and themes to the ways Kuna joke about one another, and thereby handle rivalry and misfortune, as well as give meaning to ambiguous persons.

J. Barre Toelken arrived at some unusual insights into Navaho Coyote stories by reflecting upon the comments of his storytelling host, Yellowman. These remarks led Toelken to reject the common view that trickster stories serve essentially to entertain and amuse audiences. Two of Yellowman's storytelling observations are particularly revealing: "Many things about the story are funny, but the story is not funny." And, "Through the stories, everything is made possible." Toelken interprets these and other remarks to mean that ". . . Yellowman thus sees Coyote less as a Trickster per se and more as an *enabler,* whose actions, good or bad, bring certain ideas and actions into the field of possibility, a model who symbolizes abstractions in terms of real entities" (1969:221).

Considered along with the classic texts from North America, the various studies of the extremely widespread African trickster traditions suggest the potential fruitfulness of a discourse-centered approach to that rich and varied material, since speech-centered events seem so critical to the constitution of the stories.

Chapter 2

1. The reader can compare these Kalapalo stories with versions published in other collections and studies of Upper Xingu mythology, especially Aurore Monod-Becquelin's comprehensive collection of Trumai mythology (1975) and Pedro Agostinho's publication of Kamaiura stories (1978). Several trickster stories appear in Orlando and Claudio Villas Boas's collection of what appear to be myth variants told by different narrators, condensed into single narratives (1970; 1973). Roque de Barros Laraia has made a study of Sun and Moon myths, comparing those from the Upper Xingu region with versions from Tupi-speaking peoples elsewhere in Brazil (1967). He proposes that what the Kalapalo know as the story of "Kwatïngï" is originally Tupi.

The first translation of a Kalapalo version of the Kwatïngï story was published in Portuguese by Jose Candido M. de Carvalho (1951). Translation of a Bakairi Carib version appears in Karl von den Steinen (1940). This language, spoken to the south of the Upper Xingu Basin, is closely related to Kalapalo.

I have not included a comparative analysis of trickster "themes" in this book, but it is interesting that stories from the northern Carib-speaking peoples living in the Guiana regions north of the Amazon show far fewer resemblances to the Kalapalo tales than do those of the central Brazilian Bororo and Ge-speaking peoples. In the collection *Folk Literature of the Bororo Indians* (1983), the theme of twins who take revenge on their grandmother appears in Nos. 98 and 99. The Bororo myth made famous by Lévi-Strauss, which in this publication is called "The Legend of the Hero Toribugu" (Nos. 104–105), has interesting formal and thematic similarities to the Kalapalo story about the two rival brothers Kangangafanga and Kangangatï. Myths 1 and 2 in this same publication have resemblances to the Kalapalo story "Fiery." The motif of the son who recognizes his father (sometimes, as in the Kalapalo story "Dyekuku's Daughter," this occurs when men present the son with arrows) is widespread in South America. (See, for example, Metraux, pp. 158–160). A number of Ge Sun and Moon myths appear in Curt Nimuendaju's monograph on the Eastern Timbira (1946).

2. See Basso, 1973, for a description of this ritual.

3. The abruptness and difficulty of the break with parents may also suggest how contacts with powerful beings can be made. I am thinking here of the image of the arduous journey, one calling for long periods of travel through unknown and dangerous country, the traveler suffering painful ordeals along the way. Here is a narrative event of great importance in South American cultures, during which the ability to control pain, hunger, weariness, and sexual passion allows the traveler to contribute uniquely to human welfare by acquiring power from supernatural beings. Or, in the context of strictly human contacts, the traveler helps his own people by participating in a new exchange relation with formerly hostile foreigners. Again, there are several moral points being made. In situations of changing productive relations, the younger sibling may represent new strategies that are alternatives to traditional kinds of interpersonal activities, although these alternatives may have dubious worth in more predictable and familiar situations.

Chapter 3

1. Comparing the analysis of what he later called "versification" with structuralism, Dell Hymes remarks in his essay "Oral Performance and Measured Verse" that "comparison in terms of transformations, motifemes, or other structural categories would miss the control over detail to which verse analysis contributes" (1981a:239).

Hymes's reanalysis of a Clackamas Chinook myth in his "The 'Wife' Who 'Goes Out' like a Man" (1981b) is a superb demonstration of how analysis of discourse structure can provide us with information about a teller's own understanding of the story, even from a great distance. This sort of treatment thus complements the structuralist's by providing information crucial to understanding the semiotic functions of the kinds of sensory imagery to which Lévi-Strauss called our attention.

2. The single exception, to my knowledge, is the article by Hymes (1985) on a Salish narrator's portrayal of Coyote, "Bungling Host, Benevolent Host: Louis Simpson's 'Deer and Coyote.'"

3. Other South American groups who make extensive use of quoted speech in storytelling are the Aguaruna, described by Mildred Larsen (1978), and the Kuna, described by Joel Sherzer (1984).

4. The use of substitution in the formal speech of Kuikuro leaders, who belong to a community closely related to the Kalapalo, has been described by Bruna Francetto (1983).

5. In segment VII, traveling by Taugi as well as by Cuckoo and his relatives underscores the contrasts between those characters' points of view.

6. On one special occasion (lines 82 and following), speech between very close relatives sounds "affinal" because the entire context is charged with affinity. In speaking to his daughter, Cuckoo's father-in-law uses a quasi-oratorical style, signaled by the form *ogiña ogi*, ordinarily used by hereditary leaders to initiate a collective action that derives from consensus of a settlement. In the present case, this indicates to the young woman that she should perform an activity already deemed appropriate by virtue of her family's consensus.

7. Except when, in line 230, Cuckoo declares that he "must relieve himself." With this remark, Cuckoo asserts his obligation to complete the affinal exchange by creating something important and valuable. The fact that thatching grass grows up from his excrement makes it an especially "affinal" gift. Just as Cuckoo's affines refer to precious gifts they offer him as if they were disgusting or of no value, so, by a kind of metaphoric inversion, even the waste of the son-in-law is treasured for its exchange value. This small element of the Cuckoo story becomes the focus of several "Disgusting Dawn People" stories (see Chapter 4), which examine affinal reactions to such miraculous gifts.

8. There are of course particular segments where more than one person is addressed by a speaker, when oratory is quoted, for example, or other contexts in which several people are addressed in turn. There is, however, always a dialogical process in these passages, exhibited by the fact that some kind of response to a statement—even silence—is indicated.

Chapter 4

1. Boas defended their publication by arguing that such tales contributed to what Fletcher believed were the more important traditions worthy of scholarly attention: those of the shaman intellectuals of a community. Boas pointed out that the "esoteric" shamanic traditions seem to have developed from the more "exoteric" popular stories, making the popular stories crucial to an understanding of the history of a people's mythology (Boas, 1902; 1936).

Chapter 5

The title of this chapter is taken from an article by Denise Paulme (1976).

The Toba and Mataco trickster Fox (as well as Hopi Coyote) might be profitably compared with Afasa. Like Afasa, both Fox and Coyote engage in adventures that inevitably end badly for them; they are tricksters with almost no culture-hero attributes, and, despite their wishes, they seem to exist outside the realm of reciprocal relations, a realm they nonetheless persist in trying to enter.

The "suffering element" that Jung points out in the Winnebago Trickster is most prominent in the Afasa stories, among all the Kalapalo narratives. Afasa dies by suffocation, has a stingray encrusted with embers slapped over his face, is hog-tied and then bludgeoned to death, explodes from the heat of a fire, and has a stinging caterpillar rubbed along a very tender part of his anatomy. Jung's interpretation of this attribute of trickster characters has some application to Afasa: according to Jung, what is learned is something about self-consciousness. It is more specifically to the Kalapalo point, however, to see Afasa as learning about the deceptive nature of human relations, what lying is all about, and of the impossibility of his ever being "just like" a human being.

Bibliography

Agostinho, Pedro

1974   *Kwarìp. Mito e Ritual no Alto Xingu.* São Paulo: Editora da Universidade de São Paulo.

1978   *Mitos e Outras Narrativas Kamayurá.* Bahia: Universidade Federal da Bahia (Colecão Ciencia e Homem).

Babcock-Abrahams, Barbara

1975   "'A Tolerated Margin of Mess.' The Trickster and His Tales Reconsidered." *Journal of the Folklore Institute,* vol. 11, no. 3:147–86.

Basso, Ellen B.

1973   *The Kalapalo Indians of Central Brazil.* New York: Holt, Rinehart, and Winston.

1985   *A Musical View of the Universe.* Philadelphia: University of Pennsylvania Press.

Bates, Elizabeth

1976a   *Language and Context: The Acquisition of Pragmatics.* New York: Academic Press.

1976b   "Pragmatics and Sociolinguistics in Child Language." In *Normal and Deficient Child Language,* edited by D. M. Morehead and A. E. Morehead. Baltimore: University Park Press.

Beidelman, T. O.

1980   "The Moral Imagination of the Kaguru: Some Thoughts on Tricksters, Translation and Comparative Analysis." *American Ethnologist* 7:27–42.

Boas, Franz

1898   "Introduction." In James Teit, *Traditions of the Thompson River In-*
(1982) *dians,* pp. 1–18. *Memoirs of the American Folklore Society.* Vol. 6. (Reprinted in *Race, Language and Culture* (collected works of Franz Boas), pp. 407–24, Chicago: University of Chicago Press.)

1902   "The Ethnological Significance of Esoteric Doctrines." *Science* 16:
(1982) 872–74. (Reprinted in *Race, Language and Culture,* pp. 312–15.)

1916 "The Development of Folk-Tales and Myths." *The Scientific Monthly*
(1982) 3:335–43. (Reprinted in *Race, Language and Culture*, pp. 397–406.)
1936 "History and Science in Anthropology: A Reply." *American Anthro-*
(1982) *pologist* N.S. 38:137–41. (Reprinted in *Race, Language and Culture*,
pp. 305–15.)

Candido M. de Carvalho, José
1951 "Relações entre os Indios do Alto Xingu e a fauna regional." *Pub-*
licações Avulsas do Museu Nacional, no. 7. Rio de Janeiro.

Carroll, Michael P.
1984 "The Trickster as Selfish Buffoon and Culture Hero." *Ethos* 12:
105–31.

Coleman, L., and Kay, P.
1981 "Prototype Semantics: The English Word *lie.*" *Language* 57:26–44.

De Civrieux, Marc
1970 *Watunna: Mitologia Makiritare*. Caracas: Monte Avila Editors.

Evans-Pritchard, E. E.
1967 *The Zande Trickster*. Oxford: Clarendon Press.

Franchetto, Bruna
1983 "A fala do chefe: Generos verbais entre os Kuikuru do Alto Xingu."
Cadernos de Estudos Lingüisticos 4:4–72. Campinas(?), Brazil.

Goffman, Erving
1974 *Frame Analysis*. New York: Harper & Row.

Howe, James, and Sherzer, Joel
1985 "Friend Hairyfish and Friend Rattlesnake, or Keeping Anthropologists in Their Place." Unpublished manuscript.

Hymes, Dell
1981a "Discovering Oral Performance and Measured Verse in American
Indian Narrative." In *"In Vain I Tried to Tell You." Essays in Native
American Ethnopoetics*, pp. 309–41. Philadelphia: University of Pennsylvania Press.
1981b "The Wife Who 'Goes Out' like a Man." In *"In Vain I Tried to Tell
You." Essays in Native American Ethnopoetics*, pp. 274–308.
1985 "Bungling Host, Benevolent Host: Louis Simpson's 'Deer and Coyote.'" *American Indian Quarterly*, Summer 1984:171–98.

Jung, Carl G.
1972 "The Psychology of the Trickster." In Paul Radin, *The Trickster: A
Study in American Indian Mythology*, pp. 195–211. New York: Schocken
Books.

Laraia, Roque de Barros
1967 "O Sol e a Lua na Mitologia Xinguana." *Revista do Museu Paulista*,
n.s. 17:7–46.

Larsen, Mildred
1978 *The Functions of Reported Speech in Discourse*. Norman, Oklahoma:
Summer Institute of Linguistics.

Lévi-Strauss, Claude
1962 *La pensée sauvage*. Paris: Libriarie Plon.
1963 "The Structural Study of Myth." In *Structural Anthropology*, pp. 206–
31. Translated by Claire Jacobson and Brooke Grundfest Schoepf.
New York and London: Basic Books.

1969   *The Raw and the Cooked: Introduction to a Science of Mythology.* Vol. 1. Translated by John and Doreen Weightman. New York: Harper & Row.

1973   *From Honey to Ashes. Introduction to a Science of Mythology.* Vol. 2. Translated by John and Doreen Weightman. New York: Harper & Row.

1978   *The Origin of Table Manners. Introduction to a Science of Mythology.* Vol. 3. Translated by John and Doreen Weightman. London: Jonathan Cape.

1979   *Myth and Meaning.* New York: Schocken Books.

1981   *The Naked Man. Introduction to a Science of Mythology.* Vol. 4. Translated by John and Doreen Weightman. New York: Harper & Row.

Lowie, Robert

1909   "The Hero-Trickster Discussion." *Journal of American Folklore* 22: 431–33.

Métraux, Alfred

1946   *Myths of the Toba and Pilagá Indians of the Gran Chaco.* Philadelphia: American Folklore Society.

Monod-Becquelin, Aurore

1975   *La pratique linguistique des indiens Trumai.* Tome II, Mythes Trumai (Haut-Xingu, Mato Grosso, Bresil). Langages et civilisations à tradition orale, 10. Paris: Société d'études linguistiques et anthropologiques de France.

Nimuendaju, Curt

1946   *The Eastern Timbira.* Translated and edited by Robert H. Lowie. University of California Publications in American Archaeology and Ethnology, Vol. 41. Berkeley: University of California Press.

Paulme, Denise

1976   "Typologie des contes africains du décepteur." *Cahiers d'études africaines* 60:569–600.

1977   "The Impossible Imitation in African Trickster Tales." In *Forms of Folklore in Africa,* edited by Dan Ben-Amos, pp. 64–103. Austin and London: University of Texas Press.

Pelton, Robert D.

1980   *The Trickster in West Africa. A Study of Mythic Irony and Sacred Delight.* Berkeley: University of California Press.

Radin, Paul

1972   *The Trickster: A Study in American Indian Mythology.* New York: Schocken Books.

Rappaport, Roy A.

1979   "Sanctity and Lies in Evolution." In *Ecology, Meaning, and Religion,* pp. 223–43. Richmond, California: North Atlantic Books.

Schultz, Thomas R., and Robillard, Judith

1980   "The Development of Linguistic Humour in Children: Incongruity Through Rule Violation." In *Children's Humour,* edited by Paul E. McGhee and Antony J. Chapman, pp. 59–90. John Wiley and Sons: New York.

Searle, John R.

1979   *Expression and Meaning.* New York: Cambridge University Press.

Sherzer, Joel
  1983 *Kuna Ways of Speaking.* Austin: University of Texas Press.
Street, Brian V.
  1972 "The Trickster Theme: Winnebago and Azande." In *Zande Themes,* edited by A. Singer and Brian V. Street. Oxford: Oxford University Press.
Tedlock, Dennis
  1972a *Finding the Center.* New York: Dial Press.
  1972b "On the Translation of Style in Oral Narrative." In *Towards New Perspectives in Folklore,* edited by Americo Paredes and Richard Bauman, pp. 114–133. Austin: University of Texas Press.
  1983 *The Spoken Word and the Work of Interpretation.* Philadelphia: University of Pennsylvania Press.
Toelken, J. Barre
  1969 "The 'Pretty Language' of Yellowman: Genre, Mode, and Texture in Navaho Coyote Narratives." *Genre* 2:211–35.
Villas Boas, Orlando, and Villas Boas, Claudio
  1970 *Xingu. Os Indios Seus Mitos.* Rio de Janeiro: Zahar Editores. (English
  (1973) translation: *Xingu. The Indians, Their Myths.* Translated by K. Brecher. New York: Farrar, Straus, and Giroux.)
Von den Steinen, Karl
  1940 *Entre os Aborigenes do Brasil Central.* (Separata da Revista do Arquivo, n.s. 34 a 58, Departamento de Cultura, São Paulo.)
Wilbert, Johannes and Simoneau, Karen, editors
  1983 *Folk Literature of the Bororo Indians.* Los Angeles: University of California at Los Angeles Latin American Center Publications.

Index of Stories

General Index

Afasa (cannibal forest monster): curing ceremony, 318–19; character in stories, 349–50, 353, 355; conversations in stories, 349–50
Affinal speech, 21n, 107n, 232, 272–73, 366n.6 (Ch. 3), 367n.7 (Ch. 3)
Akiña (see stories, Kalapalo)
Akiñatunda (see storytelling, Kalapalo)
Anetaü (see hereditary leaders, Kalapalo)
Anetu taginunda ("the talk of a leader"), 109n, 230–32
Astronomy, 40, 140, 152–53, 293, 359–61
Augïnda (see deception, Kalapalo)

Babcock-Abrahams, Barbara, 364n.2
Beidelman, Thomas O., 5, 364n.2
Boas, Franz, 4, 298, 363n.1
Brinton, Daniel, 5

Campo cerrado habitat, 10, 22n, 107n, 108n, 139
Combs, 295–96
Conversations, Kalapalo (See also quoted speech), 235–40, 242–43, 285
Coyote (Hopi), 367
Coyote (Navajo), 298, 365n.2 (Ch. 1)

Deception, Kalapalo: concealment and, 352–53, 355; contrasted with English-speakers' concepts of, 240–42; eroticism and, 295–98, 349, 351–52; gender and, 225–26, 316; illusionary sensibility and, 2–3, 356–57; language and, 9, 232–34, 296–97; overstimulated emotions and, 275–76, 299–300, 352–53; in speech of hereditary lead-

ers, 230–32; in stories, 2–3, 8, 229–30, 352–53; Taugi and, 175, 207; tricksters', 229
Disagreement, Kalapalo, 238–39
Disgusting Dawn People, stories of, 298–300, 354

Evidence: absence of marking in Taugi's speech, 354; feelings and, 243; hearsay marker, 299; in Kalapalo speech, 232, 235–36, 237, 243; verification and, 240
Evans-Pritchard, E. E., 363n.2

Feelings (emotions): in Afasa stories, 349; of Cuckoo character, 272; conversations and, 351–52; evidence and, 243; Kalapalo detachment, 355; in Kalapalo narratives, xv, 1–3, 9, 23–24, 226, 229–30, 351–52, 355; of listeners to Disgusting Dawn People stories, 299–300; overstimulation of, by tricksters, 275–76, 299–300, 352–53; sound symbols and, xvii; tricksters' speech and, 229–30
Fox (South American trickster), 367
Funita ("loving," "cherishing," "compassionate"): dangers of, 216–17; expressed during accusations of witchcraft, 239, first women of, 24

Goffman, Erving, 241, 269

Hereditary leaders, Kalapalo (anetaü), 23, 109n, 134n, 230
Human beings, interactional contrasts with powerful beings and, 351, 355;